A
shilling
for
your
scowl

The history of a
Scottish legal *mafia*

JAMES SHAW GRANT

The publishers acknowledge subsidy from the Scottish Arts Council
towards the publication of this volume.

First published in Scotland in 1992 by Acair Ltd, 7 James Street,
Stornoway, Isle of Lewis

Designed and typeset by Acair Ltd.

Printed by BPCC Wheatons Ltd, Exeter

ISBN 0 86152 898 0

ACKNOWLEDGMENTS

The writing of this book would not have been possible without the help of many people. In particular I wish to acknowledge the assistance of the Scottish Arts Council in the form of a grant towards the cost of research. Others to whom I am indebted for advice, information, permission to quote or the use of photographs, include: Mr Iain F Maciver and the staff of the National Library of Scotland; the staff of the Scottish Record Office; the late Dr I.M.M. MacPhail; Rev Donald Macaulay, Bernera; Mr A.M. Matheson, formerly Convener of Comhairle nan Eilean; Mr Murdoch Macleod, Stornoway Pier and Harbour Commission; the Rt. Hon Donald Stewart, P.C.; Mr Malcolm MacIver, Solicitor; Mr John Barron of Messrs Innes & Mackay, Solicitors, Inverness, Mrs Janet Hunter; Prof. Derick Thomson; Mr and Mrs C Scott Mackenzie; Comunn Eachdraidh, Uig; Lodge Fortrose No 108 Stornoway; Mr B.P. Hutton, editor of *Masonic Square*; Mr John E. Farmer, County Librarian, Cornwall; Mr Frank Thompson; Mr Richard Langhorne; Mr Donald Smith, Factor of the Stornoway Trust Estate; the Guildhall Library, London; the British Library; Mr A.M. Morrison; the Crown Estate Commissioners; Mr Edward Young, formerly Rector of the Nicolson Institute; Cambridge University Library; Mr Bill Lawson, Northton; W. Matheson; the late Donald MacDonald; J.H.M. Mackenzie for the perusal of the invaluable diary of John Munro Mackenzie; and the *Stornoway Gazette*. I am specially indebted to the staff of Acair Ltd and to my late wife Catherine Mary Grant, who shared with me many dusty hours in the Scottish Record Office, and brought to light some of the more significant documents in the tangled story of the relationship of Munro, Ross and Skinner, with each other and with the people of Lewis.

Contents

1. FACTOR DEVOURED BY A WORM

Donald Munro, who was Factor, or Chamberlain, of the Island of Lewis in the middle years of last century, was the most hated man in the island's history.

During his lifetime he was excoriated in a Gaelic poem, ironically entitled *The Spirit of Kindliness* (*Spiorad a' Charthannais*), which concludes with a worm greeting his corpse as a juicy morsel, "since he made hundreds thin to feed himself for me."

He is exposed less savagely, but in some ways more effectively, in a long forgotten Victorian novel, which, again ironically, is dedicated to him. As literature it is poor but it deserves to be remembered as a valuable social document: one of the curiosities of Scottish literature.

Almost every family in the island has its own tradition of a particular injustice or indignity inflicted by Munro on one of its members.

In my wife's family it is the story of a forebear — Murdo Smith (*Murchadh Chaluim Tàilleir*) who returned from a fishing trip to find the Factor's men stripping the thatch from the house in Skigersta in which his young wife was sheltering. She was Margaret Mackay, reputed to be the last child born on the Island of North Rona.

Murdo put his wife and his belongings into a boat and made his way to Tong where he was lucky enough to get a croft, but the malevolence of the Factor followed him there.

When the rent fell due, he walked to the village of Back, several miles distant, to pay it. Munro refused to take it because he was a few minutes late. He was ordered to be in time at the next collection, the same day, at Aignish, on the other side of Broad Bay.

Munro drove off in his gig for Aignish, while Murdo, who had neither horse nor gig, took off his shoes and raced across the sands, against tide and clock, knowing that failure would cost him a fine, or perhaps the loss of a second croft.

Munro's oft repeated threat *"Cuiridh mi às an fhearann thu"* — "I'll take the land from you" — has become proverbial. The phrase he used when fining tenants if they were surly when they paid the rent — *"Tasdan air do dhrèin"* — "A shilling for your scowl!" — is also remembered with bitterness.

In my own family there is the same tradition as in my wife's of petty harassment. My grandmother was fined because she had peats in front of the house when Munro went marching by at the head of the Local

Volunteer Company of which he was Commanding Officer. The peats offended the dignity of the parade!

More substantially, the family remembers how Munro pursued it through the Courts for over thirty years in a maze of trumped up law suits which surpass the notorious case of Jarndyce v. Jarndyce in Dickens's *Bleak House.*

My granduncle, my great grandmother, and my grandfather were successively bankrupted in the process. My grandaunt and my granduncle were imprisoned for debts they didn't owe. Their children had to buy back the family home at a public roup in Edinburgh, although it had been taken from their parents quite illegally.

The sorest blow of all was the loss of their twin daughters, who perished as infants from neglect and malnutrition, because of the inhuman behaviour of those whose duty it was to protect the innocent and maintain the peace.

Despite the passion which these injustices inevitably arouse, even after the lapse of more than a hundred years, I feel constrained to ask whether the oral tradition has maligned the man.

Certainly, in some respects, the tradition has passed from history through legend into myth. I have been told, with great authority and circumstantial detail, how Munro eventually lost his job, emigrated to Canada and was starving on the streets of Toronto when his life was saved by one of the crofters he had evicted.

The story is completely untrue.

Munro died in his bed, in Stornoway, in a room with which I was very familiar in my youth. At the same time the true circumstances of his end had even more of divine nemesis, or at least of irony, than is suggested in the myth.

The questions that must be asked are these: was Donald Munro worse than other factors of his time or was he a typical representative of a harsh oppressive age? Did he exceed the authority conferred on him by his employer or was he a faithful servant diligently carrying out the instructions he received?

If we compare events in Lewis with what was happening at the same time in the neighbouring island of North Uist we find that Munro was representative rather than an aberration.

If we compare the policies he pursued with those of his immediate predecessor and his immediate successor as factors in Lewis, we are forced to the conclusion that he was carrying out the settled policy of the proprietor, Sir James Matheson. That, in itself, raises other questions because Sir James was widely regarded in his day, and by historians since, as a model landlord and one of the great benefactors in Highland history.

Even so Donald Munro was unique.

Paradoxically, he was unique in that he was not alone. He was the godfather of a little legal mafia of cousins, operating together in the law courts in Lewis and Edinburgh, who held a community of more than twenty thousand people in thrall for a generation.

Even if we leave his relations out of the picture for the moment, he was also unique in the extent of his personal power.

At the summit of his career, he held nearly thirty public offices. He was simultaneously Procurator Fiscal and Factor for the whole of Lewis — two incompatible offices — while as Captain of the Militia he had behind him the only military force in the island, and did not scruple to use it, at least in threat.

He was one of only two solicitors practising in the island. The other was his cousin and partner, William Ross. He was chairman of the four Parochial Boards, and legal adviser to the boards of which he was chairman. He was chairman of the four island School Boards, vice-chairman of the Harbour Trustees, the chief magistrate of Stornoway, deputy chairman of the Road Trust and a director of both the Gas Company and the Water Company.

He appeared in the Sheriff Court in two different capacities — solicitor and procurator fiscal — but he also sat on the bench himself as a Justice of the Peace. He also held the ancient appointment of baron bailie although, latterly at least, he did not convene courts in that capacity. He was also a commissioner of supply and a commissioner under the Income Tax acts.

The only office he held which was not capable of being exercised oppressively against the people whose destinies he controlled was the captaincy of the Matheson Cricket Club; an organisation ill suited to the Hebridean weather and unrelated to the interests of the indigenous community.

It is significant that, although he was for many years an active member of the local lodge of Freemasons — Lodge Fortrose No 108 — he never seems to have held high office, and the very active Stornoway Literary and Debating Society, which was patronised by his employer, Sir James, year after year blackballed Munro from membership.

In the areas in which there was some element of democratic choice Munro was rejected, even at the height of his power, not only by the

Many of those who figure in this book were drawn together for the laying of the foundation stone of Lews Castle, and are represented in a painting of the ceremony in Lodge Fortrose No 108, Stornoway. Slightly aloof from the rest are Sir James and Lady Matheson (Nos 32 and 33 in the key). Not far away (No 28) is Donald Munro, Procurator Fiscal but not yet Factor. (Courtesy of Lodge Fortrose No 108, Stornoway.)

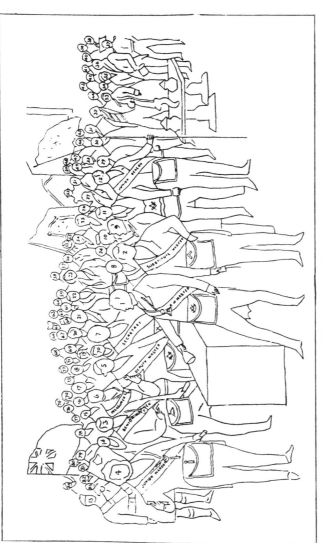

KEY TO THE MASONIC PICTURE.

Others in the group are James Robertson MacIver (No 2), Norman MacIver, shipowner and banker (No 5), Colin Morison (No 6), Hugh Brown (No 25), Roderick Nicolson, shipowner (No 31), Rev Roderick Nicolson, his son (No 71), Sheriff Andrew Lothian MacDonald (No 36), John Munro Mackenzie (No 41), Capt Donald Mackenzie (No 50), Capt Benjamin Oliver (No 35) and John Scobie (No 42), the Chamberlain who added to the crofters' rents the meal "gifted" by Sir James during the famine. (Courtesy of Lodge Fortrose No 108, Stornoway.)

Gaelic-speaking crofters in the rural areas but by the English-speaking, or bilingual, business and professional community in the town of Stornoway.

The fact that Munro was Chief Magistrate does not undermine that assessment. The people of Stornoway had to fight hard against the Estate to get Police Burgh status for the town. Acceptance of the Estate's representative as Chief Magistrate was part of the price they paid.

Munro was also unique among the oppressive factors of his day in the personal pleasure he derived from gratuitous acts of malevolence. This we know, not only from the oral tradition, and the contemporary Gaelic poem by John Smith, the Earshader Bard, from which I have already quoted; we have the written testimony, from beyond the grave, of one of his own subordinates, rediscovered for us by a chance annotation in shorthand in a newspaper cutting book kept by my father.

It is not Munro's uniqueness, however, that gives his career importance. It is the fact that he was the natural product of a flawed system of legal administration. A system which was admirable in its intentions and effective in most of its procedures, but in which one essential element — the provision of solicitors — was left to the free play of market forces. On the periphery, in the Outer Hebrides, the market was weak, or non-existent, and failed to sustain the competition which an adversarial system demands.

This gives the life of Donald Munro contemporary relevance in an age in which the market is regarded as the most effective social regulator even in the areas where, for geographical or commercial reasons, the market manifestly does not work.

His ultimate downfall may be a portent of more than local or historical significance. It was brought about by one of the most remarkable "risings" in Highland history. The "rising" was completely peaceful in so far as those directly involved were concerned, but was so badly handled, by Munro and his associates, it precipitated a riot among the bystanders. The so-called Bernera Riot of 1874 was the ultimate condemnation of a system of oppression which inevitably produced violence by its own excesses and ineptitude.

In order to take up the contemporary theme of the market which failed to function, and to set the scene for the rise of Donald Munro and his associates, it is necessary to go back to 1788 when, as those in authority saw it, the legal system of Scotland was reformed, and the rule of law came to the Western Isles for the first time in history.

2. NO MARKET IN SOLICITORS

The reform which gave Lewis its first Sheriff Court was a by-product of a dispute about pay.

In 1788 the Scottish Sheriffs wanted a rise. Instead the Government relieved them of the cost of paying the salaries of their Substitutes.

Under the old system, the Sheriffs, looking to their own financial interest, appointed as few Substitutes as they could get away with, and the remoter parts of the country were scandalously neglected.

Once that financial disincentive was removed, the Sheriffs began to give some attention to the facts of Scottish geography.

The only regular connection between Stornoway and the mainland was via Poolewe. A "packet" sailed every Wednesday and Saturday "weather permitting". From Poolewe the traveller had to make his way down Loch Maree by boat, and then get the "mail car" — presumably a gig — to Dingwall.

There could have been no other area in Britain where nearly half the population of a county was separated from the county town and the Sheriff Court by so difficult a journey.

West Uig, then one of the most prosperous parts of Lewis, with a seaborne trade of its own, was even more inaccessible from Stornoway than Stornoway was from Dingwall. So far as Uig was concerned, there might just as well have been no courts of justice at all.

Lewis was even more isolated from the higher courts in Edinburgh.

Portree was the terminus of the steam-packet service from Glasgow. When the Lewis-bound traveller had got as far as Skye, he had the option of working his way by a leisurely coaster to Poolewe and completing the journey from there by the twice weekly packet, or hiring a sailing boat to take him direct to Stornoway. As direct, that is, as the vagaries of wind and tide permitted.

Seen from Edinburgh or London, the placing of a Sheriff Substitute in Stornoway was almost a missionary enterprise: civilisation reaching out to bring the benefits of a sound judicial system to the barbarous Islanders. The historical facts are somewhat different.

Under the old Lordship of the Isles there had been an established legal system in the Hebrides. Not much is known about it. The laws were probably transmitted orally rather than set out in written statutes. They may have been administered somewhat arbitrarily. But, at least, there was a law-giver, someone to resolve disputes, in each of the major islands.

Justice was accessible to the people. The Morisons of Ness in Lewis, who had been hereditary Breves, were still regarded as such for more than a century after the Lordship of the Isles, from which they derived their authority, had disappeared. They are remembered with respect even today.

The reform of 1788 merely filled a vacuum which central government itself created when the Lordship of the Isles was forfeited in 1493.

Attention was drawn to the vacuum by the Church of Scotland Synod of Glenelg at its very first meeting in July 1725.

The Synod was set up by the General Assembly to cover the Islands and the North West Mainland, which had previously been almost totally neglected by both Church and State. Its first act, apart from essential administrative decisions, was to address a petition to the Government asking that "fit persons" should be commissioned to reside "in some of those places at greatest distance to see the laws duly executed."

Sixty-three years later, when the Synod's plea was eventually listened to, the Sheriff of Ross & Cromarty — Donald Macleod of Geanies — put it on record that "many instances" had occurred of Defenders being put to "unnecessary trouble, hardship and expense" by Pursuers who, "from improper motives," and "without serving any good purpose" cited them to appear in distant courts. He makes clear that this oppression, by due process of law, occurred in both criminal and civil cases.

So far as the Western Isles were concerned, the legal system, prior to 1788, and as we shall see, for a long time after 1788, was itself a primary instrument of injustice inflicted on innocent people.

The reform of 1788 was long overdue but, unfortunately, in spite of Donald Macleod's good intentions, it was more token than real.

The Sheriff Substitute appointed to Stornoway was George Munro, a writer (or solicitor) in Dingwall who continued to reside and practice there.

At the first court held in Stornoway, he accepted the nomination of his own apprentice as Sheriff Clerk Depute "within the island of Lewis," a description which defined his jurisdiction rather than his place of residence.

In the following month, finding it necessary to appoint a Procurator Fiscal, he gave the job to John MacAllan, another writer in Dingwall.

He also decreed that actions against Defenders within a computed mile of Stornoway would proceed on a day's notice, and against Defenders in other parts of Lewis on two days' notice. This, it was explained, was "for the greater despatch of business" but, quite clearly, it was intended to reduce to a minimum the length of his visits to the island in which he was supposed to administer justice.

To answer a summons in the Court in Stornoway within two days, a Defender in many parts of Lewis would have to leave home as soon as he received it without time to order his affairs, or consult his friends.

Lewis had been given a Sheriff and a Sheriff Court but the administration of justice was still firmly located in Dingwall.

In the regulations for the administration of the new Courts, Donald Macleod of Geanies drew attention to the fact that there was an insufficient number of legal practitioners resident in Fortrose to service the Sheriff Court there, so the people of Fortrose were authorised, if they wished, to treat Tain or Dingwall as their local court.

The same difficulty arose in Lewis, even more acutely, but the Sheriff does not mention it. We can only assume that Lewis was "beyond the pale" and what happened there did not really matter anyway.

The legal reforms of 1788 were completely frustrated on the periphery of Scotland by the fact that one essential element in an adversarial system — the availability of skilled legal advice for all parties to a dispute — was left to the free play of market forces.

For the best part of a century after Lewis, belatedly, got a Sheriff Court of its own, there was never a period of ten consecutive years, I believe not even five, in which there were two independent legal agents in the town of Stornoway, so that one litigant in every civil case, and the accused in every criminal case, was unrepresented, except on the rare occasions when relatively wealthy people, faced with major litigation, were able to buy in legal advice from across the Minch.

Because of the lack of qualified legal agents in Stornoway, the Court had great difficulty, over a long period of years, even in finding suitably qualified people to act as Procurator Fiscal.

The idea of having a Procurator Fiscal based in Dingwall soon proved unworkable. The Sheriff-Substitute appointed to Stornoway found it necessary to have a Procurator Fiscal resident within the island, even if he wasn't there himself.

He appointed Donald Ross, tacksman of Mid Borve. No indication is given that Ross had any qualifications or aptitude for the post. The name Ross is not indigenous to Lewis, but it is very common around Tain and

Dingwall. The presumption must be that the appointment rested on some link of blood or friendship or the recommendation of a mutual acquaintance.

In the following year Ross's appointment was terminated, ostensibly because it was found inconvenient to have a Procurator Fiscal residing in a rural area rather than in the town of Stornoway. The new appointee was Alexander Anderson. Again there is no indication of qualifications or aptitude beyond the fact that he was "a residenter in Stornoway."

Anderson did not last long either and the normal situation thereafter was that the Mackenzies of Seaforth, who owned Lewis, as a sort of overseas colony of their mainland estates, retained a solicitor in Stornoway who was also appointed Procurator Fiscal.

In some ways the position was worse than it had been before the reform which gave Stornoway a Sheriff Court. Defenders in civil actions and the accused in criminal actions were still generally without legal representation, but the Pursuer in both the civil and criminal courts was now represented on the spot. Life had become considerably easier for Pursuers, but, if anything, it was more difficult than it had been for Defenders.

The evils of the situation were intensified when, as happened repeatedly, the Seaforths' legal agent in Lewis was also the Chamberlain, or Factor, and the post of Procurator Fiscal was added to this intense concentration of legal and administrative power.

Eventually the concentration of power became an accepted feature of the island scene, with disastrous consequences for the people who had to endure it and for the reputation of the courts.

A temporary break in the pattern occurred when Thomas Buchanan Drummond was appointed Procurator Fiscal in May 1834. He was not, at that time, a retainer of the Seaforths and seems to have had some considerable legal experience. His petition to be admitted to practise before the Stornoway Court describes him as "having been regularly bred to the law profession and qualified to act as a procurator before any court of law in Scotland," which is no doubt true, although it was written by himself.

Whatever his qualifications, Drummond was a man of very inept judgement.

One of his first acts on taking up office was to write a long letter to Seaforth suggesting that the inhabitants should be roused from "their present state of idleness and misery" by changing the name of Stornoway to Port Royal, and importing Irish navvies to show the islanders how to work. The name Stornoway, he complained, "sounds harsh to the ear of all lowlanders" and "gives strangers a wild idea of this country."

He chose the name Port Royal, in honour of William IVth, the Sailor King, who had visited Stornoway in 1793. He seems to have been quite unaware that Portree, the "capital" of the neighbouring island of Skye, was already named Port Royal, in the indigenous language of the people, and in honour of a much more important monarch in Highland terms — James Vth, who in 1540 had sailed to the islands with a fleet of 12 warships on a very bellicose mission of peace.

Drummond had some sensible ideas too but they were lonely swimmers in a vast ocean of nonsense.

He recognised the importance of opening up the island with roads, and improving communications with the mainland. He urged the need for a jail, a Court house and proper public offices. He anticipated history by 150 years when he recommended the amalgamation of the Western Isles into a new county. But he also wanted Seaforth to restructure the island's crofts and farms with a mathematical precision which took little account of topography and on a scale which would have made the Sutherland clearances look like a picnic.

He was one of those instant reformers who can see only the end result with none of the incidental difficulties of getting there. He offered to write a book about Lewis and, being "already the author of several works," he guaranteed that "strangers from all corners of the country will pour into the place and be induced to reside here." "The seas and rivers here, as well as the lands, abound with everything necessary for man's existence yet all these mercies are, as it were, neglected by the inactivity of the natives" but, if his advice was taken, the "bareness and misery" of the island would be replaced by "beauty and fruitfulness."

He told Seaforth he had consulted some of the "most respectable merchants" and that his plans had their approbation. One can see him scurrying round the modest villas of the little town, explaining to the merchants and ship's captains home from foreign voyages that all their island needed, to make it into a modern Eden, was a change in the name of Stornoway and an infusion of Irish blood. I wonder what they said behind his back?

Whatever it was, I think it unlikely that the presence of Thomas Buchanan Drummond in Stornoway did very much to gain respect for the courts and the general process of justice. Even his letters to Seaforth, seeking his aid, were injudicious.

To enhance his own status in the great man's eyes he belittled the townsfolk by suggesting that they were critical of Seaforth's policies for the place, but then went on to suggest, in a hectoring tone which none of the locals would venture to employ, that Seaforth should use his influence as a member of the government to "ask and obtain all the good that possibly can be obtained for this place."

For himself he sought neither fee nor reward — or at least so he protested— but he asked that Seaforth would do him the justice of "intimating to his Majesty that it was I, an humble individual, that suggested" changing the name of Stornoway to Port Royal, in honour of the King.

However inept Drummond may have been; however much the locals may have laughed at him; the presence in the town of a solicitor independent of the proprietor was of considerable importance.

In a later letter to Seaforth, Drummond, acting as solicitor for a group of business men, urged him to seek Parliamentary powers for the development of Stornoway as a commercial port, regulated by an elected harbour authority. The neglect of the harbour was a long running grievance, and the prosperity of Stornoway was seriously compromised, for fully half a century, by the preoccupation of proprietors with their own careers in London, or abroad, or their wives' aesthetic dislike of a messy business like the curing of herring.

Unfortunately Drummond's independence of the proprietor was relatively short lived. Less than a year after his letter to Seaforth, as spokesman for the frustrated business men of Stornoway, Drummond was accepting from Seaforth an appointment to be both his Baron Bailie and his political agent: an odd assortment of offices for a Procurator Fiscal to hold.

Buchanan clearly had some qualms. He replied "I have never received any letter from the Lord Advocate stating that as Fiscal I was not entitled to act as an agent in Political matters" but speculated that the power to prevent him might lie with the Sheriff rather than the Lord Advocate. Even if that were the case, he did not see it as an insuperable obstacle: he could distance himself from politics by using Seaforth's Factor as a screen.

He offered to take on the two jobs for £100 per annum, plus expenses — a tidy salary in the money values of the time — and assured

Seaforth that he would arrange matters, "so as your own or your friends interests in this quarter will always be duly and properly attended to."

The Baron Bailie courts had been in decline for many years. At one point in the distant past the Baron Bailies had a limited right of capital punishment but, by the date of Drummond's appointment, their function was primarily to settle minor quarrels among tenants and to collect fines levied for non-attendance at the head court. They tended to survive longer, perhaps not unnaturally, in the remoter parts of the country and, when properly conducted, could have served a useful purpose, somewhat similar to the Scottish Land Court in our own day. There was still a Baron Bailie in Lewis forty years later, although he protested that he no longer held courts, and the appointment of a Baron Bailie was attended with considerable formality. The Commission of John Munro Mackenzie, who was appointed Baron Bailie of Lewis more than twenty years after Drummond, authorises him "to fence hold and continue Baron Bailie Courts as he shall think proper, to administer justice in all causes, to place and displace, appoint and remove all officers and members of court when necessary and generally to do any other thing which any Baron Bailie may lawfully do by the law and practice of Scotland."

In 1835, in Lewis, when Drummond assumed the office, it was certainly not a sinecure, especially after the proprietor, from whom the appointment was held, and to whom alone the Baron Bailie seems to have been responsible, accepted an appointment as Governor of Ceylon and removed himself even further from events in Lewis than he had been as a member of the Government in London.

In 1837, according to a directory published in that year, there were two "writers and notaries" in Stornoway, but this breach in the monopoly situation was short lived, and, even while it lasted, it was vitiated by the incestuous relationship which existed within official circles. The other "writer and notary" was Roderick Mackenzie, the town clerk of Stornoway, who was Drummond's clerk in the Baron Bailie court.

In the following year Thomas Buchanan Drummond died and Stornoway was left with no qualified legal practitioner at all. Whether this implies that Roderick Mackenzie had left, or that his qualifications were less substantial than the almanac implied, is not clear. The consequence, however, is clear enough: a further concentration of civil and administrative power in inappropriate hands.

On 25th April 1838, Thomas Knox, factor for the Seaforth Estates in Lewis was appointed Procurator Fiscal "there being at present no legal practitioner resident in said island." The minutes indicate that the appointment was regarded as an emergency one, the Sheriff Substitute finding it necessary to "appoint some proper person (not being a legal practitioner)."

Two months later, the powers of the Factor were strengthened still further: the proprietors petitioned the court to permit him to plead in civil actions as well, despite the fact that he was not qualified to practice before the Court at all. The Sheriff agreed, somewhat reluctantly.

While that solved the problem for the estate in initiating legal actions, it meant that the tenants were more defenceless than ever in resisting any arbitrary use of the Factor's power.

It is impossible to assess the extent to which petty oppression, or outright injustice, flourished while the operation of the legal system was hampered by a lack of qualified agents to appear before the courts. The measure is not in the cases which are recorded but in the harassment submitted to in silence, because there was no one available to advise or support the harassed. The records do, however, give us an occasional glimpse of the tip of the iceberg.

Sheriff Robert Sutherland Taylor, who presided for a short time in the Stornoway Court around 1840, commented thrice, within the space of two months, on the problems arising from "the circumstances of this Court, where the Respondents have not access to professional legal assistance except at a great distance," but, in each case, refused to delay proceedings, because there was "no remedy consistent with the expeditious discussion" to which the cases were entitled.

Two of the cases were actions for removal at the instance of the Seaforths, and it seems reasonable to assume that, whatever the urgency with which the estate wished to get vacant possession of its property, the tenants being evicted would suffer more from undue haste than the estate from undue delay.

The problem of defendants in the Stornoway Court, over a period of nearly a hundred years, was put more forcefully in the pleadings submitted by a tailor, Murdoch Matheson, threatened with the loss of his horse.

Matheson, who combined with his tailoring a modest business as a carter, sent his grey horse to graze on the Tong moor in the spring. The horse strayed but, some weeks later, Matheson heard there was a grey horse wandering along the fences of Arnish Farm. He sent his wife and a servant to collect it. They recognised the horse and the horse recognised them. They brought it home. It was so domesticated it used to wander into the house in search of food.

At that stage one of the leading businessmen in Stornoway, Roderick Nicolson, shipowner, merchant and tacksman, raised an action in the Sheriff Court claiming the horse as one of his, which, about the same time, had strayed from the moor in Lochs.

Nicolson engaged the only solicitor available, and might well have won his action — and the horse! — by default, but for the fact that a friend, who could write, came to the tailor's assistance, pointing out to the court that Nicolson's horse had been seen on the moor at Lochs sometime after Matheson's horse was reported at the boundary of Arnish Farm, and "unless he were a Pegasus he could not be one and the same animal."

Matheson's pleadings, a beautifully written document, describing Nicolson's action as vexatious, concludes: "He is a poor, illiterate man without legal advice or assistance, depending for his own and his family's subsistence on the services of the animal of which the Petitioner so unjustly seeks to deprive him. On the other hand the Petitioner, with whom he has to contend in defending his lawful property, is a rich man and has employed the only procurator in the place to conduct his case He had the greatest difficulty in getting a person to undertake the writing of these answers and, were it not that he has the greatest confidence in the goodness of his cause and your Lordship's impartial judgment, he would, in all probability, sit down in despair and suffer the Petitioner to carry away his property without opposition."

Matheson's answers were "drawn without fee or reward by H. Brown" and signed by Matheson with a cross.

Hugh Brown is a rather shadowy figure who first appears in the Sheriff Court records as "a messenger." In December 1815 he was appointed Procurator Fiscal although he does not appear to have had any legal qualification.

The records are sparse and incomplete, but he was still Procurator Fiscal in 1824 when he is mentioned as concurring in an action by William and Roderick Morison, Lloyd's agents in Stornoway, against tenants in Lemreway, for destroying a mast and beam from an unnamed wreck, for which they had to pay fines ranging from 10/- to £4 together with £8.7 of modified expenses. In 1833 Brown ceased to be Fiscal, in circumstances which will be examined later.

Even when he was Fiscal, Brown does not seem to have been admitted to practice in civil cases, which, no doubt, explains his anxiety to make clear that he had acted for Matheson "without fee or reward." And the question must be asked whether he would have acted for Matheson in any circumstances if Matheson's opponent in the case had been the all powerful Factor, representing the Seaforths, rather than a Stornoway merchant.

Two years earlier the same Roderick Nicolson, as farmer of Upper Coll, applied for an interdict against the 36 tenants in the club farm of Nether Coll, prohibiting them from grazing their stock on the seaweed along the shore.

The tenants of Nether Coll had around 300 black cattle and the seaweed was an important part of their winter feed. They were taken down to the beach as the tide went out and allowed to graze until the flood began. Three hundred black cattle on the sands at Coll would have been a sight worth seeing.

There was only one legal agent in Stornoway at that time, and, as Nicolson had engaged him, the 36 tenants were unable to get advice. They lost the case by default, and suffered the further injustice of having expenses awarded against them so that they had, in effect, to pay for their own improper exclusion from a perquisite of their holdings which they had enjoyed from time immemorial.

Shortly afterwards the Factor, Alexander Stewart, was sacked by the Seaforths for undisclosed reasons. He immediately set up business in Stornoway as a "writer and Notary Public." On 16th June 1832, he was admitted to practice in Stornoway Sheriff Court. His application states that he had served a legal apprenticeship with William Laurie, Procurator in Lanarkshire.

In this way, for a short time, there were two qualified legal agents in Stornoway and the effect on the administration of justice was immediate.

The discontented tenants of Nether Coll sought the help of their old enemy, the ex-Factor, and the case about the seaweed was re-opened.

Stewart informed the court that, at Whitsunday 1830, the 36 tenants in Nether Coll had been given a nine year lease by the Seaforth Trustees which obliged them to carry out extensive improvements, including the erection of new houses and offices, at a considerable distance from their arable land, "in order to increase the value of the farm to the landlord."

It had always been use and wont in the Island for tenants' cattle to feed along the shore, without interruption or molestation, he said. The new lease confirmed that right but, as a result of their exclusion by

Nicolson, the Nether Coll cattle were "now in a state of starvation from which, if they do ever recover, their value must be greatly reduced."

Even if one assumes that Stewart overstated the effect of the exclusion on his clients' cattle, it is clear that they suffered a considerable injustice because of the unavailability of competent legal advice, when the case against them was first raised.

Moreover, the injury to their interests would have been permanent, and no record of it would have survived, but for the timely dismissal of the Factor.

We have no way of knowing how many similar incidents arose over the years when there was no dismissed and disgruntled Factor around to secure the justice which the normal process of law in Lewis, at that time, failed to deliver.

3. ENTER THE GODFATHER

The hardships inflicted on unrepresented litigants in the Stornoway Courts may have been modified to some extent by the chance that, for almost 30 years, from 11th March 1813, the bench was occupied by a sympathetic Sheriff-substitute — John Mackenzie.

So far as I know, he was the only Sheriff-substitute in the two hundred years existence of the Stornoway Court who had any real knowledge of the island and its people prior to his appointment. He was a son of John Mackenzie of Letterewe and had his own estate on the mainland, but, as a young man, he had been a writer in Stornoway, and for a time had been Sheriff Clerk to the Stornoway Court. His wife was a daughter of Rev Hugh Munro, a well known minister in the parish of Uig.

Because of his local ties Sheriff Mackenzie was, however, open to pressures which an outsider would have escaped.

Shortly before Alexander Stewart's dismissal as Factor, for instance, the Sheriff went with Lewis MacIver, the tacksman of Gress, on a visit to the celebrated seal cave, the entrance to which is so narrow that a special boat had to be built for access. The boat was unstable and MacIver and the Sheriff were thrown into the water. They were quickly rescued but Mackenzie, who was a frail old man, was badly shaken. He was hurried to MacIver's home at Gress and put to bed.

While the Sheriff was in bed recovering, Stewart arrived on horseback to get his signature to a summons for debt against another leading figure in the community, Dr Macaulay, who was a tacksman and merchant as well as a doctor: a thoroughly unpleasant character who had once threatened to kill a Sheriff Officer with a shovel, and who was much more interested in his business ventures than in his patients, if he had any.

The Sheriff, with his mind on his recent escape from drowning, commented to the Factor that he was delighted to be able to sign the document. The Factor, knowing there was an old animosity between the Sheriff and the Doctor, fanned the flames by reporting the Sheriff's comment to Macaulay, without revealing the circumstance to which it referred.

The Sheriff's usefulness was also diminished by his pre-occupation with his mainland farm. There were many occasions, even in summer, but especially in winter, when he was cut off from Stornoway for days, or even weeks, at a time.

He was, for instance, absent from his jurisdiction when the

mutineers of the *Jane* were arrested, and charged with murder and piracy. In national terms, it was much the biggest case to arise during his thirty year tenure of office but he appears to have played no part in it.

The schooner *Jane*, owned by a merchant named Moses Levy, sailed from Gibraltar, on an evening in May, 1821, for "the Brazils" with a cargo of sweet oil, paper, beeswax, and aniseed. Beneath the beeswax were hidden 38,180 Spanish hard dollars, which may have been intended to finance the revolutionary struggle then taking place in South America. The casks containing the dollars were loaded late in the evening, after the other cargo, and their great weight caused speculation among the crew.

In the course of the voyage, the Captain, Thomas Johnston, a Scot, was indiscreet enough to reveal the truth to the mate, Peter Heaman, a man of rather dubious background who came from Sunderland or Shields.

Heaman, together with the French cook, Francois Gautier, organised a mutiny in mid Atlantic, murdering the Captain and another member of the crew.

They sailed north to the Hebrides and scuttled the vessel in the Minch, hoping to land on the Scottish mainland and pass themselves off as the shipwrecked crew of a Scandinavian vessel outward bound for New York.

Contrary winds drove the mutineers ashore at Swordale in Lewis. The dollars were found by customs officers, secreted among their belongings or buried under the shingle of the beach. The Maltese cabin boy, Andrew Camelier, turned King's evidence. Heaman and Gautier were convicted of piracy and murder, in the High Court of Admiralty in Edinburgh, and publicly executed on Leith sands: the last pirates to suffer the death penalty in Scotland.

The trial of the mutineers of the *Jane* aroused widespread interest among lawyers because of the issues it raised concerning the jurisdiction of a Scottish court to try foreign seamen, for a crime committed on a foreign vessel, on the high seas, thousands of miles from the Scottish coast.

From the Lewis point of view the most significant feature of the affair is that the arrest of the pirates was accomplished because of the efficient arrangements made for the protection of the revenue, not because of any particular efficiency in the general administration of the law.

There was a well staffed Customs House at Stornoway and a revenue cutter stationed at the port. Capt Benjamin Oliver of the *Prince of Wales*, who brought the pirates to Leith, captured 11 smugglers between 1815 and 1829: cutters, ketches, luggers, sloops and brigs, with crews ranging from 5 to 29. Altogether 127 individuals — mainly foreign — were arrested. Another 19 escaped, but their cargo of gin was seized.

The same degree of protection was not given to the King's subjects as to the King's revenue.

When the mate and cook of the *Jane* were arrested, the matter was in the hands of the Surveyor of Customs, although the offences had nothing to do with his department, and he had to rely on the crofters round about to guard the criminals overnight. The crofters were told to stave the pirates' boat and bind the crew if they tried to escape. The murderers were not arrested until the following day, when the Surveyor sent his son from Stornoway with a party of men to secure them. They were then lodged in an hotel on the South Beach, for want of a jail, and examined by four J.P.s, in the absence of the Sheriff.

While the mutineers were in jail in Edinburgh, awaiting their trial, Mrs Stewart Mackenzie of Seaforth sought to have Sheriff John Mackenzie removed from office because of his long and repeated absences from his jurisdiction.

Mrs Mackenzie was popularly referred to in the North as Lady Hood Mackenzie. As the young bride of Admiral Sir Samuel Hood, she had been the toast of London society and made a notable journey across India in a palanquin, like a queen. On her return from India — as Sir Walter Scott, a close friend, records in his poetical "Farewell to Mackenzie" — she lost her husband, her father, and her brother, all within a space of six months. As a result, she found herself, a young widow, saddled with the administration of the vast Seaforth estates: as foretold in the best known prophecy of the Brahan Seer, with which Sir Walter Scott claims to have been personally familiar long before the sudden spate of family deaths which brought about its fulfilment

The young widow married James Alexander Stewart of Glasserton, eldest son of Admiral Keith Stewart, and grandson of the Earl of Galloway. He added the name Mackenzie to his own and undertook the administration of the Seaforth Estates on his wife's behalf. On occasions, however, Mrs Stewart Mackenzie intervened directly in matters in which she had a special interest.

It is perhaps significant that, when she wrote Donald Macleod of Geanies, the Sheriff Principal (as we would designate him nowadays), seeking the dismissal of the Sheriff-substitute, he temporised, and sought the views of her husband.

In addition to her complaint about Sheriff John Mackenzie's

non-residence in Lewis, it is clear she was angry because he had given a decision against her which was overturned on appeal to the Court of Session. In the circumstances, her attempt to have him removed from office possibly tells us more about the relationship between the Estate and the Courts, as she perceived it, than about John Mackenzie's qualities as Sheriff Substitute at Stornoway.

Not content with trying to get John Mackenzie out, she attempted to get her own nominee in: James Adam, her Factor in Lewis.

Presumably he would have ceased to be Factor, if he were appointed Sheriff, but clearly his appointment, as her protege, would not have made for even-handed justice between proprietor and tenant.

Whether because of advancing years, or awareness of Mrs Stewart Mackenzie's machinations, John Mackenzie sought to divest himself of the office of Sheriff Substitute in favour of his nephew, Murdo Robertson.

Murdo's qualifications for the post were rudimentary. He had worked for a couple of years with a writer in Aberdeen, and later held a temporary clerkship in a law office in Edinburgh.

His strongest card was the influence he could bring to bear. In addition to being a nephew (by marriage) of the Sheriff Substitute, he was a full nephew of Lewis MacIver, the most influential merchant and tacksman in Lewis at the time, and a son of James Robertson, Collector of Customs, who was a key figure in the island community for many years.

Mrs Stewart Mackenzie retorted, in a letter to the Lord Justice Clerk, that the young man's "notions of law and justice" were not very clearly defined and that his connections with the principal tacksmen in the island were much too close.

"The Island of Lewis is perhaps the only part of Great Britain now actually groaning under the oppressive system of middlemen," she told the Lord Justice Clerk, intimating the intention of her husband and herself to reside in Lewis for a number of years to deal with the situation.

They did reside in Lewis for a time, and tried to raise finance for the development of the island by the issue of their own currency: Twenty Shilling Notes, payable on demand at the counting house in Stornaway, (sic), and signed by J. A. Stewart Mackenzie. This expedient was probably made necessary by the fact that both the Seaforth and the Glasserton Estates were heavily burdened with debt.

The Mackenzies did bring "the oppressive system of middlemen" to an end, and, long after she had sold the island, "Lady Hood Mackenzie" was revered in Lewis for it.

The reform, however, was only partially successful. The middle-men remained as farmers, now competing with their old sub-tenants for a very limited acreage of arable land. More importantly, Stewart Mackenzie and his wife left Lewis, when he became, successively, a Member of Parliament, a Junior Minister, Governor of Ceylon and High Commissioner in the Ionian Islands, with the result that Lewis passed into the control of trustees.

The old tacksmen, with all their faults, had been modest entrepreneurs, providing a little work and leadership in their communities, but trustees, by definition, were dedicated to maintaining the *status quo*, avoiding all risk and squeezing as much rent as possible out of crofters and farmers alike. No worse fate could befall a Highland estate, crying out for commercial development, than to come under the dead hand of legal Trustees in Edinburgh.

Although Mrs Stewart Mackenzie did succeed in getting rid of the tacksmen, with rather different results from those she intended, she failed in her attempt to get rid of Sheriff John Mackenzie. The authorities appear to have been unwilling to dismiss him — presumably they had no grounds, in spite of the lady's complaints — and he abandoned his intention to resign when he realised he had no hope of establishing a family dynasty.

While the battle over his personal position was still in progress, the Sheriff was called on to deal with an unusual application to the Court, which casts its own light on the bizarre manner in which justice was administered, in the Western Isles, in the early years of the nineteenth century.

While the mutineers of the *Jane* were awaiting trial in Edinburgh, Donald Macleod, a mason from Bayhead, was in the tolbooth of Stornoway, awaiting trial on charges of malicious mischief and theft. Because of the cumbersome "colonial" system of administration, it took the Sheriff Court in Stornoway a good deal longer to deal with these petty offences than it took the High Court in Edinburgh to try the mutineers and send two men to the gallows.

Macleod had set a boat adrift and stolen some bedclothes from it. He admitted the charge, when interrogated on the 13th of August, but was told he would be detained in the tolbooth until April of the following year before being tried and sentenced.

In desperation he got a friend — Hugh Brown? — to address a petition to the Sheriff-substitute, drawing attention to the deplorable conditions in which he was kept. He asked the Sheriff "to banish him from the county for such a number of years and under such a penalty as your Lordship may see proper to inflict and grant him his liberty for banishing himself."

The Sheriff acceded to this peculiar request, and banished the mason for seven years!

A few years earlier, in 1818, another prisoner, weary of the law's delays, achieved his release in an even more unusual manner.

Alexander Macdonald, a sub tenant at Begnigary, admitted stealing a quantity of "oat and bear" seed from a neighbour's barn, because of want and necessity. He was languishing in jail, awaiting trial and a sentence, which would probably have involved a public whipping and a long banishment from the island.

At last he petitioned the Sheriff, expressing the hope "that your Lordship will consider that he has already been sufficiently punished for his crime by being confined so long in this jail, and, as he is given to understand that there is no Common Executioner at present in the Town of Stornoway, he is willing to accept this office for his liberation, and on condition that a reasonable provision will be made to maintain himself and family."

The Sheriff granted the petition, and found the prisoner entitled to the "fees, perquisites and emoluments" of the office, provided he would "consider himself bound to perform" the duties, "whenever he is called upon to do so."

The post of Common Executioner must have been extremely unpopular in Stornoway to make such a bargain acceptable to the Court. A bargain, incidentally, which anticipated *The Mikado* by nearly a century.

These unusual arrangements were made while Sheriff Mackenzie was on the bench and Hugh Brown was the Procurator Fiscal. They suggest that the wheels of a creaky system were being oiled by a little common sense and local knowledge, but the partnership came to an end in 1833.

In that year Donald Macleod of Geanies was gently — perhaps not so gently! — eased out of the office of Sheriff of Ross & Cromarty which he had occupied for nearly half a century.

Although he had been an advocate for a short time in Edinburgh, Macleod was more of a country gentleman than a lawyer. It was said of him, around the time of his retiral, that he was respected for everything "except his knowledge of the law." He was in ill health and quite incapable of performing the duties of his office.

Quite apart from that, the Lord Advocate was anxious to get rid of him, because the legal system in Scotland was once more being improved and higher standards were now demanded of Sheriffs than Macleod could possibly meet.

It was rather an unseemly and a sad little episode.

Macleod was reluctant to go unless he was assured of a pension equal to his full salary. The Government was reluctant to pay a full pension as well as the salary of the incoming Sheriff. Macleod held his commission for life and wouldn't budge. The new Sheriff — John Jardine — had been chosen and was impatient to get his hands on the salary, but his appointment could not be announced while Macleod was still in post.

While Jardine fretted in the wings, there was considerable jockeying by others to get the preferment for friends or clients of their own. It was suggested, for instance, that Jardine's horsemanship was unequal to the rigours of the post: he was too old and fat to go riding round the Highland countryside. The Lord Advocate thought otherwise, and stuck by his nominee. Pressure was applied to the dying man, through his family, and eventually he resigned.

Sheriff Mackenzie's commission lapsed with Donald Macleod's resignation but John Jardine re-appointed him, which suggests that he was still acceptable to the authorities in Edinburgh, despite the attempt by the Seaforths to unseat him.

The same, however, was not true of Hugh Brown. At his first Court after his own re-appointment, Mackenzie installed Andrew Mercer as Procurator Fiscal.

The Records give no indication what happened to Brown. Presumably he did not have the qualifications now demanded of Fiscals in Scotland, and had to go, irrespective of the fact that he had filled the post very adequately for many years.

The standard of professionalism in the Scottish Courts was being raised in national terms, but, as so often happens, what worked at the centre caused problems at the periphery.

The appointment of Andrew Mercer to be Procurator Fiscal at Stornoway was not a success.

A few months after his appointment, he quarrelled with Dr Macaulay, whom we have already met and will meet again. Mercer sued Macaulay for defamation and damages.

In view of Dr Macaulay's reputation, the presumption is that

Mercer was in the right, but he made the mistake of pursuing his private quarrel in his official capacity as Procurator Fiscal.

The Sheriff rebuked him for the confusion of roles, and, in the following year, the egregious Drummond was appointed in his place, although Mercer still continued to appear for a time as a solicitor.

It would be difficult to argue, from the evidence we have, that the replacement of Hugh Brown, by either Mercer or Drummond, was in the public interest, even if they were better qualified on paper, and, when Drummond died, the situation deteriorated still further with the appointment of Thomas Knox, to be both Chamberlain and Fiscal.

It became completely ridiculous when Knox was absent from Lewis for a period and Brown was temporarily recalled as his replacement.

Knox was less experienced in the Courts than Brown and utterly unsuitable for the office, having regard to the other major appointment he held. Maintaining the quality of justice was clearly not the basis on which appointments were made.

The long reign of Sheriff John Mackenzie came to an end in July 1841, when he resigned because of old age. The family association with Lewis was, however, renewed a few years later when his son, John Munro Mackenzie, became Chamberlain, and an Honorary Sheriff Substitute.

It was renewed again, more than a century later, when the Sheriff's great great grandson — J. H. M. Mackenzie became owner of the largest firm in the Harris Tweed industry, and proprietor of the little estate of Scaliscro in the west of Lewis.

The family still cherish the Sheriff's beautiful embroidered Georgian waistcoat, a work of art which suggests that he must have been, in his younger days at least, something of a dandy.

Four months after Sheriff Mackenzie was succeeded on the bench by James Robertson SSC, administration of the law in the Island of Lewis entered an entirely new phase.

On 5th November, 1841, Donald Munro "sometime writer in Tain, but later residing in Edinburgh," was admitted to practice in the Stornoway Court and "having taken the oaths to government and *de fideli administratione officio*," was appointed Procurator Fiscal.

Hitherto the deficiencies in the legal system in Lewis had been largely negative, arising from the shortage of qualified solicitors, which left accused people, and respondents in civil cases, without representation, and had sometimes led, for short periods, to the amalgamation of the incompatible offices of Fiscal and Factor.

Donald Munro.
(Courtesy of Sheriff C. Scott Mackenzie.)

Now a key position in the legal system, and in the life of the island, was occupied by an ambitious and arrogant man who systematically set about accumulating power and flaunting it in the faces of the people whose lives he dominated.

When he arrived in Lewis, Donald Munro was Procurator Fiscal, estate solicitor for the Seaforths, a Notary Public and the only legal agent in the island.

Ten years later, on 21st February, 1851, he was joined by his cousin, William Ross, and thereafter conducted his private practice as Munro and Ross.

In admitting William Ross, Sheriff George Deas added a cautionary note to his interlocutor: "as the applicant has only been examined by the single Procurator practising before the Court at Stornoway, the Sheriff thinks it the safer and better course to admit the applicant in the meantime as a practitioner in that district only, leaving him to apply of new if he shall afterwards desire to practice elsewhere in the Sheriffdom."

Clearly Sheriff Deas, only recently arrived in the island, had some reservations about the situation which confronted him. He also, apparently, subscribed to the view not uncommonly held by central government over the centuries that what might not be good enough for other parts of Scotland would serve quite well in the off-shore islands.

Shortly after his arrival, William Ross was appointed Deputy Fiscal to his cousin, then Joint Fiscal with him, and when, in 1874, Donald Munro was belatedly stripped of his commission because of a scandalous abuse of power, which had come to public notice, he became sole Fiscal, while remaining a partner of his discredited cousin in their private business.

The arrival of William Ross in Stornoway suggests that the business of the island had grown to the stage at which it would support two solicitors. If a rival to Donald Munro had set up his plate, many of the island's later problems might have been averted. Unfortunately, the arrival of his cousin as a partner merely served to increase his stranglehold on the life of the community.

Four years after William Ross arrived in Lewis, Donald Munro was appointed Chamberlain, or Factor, by Sir James Matheson, without relinquishing his private legal practice, his Fiscalship or any of the nearly thirty appointments I have already listed.

William Ross did not acquire quite so many offices as his older cousin and senior partner, but he did add quite considerably to the power of the mafia.

He was Secretary and Treasurer to the Harbour Trust of which Donald Munro was virtually chairman, being vice to Sir James Matheson, who was seldom present and whose doer he was. Ross was also Clerk and Treasurer to the four School Boards over which Donald Munro presided and for a time Inspector of Poor, for the parish of Stornoway.

His son John, served an apprenticeship with Munro and Ross, and, after a period in Edinburgh, became joint Procurator Fiscal with him.

The Sheriff Clerk Depute was also John Ross by name, and a native of Tain, but he was not a relative, was a highly respected member of the community, and was generally referred to as "Little Ross" to distinguish him from the others.

John Rose, a nephew of Donald Munro, was a clerk in the Chamberlain's Office and Ground Officer for the Parish of Stornoway, which gave him a detailed knowledge of what was happening in the townships and considerable executive authority over crofting affairs.

Another employee in the Chamberlain's Office — although not, I think, a relative of Munro — collected the Poor Rates for the island, and still another was agent for the Royal Mail Steamer *Ondine* plying between Stornoway and Ullapool daily in summer and thrice a week in winter.

Another cousin of Donald Munro, William Ross Skinner, was an S.S.C. in Edinburgh. When the Chamberlain's operations became too complicated to handle at the local level, Skinner acted in the higher courts. He was not, however, the Edinburgh agent for the Matheson estates. He only acted in Donald Munro's personal ploys.

In a small community some degree of pluralism is bound to occur in the filling of public offices which are necessarily part-time, but the concentration of power within the Chamberlain's Office in Lewis was unique in Scotland, as was the control exercised by the Chamberlain and his relatives over the judicial process, both civil and criminal.

A strong Sheriff Substitute could have mitigated the grosser evils, but the available evidence suggests that, for a long period after the retirement of John Mackenzie, that essential restraint on arbitrary power was lacking.

Such was the situation in the early 1870's when, after thirty years residence in Lewis, Munro's power was at its peak. It was built up steadily from his arrival in the island, as he gathered offices of trust and authority into his own hands, or the hands of his relatives and employees. It altered dramatically after his fall. The relationship between the members of the family, and the relations of each with the public were also altered by the rise and fall of the Chamberlain.

We are examining not a situation but a process. A process in which Donald Munro and his little mafia acted as if they were prime movers, disposing of others like pawns on the board, but in which they were themselves the pawns on a larger board, on which the people of Lewis conducted a notable struggle against a well-intentioned but misguided and despotic landlord, and a remote, uncaring, and often ill-informed, government.

Donald Munro made his first public impact on Lewis very shortly after his arrival, in an incident which shows some aspects of his character, but has wider significance, because it illustrates an historical change in the hierarchy of power within the island.

4. BETTER THAN THE BAYONET

Donald Munro arrived in Lewis in November 1841. A few months later he was involved in his first conflict with the crofters, or, at least, with the crofters' wives.

On June 15th, 1842, the *Inverness Courier* reported that "Another of these painful scenes, which lately have been too prevalent, connected with the removal of Highland cottars, took place at the farm of Loch Shell, parish of Lochs in the county of Ross.

"The farm has been taken by an extensive sheep farmer from the south and, with the view of carrying out rural improvements, the occupiers of the soil were summoned to remove.

"The Sheriff, Procurator Fiscal and Factor with a party of ground officers, constables and others proceeded to the spot and commenced throwing down the huts.

"A number of women then rushed upon the party and drove them off the field without committing any bodily injury except a little rough handling to one of the officers."

The Sheriff, R. S. Taylor, seems to have been impressed by the vehemence of the resistance. Instead of using the force at his disposal, he parleyed with the women. Surprisingly they complained more about the reason given for their removal, than the removal itself.

Their men, they said, had been accused of stealing sheep from a neighbouring farm, but no instance of sheep stealing had ever been proved against them. They resented being driven from their homes as thieves!

The accusation rankled long after the Loch Shell villages had disappeared in the process of so-called rural improvement.

Forty years later, the Parish Doctor, Roderick Ross, whose grandson, Iain Macleod, was Chancellor of the Exchequer in Edward Heath's government, told the Napier Commission there was no serious crime in the district. "We have a policeman among us," he added. "The Commissioners, especially the Lord Lieutenant, should be informed how he was appointed and how he gets on since his appointment.

"A mainland farmer took a lease of a farm here, once upon a time. I suppose some wag got him to believe that it would not be safe for him to trust himself or his sheep at Lochs without the protection of the gentleman in blue. So he took a novel and highly ingenious method of getting one appointed. He got all the old stories he could collect about the plundering days of the good old Rob Roy times, when 'each one took who could', and made out clearly to his own satisfaction and, a greater pity, to that of the County Commissioners, that Lewis was a dreadful place, and that Lochs especially was unsafe. So he got his policeman, but he has not got his thieves. For all the officer gets to do here he might be far more beneficially employed for society taking observations on the top of Ben Nevis."

Whether Sheriff Taylor was impressed by the women's protestation that their men were guiltless of sheep-stealing, or whether he began to suspect — as was the case —that he was on the wrong side of the law himself, he withdrew his little army and consulted the Lord Advocate, who despatched Sheriff Principal Jardine to Lewis to investigate.

As a result of the Sheriff Principal's intervention, the proposed evictions were postponed for a year. The crofters gave an undertaking to go voluntarily at Whitsunday 1843, and no punitive action was taken against them for their resistance.

The failure to prosecute in what was, by the standards of the day, a very serious case of deforcement is, on the face of it, surprising. The explanation would seem to be that Donald Munro had involved his superiors in a very questionable, if not illegal, act.

Munro cannot be held solely, or even primarily, responsible for the evictions. As local solicitor for the Seaforths in Lewis he was a relatively minor figure in the chain of command.

The proprietors were abroad. J.A. Stewart Mackenzie, M.P., grandson of the Earl of Galloway, who had married the Seaforth heiress, Lady Hood, was British High Commissioner in the Ionian Islands. The decision to clear the area was taken by the Seaforth Trustees in Edinburgh. Munro's contribution was an element of gratuitous arrogance, which was his hallmark.

As local solicitor for the estate, he applied to the Sheriff Court, and obtained, summary ejection orders against 36 heads of families in the villages of Lemreway, Eishken and Orinsay. As Procurator Fiscal, he organised the expedition to implement the ejection orders by force.

As the solicitor concerned, he was well aware that the decrees he obtained became effective only "at the separation of the crop from the ground," which, in Lewis, would have been October, yet, as Procurator Fiscal, he gave the protection of the Crown to the attempted destruction of the crofters' houses on the 2nd of June, more than four months before the Court orders became effective.

The participation of the Sheriff in this unlawful act is surprising.

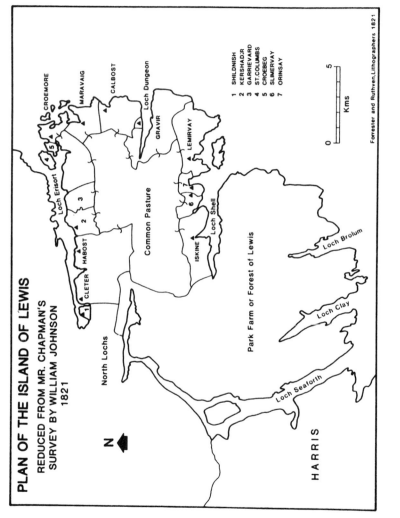

PLAN OF THE ISLAND OF LEWIS

REDUCED FROM MR. CHAPMAN'S
SURVEY BY WILLIAM JOHNSON
1821

N

HARRIS

Loch Seaforth

Loch Clay

Loch Brolum

Park Farm or Forest of Lewis

North Lochs

Common Pasture

Loch Shell

ISKINE

LEMIRVAY

GRAVIR

Loch Dungeon

CALBOST

MARAVAIG

CROEMORE

Loch Erisort

CLETER

HABOST

1
2
3
6

4
5

1 SHILDNISH
2 KERSHAD:R
3 GARRIEVARD
4 ST.COLUMBS
5 CROEBEG
6 SLIMERVAY
7 ORINSAY

Kms

0   5

Forrester and Ruthven,Lithographers. 1821

This plan of part of the Island of Lewis in 1821 shows the old settlements along the shores of Loch Shell from which the tenants were evicted shortly after Donald Munro's arrival in Lewis, precipitating the first clash between him and the crofters. (Original map courtesy of the National Library of Scotland.) (Re-drawn map courtesy of Professor Caird.)

38

The explanation probably lies in the fact that Robert Sutherland Taylor had just taken up duty as Sheriff-substitute in Stornoway and may well have accepted the guidance of the Procurator Fiscal, without considering it necessary to look back through the Court records to check the actual terms of his predecessor's decree.

It is an error the Sheriff would not have fallen into if there had been an independent solicitor in Lewis to represent the crofters against the harassment of the estate and its agents, or if the office of Procurator Fiscal had been separate from that of legal adviser to the estate.

The important point is not that Donald Munro was by nature a tyrant, (which he undoubtedly was) but that the legal system, as it operated in the Western Isles for a large part of last century, gave him the opportunity to be a tyrant.

The evictions aroused great resentment among all classes in the community. There was no legal agent to whom the crofters could turn for advice, but the leading businessman in the island, Lewis MacIver of Gress, shipowner, merchant and tacksman, took up their cause. Munro drove a hard bargain with him.

The agreement between them, signed on 28th June, just after Sheriff Jardine's visit, obliged the tenants to remove by the 1st of May 1843. They had to pay the rent up to that date, although it was necessary for them to dispose of their stock in the preceding autumn when they were still saleable, and they were prohibited from sub-letting the grazings to anyone else when the grass began to grow again in spring.

MacIver, as their representative, had to make himself personally responsible for every penny of rent, if they defaulted, and, in addition, to pay a penalty of £50, if the conditions imposed on the crofters were not fulfilled "in all respects."

The crofters had to go without any fresh ejection order from the Court but, as an extra safeguard, MacIver had to sign an undertaking that the warrants of ejection already obtained were still in force "for all lawful purposes."

While MacIver was held bound by his signature to pay the rental of £70, and perhaps a penalty of £50, Munro was committed to nothing, unless the agreement MacIver had signed was approved by the Seaforth Trustees and Walter Scott, the incoming farmer. If, at that stage, either the Trustees or the farmer demanded an even more formal agreement, MacIver was bound, in advance, to sign it.

Two days later Walter Scott, the incoming sheep farmer from the

Borders, signed the agreement and a note in Munro's hand records that the Seaforth Trustees had also approved the terms, but there is no signature binding the Trustees to anything.

That was by no means the end of the matter.

In March of the following year MacIver, wrote, in reply to a letter from Munro which does not seem to have survived, that he was prepared to sign "the deed of professed agreement," which Munro had sent him, provided there was "a slight alleviation of the conditions."

It is not clear from the surviving papers how the terms of the agreement came to be renegotiated, but MacIver must have been able to exert some influence with the Seaforth Trustees, because the crofters were now permitted to sow a crop in 1843, and retrieve it at harvest time, although they were still obliged to quit their homes in early summer. The particular point at issue was the circumstances in which they could return for the harvest.

Although the tenants, with their families, stock and personal possessions, had to leave by 1st June 1843, one person in each family — nominated by the Factor! — was allowed to remain to protect and weed the growing crop.

These watchmen, however, were not permitted to live in the abandoned family houses: the agreement makes it clear they were obliged to live in the barns. The houses, presumably, were to be destroyed as soon as they were vacated.

The rest of the family were permitted to return to cut the corn and lift the potatoes, but only "as fixed by the Chamberlain."

It was against this last provision Maciver protested most vehemently. There must be some flexibility, he argued. The evicted tenants could only remove the crops "when the weather will permit of them going, with their small boats, for loads of top weight."

What a picture that conjures up!

Thirty six families trying to secure the harvest, within strict time limits, in the uncertain Hebridean weather, and moving large quantities of barley and oats, in the sheaf, in open boats, at the time of the equinoctial gales, on a date arbitrarily decreed by the Factor, without regard to wind or weather.

More than a hundred years after Donald Munro tried to impose these intolerable conditions on the crofters of the Loch Shell villages, I heard a fisherman from Orinsay, which was re-settled after the First World War, tell a Fatal Accident Inquiry in Stornoway. "We were taught by our fathers, when we were very young, to be careful in Loch Shell with the W.S.W wind, because it was bad with round black squalls."

The squalls which drowned six heads of households, out of a village of fourteen families, within a month, in 1945, were blowing just as surely in 1843.

Moreover, the men who lost their lives in 1945 were at sea voluntarily, having made their own assessment of the prevailing conditions and still got it wrong, while the crofters of 1843 were told they would have to put to sea, whatever the conditions, on a day determined in advance by an official sitting comfortably in an office in Stornoway, many miles away.

Long before the date for the removal of the crops came round, Munro began to tighten the screw still further.

As in most of the Lewis removals under the Seaforths, the dispossessed were not being thrown entirely on the world. They were offered holdings in other villages, where they could begin again from scratch, building houses and barns, and breaking in the virgin moorland to create new crofts, from which they could be once again evicted, if they offended the landlord or his factor, or it seemed likely that an incoming tenant would offer a higher rent for the fertile strips they had created.

In some ways this system of transplantation — although immorally exploitative —was less inhuman than the complete clearances which took place in other places, but it gives a special quality of bitterness to the folk memory which informs the people of Lewis of these bygone events.

People who are scattered to the four winds may carry their resentment with them but, in the course of a few generations, it is gradually dissipated: perhaps even romanticised.

In Lewis, however, the evicted generally remained in the island, in compact communities, where individual memories reinforced each other round the ceilidh fire, and where, to the resentment of those evicted, was added the almost equal resentment of those whose holdings were diminished to accommodate them, in the villages on which they were imposed.

While Donald Munro was beforehand with preparations for the evictions, to the extent that he tried to carry them out nearly six months before the legal date, he was correspondingly dilatory in making arrangements for the accommodation of the dispossessed.

On the 29th of May — just three days before they were due to leave their homes — the tenants came to Stornoway in a body to find out where they were supposed to be removing to. No one had bothered to tell them.

Even when they came to Stornoway they didn't get an answer.

Munro was unable, or unwilling, to move without instructions from the Chamberlain, and he was in Edinburgh consulting the Trustees. The crofters had to hang around the town for three days until he returned and assigned the majority of them crofts elsewhere in the parish of Lochs.

Two of the evicted crofters — Donald Maclennan and Malcolm Macleod — were not given crofts even then.

There is no indication why the estate singled them out for harsher treatment. Their families are described as being "weak and numerous" which would seem to be an argument for greater clemency. On the other hand, it might have suggested to the Estate officials that they were likely to be bad payers.

In any event, Maclennan and Macleod took the only course open to them: they went back to Loch Shell and occupied what was left of the homes they had been evicted from.

Within a week Donald Munro raised a fresh action in the Court for their eviction. At the same time he demanded from Lewis MacIver the penalty of £50.

MacIver was not at home to deal with this challenge: he had gone to England on business. He was represented in Court by his son James, whose subsequent history would suggest that he lacked his father's business ability. In this case, however, he represented his father as effectively as if he had been a trained lawyer. His answers to Munro's petition read like the work of a professional. My guess is that they were the work of a professional.

We know from the reminiscences of James's brother, Evander, — *Memoirs of a Highland Gentleman* — that, around that time, the retired Sheriff, John Mackenzie, who was their granduncle, drew up their father's will. It is not improbable that James, faced with a difficult legal problem in his father's absence, sought help from the same source and got it. Apart from the family interest, Mackenzie, as I have suggested earlier, seems to have been a much needed moderating influence in Stornoway Sheriff Court throughout his long tenure of office.

In his answers to Munro's petition, James MacIver argued vigorously that the two offending crofters had kept their part of the bargain "as far as it was possible for any human being in their distressing circumstances," and that they had as good a claim to be accommodated as the other tenants.

He also argued that the offering of lots, or crofts, to the others had been agreed without the involvement of Lewis MacIver, who was consequently released from the contract, and that Lewis MacIver had conferred a favour on Seaforth's Trustees, by negotiating an agreement with the crofters that they would leave voluntarily, which was more acceptable "than forcing them out by a party of soldiers at the point of the bayonet."

As soon as the new summonses were served on them, Maclennan and Macleod moved out and sought shelter with friends.

Munro thus achieved his main objective — indeed the only rational objective — before the case came before the Court. But he still persisted. He was determined to extract from Lewis MacIver the expenses of a quite unnecessary court case, and the penalty of £50.

He succeeded in so far as the expenses were concerned, but failed to get the £50. Sheriff Taylor, sensibly, took into account the difficulties MacIver and the crofters faced because they had "no ready access to professional legal assistance except at a great distance."

The MacIvers, father and son, were in fact acting as amateur lawyers on behalf of a group of people who had no access to a solicitor; who could not have paid a solicitor even if one had been available; and most of whom could not read, write or speak English, and could no more understand the legal documents which determined their fate than if they had been written in Hindustani.

Rev Robert Finlayson estimated in 1833 that there were only 12 people in the parish of Lochs who could write, and only a few males who could speak broken English.

It is not that they were averse to education: 50% of those between 12 and 24 could read Gaelic, thanks to the activities of the Gaelic Schools Society. This, to the discredit of the Scottish educational system, was a higher percentage than could read Gaelic a hundred years later, after seventy years of compulsory state education.

The destruction of three villages, with four hundred inhabitants, was represented, according to the *Inverness Courier*, "as rural improvement." There was, however, no element of improvement involved, even on the narrowest commercial criterion of profit.

The crofters were not in arrears with their rent. The incoming sheep farmer was not offering more than they were already paying. The new use of the land was purely extractive, leaching away, in the form of wool and mutton, the fertility the crofters had built up through generations of diligent cultivation.

The tenants being removed were not incompetent agriculturalists who had been misusing the soil. Their agricultural activities, in fact, were subordinate to their main source of income as fishermen, and, occasionally, pilots, guiding stricken vessels into the shelter of Loch Shell or the even safer anchorage of Stornoway.

Finlayson, in the "New Statistical Account" says there were boat builders in the parish as well as the more domestic craftsmen like weavers and tailors.

William Matheson, lecturer in Celtic at Edinburgh University, referring to a period seventy years earlier, has pointed out that there is a letter in the Library of Congress referring to a party of Lewis emigrants who arrived in America "in Malcolm McNeill's brig."

Malcolm McNeill was a brother of Donald McNeill of Ardmeanish, who held a tack of the whole of the Parish of Lochs south of Loch Erisort, through the influence of his father-in-law, Colin Mackenzie, who at that time was the Lewis Factor. The brig was built in Loch Odhairn, just north of Loch Shell, and was reputed, in oral tradition, to hold the record for a crossing of the Atlantic from Quebec.

Whether the claim to a record was justified or not, the fact that a vessel could have such a reputation implies a frequent, if not regular, traffic between the fiords of Pairc and the New World, which raises a number of presumptions about the economy of the crofting areas which writers on Highland history have been singularly slow to face up to.

In many ways Lewis MacIver and his son were unlikely champions of the Loch Shell villagers. Lewis MacIver, in particular, had the reputation of being himself an oppressor of the poor.

"Lewis MacIver of Gress seldom needed an excuse for removing his tenants," writes Donald Macdonald in his history of Lewis. "A shrewd business man he showed little consideration for anyone who interfered with his plans."

In that comment Donald Macdonald was drawing on the oral tradition of the area of which he was a native, but he supported the oral tradition with a quotation from papers preserved in the Seaforth Muniments, which show that in 1822 MacIver's tenants in Gress complained to Seaforth of having been dispossessed of their lands twice in as many years and sent to "the edge of the town for no known reason" although they "had paid their rents on the Day."

The Sheriff Court records show that, shortly before he took up the cause of the Loch Shell crofters, Lewis MacIver was pursuing through the courts a Brenish man, Malcolm Macleod, who was emigrating to Canada. MacIver asked that officers of the Court should search the *Lady Hood*, then lying at Stornoway, loading for Quebec, seize Macleod and have him incarcerated, "within the Tolbooth of Dingwall," all for a debt of £1.4.7. Even when the debt is multiplied up to its modern equivalent, it seems a trivial sum for which to prevent a fellow islander from making a new start in life.

Midway in time between the complaint of the tenants in Gress and MacIver's pursuit of the man from Brenish, we find him pleading with the Seaforth Estates for a lease of at least seven years of the village of Back "as I possess it."

"I pay as much rent as the tenants offered for it and not a shilling in arrears," he boasted, claiming further that he was importing "shelly sand" from Bernera to improve the land, and, given a lease, would have "Back as well improved as any tenant's holding in the land."

Clearly he was an energetic improver who was adding to the wealth of the island, but, equally clearly, he was not prepared to let anyone stand in his way.

He made no claim, it should be noted, that he could improve the land above the level ordinary tenants achieved. He merely said that he could equal them. However primitive their methods, the Island crofters were land improvers *par excellence:* converting virgin moorland into arable from which the landlord could profit.

The difference between MacIver's attitude to the crofters in Back and Gress and to the evicted crofters of Loch Shell reflects a difference in his relationship with them.

On his own doorstep in Gress, he was in competition with his crofter neighbours for the very limited arable land on which their economy depended in a way his did not. In Loch Shell, he was in a commercial partnership with the crofters as fishermen, relying on them to supply his requirements as a curer. At that time the fishermen contracted with a curer season by season: it was nearly half a century later before the practice of selling the catch by auction was introduced.

In a small community, anyone wielding as much power as Lewis MacIver did — subject though he was to the even greater power of the proprietor — must have been seen in an ambiguous light by his poorer neighbours. When he was leaning on the crofters, he was an intolerable bully, but, when they were leaning on him, he was a tower of strength. His closest neighbours had the most unfavourable view, but even they must have seen him in a different light at different times, according to the relationship in which they stood to him at any particular moment.

The crofting and the business communities were not opposed to each other: certainly not at all times and in all circumstances. Their interests were interlocked, and both were bound within the conditions and conventions of their day. There was a reciprocity, as well as an antagonism, which is sometimes overlooked when we apply the yardstick of our own experience to a very different situation.

Relationships are always more complex than oral tradition remembers or class theories postulate. However oppressive he might have been in another context, in the affair of Loch Shell Lewis MacIver was a white knight, defending the crofters against the worst excesses of the Estate Solicitor.

Donald Munro did not forget the fact and, when the opportunity appeared to offer for revenge, he tried to take it.

Significantly, Munro the solicitor for the Seaforth Estates, sought his revenge by using the power of Munro the Procurator Fiscal.

Early in the following year, Lewis MacIver had a violent quarrel with the Collector of Customs, Mr Macleay, who accused him publicly of smuggling.

There may have been some truth in the allegation. MacIver was a shipowner with a considerable foreign trade, and the illegal importation of spirits of all kinds, through the Faroe Islands, was rife along the whole west coast of Scotland.

True or false, MacIver resented the imputation and challenged Macleay to a duel.

They were both so angry they set off, without waiting to get seconds or a referee, to a field about three hundred yards west of Goathill Farm House. On the way, they met the tenant of the field, a master tailor named Mackenzie, and pressed him into service to hold their coats while they shot it out.

They both fired and missed.

Cooled by the experience, MacIver did not ask for a second shot, and Macleay, a much younger man, apologised. They went off together to MacIver's town house, at the corner of Kenneth Street and Church Street, where the Police Station stands today. There they drank each other's health, probably in whisky illicitly distilled, or brandy illegally imported.

Stornoway laughed with delight at the little comedy involving two important and rather pompous figures.

Donald Munro saw it rather differently. He obtained statements from the tailor, who is described as a pugnacious little man, and from one or two passers by who heard the shots but did not see the duel. He reported the matter to Crown Office in Edinburgh, asking for authority to prosecute the duellists. Much to his chagrin, Crown Office returned the papers, instructing him to take no further action.

Shortly afterwards, Macleay was quietly moved to a similar post in another seaport.

Lewis MacIver was addicted to quarrelling.

There is a lengthy correspondence in the Seaforth Muniments dealing with a row he had with Sir Thomas Johnstone, who had a sporting let from the Seaforth Estates in 1833.

When MacIver called on Johnstone to see if he could "administer to his comforts," he was brusquely told to come back on Sunday "to make arrangements about the house." MacIver retorted that "we are not in the habit of making any bargains on Sunday in this country." Johnstone called him a humbug. MacIver admits the rebuff "raised my Highland blood" but, unfortunately, the papers do not disclose what he said, although some weeks later, when called to account by Seaforth, he was still ranting about Johnstone's 'folly,' 'vanity' and 'absurd aristocratic notions.'

He is also said to have fought another duel, around the year 1820, on Tong sands. His opponent on that occasion was Stewart, the Lewis Chamberlain, who was later dismissed by the Estate. The quarrel arose when Stewart began to unload a cargo of coal at a pier privately owned by MacIver.

In the heat of the argument, Stewart, a much taller man, took the palm of his hand sharply down on MacIver's head, driving his top hat as far as his chin. MacIver flew at him. Stewart struck him with his malacca cane. Blood flowed and MacIver was led away by the by-standers.

That night he issued his challenge and they met next day on the sands. MacIver fired first and missed. Stewart, reputed to be a deadly shot, blew away MacIver's whiskers from the left side of his face.

The story of the duel with Stewart rests on the oral reminiscences of an old man in the Point district, who claimed to have been an eye-witness, as indeed he may have been, although the picturesque touch about MacIver's whiskers probably owes more to his abilities as a raconteur than the accuracy of his recollection.

The story of the second duel is more firmly based on a newspaper article written by John N. Anderson, a notable Provost of Stornoway, who worked as a young man in Munro's office and had access to the papers.

Anderson suggests that Munro's anxiety to prosecute was sharpened by the fact that, at that period, the Procurator Fiscal was paid by results.

When eventually he was put on a fixed salary of £500 — the same as the Sheriff-substitute — crime in Lewis began to dwindle until it reached the point at which the local prison was closed by the Prison Commissioners and sold to the County Council of Ross & Cromarty for £25, although it had cost over £2000 to build in 1832.

Donald Munro and Lewis MacIver were both domineering and disagreeable men. Like two cockerels on one dunghill. A small town, even a sizeable island, could not hold them both at peace.

There was more to it, however, than a clash of personalities. One belonged to an emerging power group, the other to a power group in decline.

MacIver represented the old class of tacksmen, who had stood between the crofters and the laird, holding considerable areas of land which they let out to sub-tenants, or worked under their own direction with their sub-tenants' labour.

The abolition of the tacksmen removed one layer of oppression from the backs of the people, as Lady Hood Mackenzie intended when she made the change, but, as the story of the Loch Shell eviction shows, there were occasions when a tacksman, in another role, could defend the crofters from the even greater oppression of remote trustees, acting through a harsh Factor, for an absentee proprietor.

The trustees were highly respectable, utterly honest, and efficient within the terms of their remit, but, by the very nature of their office, they were unable to show clemency, or take commercial risks. They contributed absolutely nothing to the real wealth or happiness of the community.

Munro's rise to power, however, did not come about because Lewis was administered by remote trustees while the Seaforth's pursued their political fortunes in London or abroad.

Very shortly after his arrival, Lewis was bought by a benevolent and developing landlord, Sir James Matheson, who was normally resident for much of the year, and sunk a lot of money in providing schools and making roads, and in industrial projects such as a brick works, land reclamation, and a chemical works to make paraffin from peat.

The most innovative of his schemes, the chemical works, might have transformed Lewis had it not been for the discovery of natural oil in USA, just as it was coming on stream. Even although it failed, it provided much needed employment, as did the schemes of public works, especially in the Hungry Forties.

In the famine years, too, Sir James supplied his tenants with meal, averting the calamity which befell the people of Ireland at that time. It was in recognition of this, in fact, that he was made a baronet.

The generosity, however, was qualified in a manner commentators at the time, and many historians since, did not fully realise.

It is in this area we must seek to discover how the servant of a benevolent master could establish a tyranny, which was bitterly resented at the time and is still remembered with hatred and revulsion.

5. HOW THE CROFTERS PAID FOR THE MEAL

The meal distributed to the Lewis crofters during the Hungry Forties was not a gift from Sir James, as many people, both then and now, have assumed.

The meal was sold to the crofters. At cost price, admittedly, and on credit, because they could not pay, but it was added to their already enormous arrears of rent.

In 1851 the Estate began to collect the debt, with far reaching consequences for hundreds of Lewis families.

Donald Munro was not the central figure in the rent collection but he did have a significant role.

Estate policy was dictated by Sir James himself, or, at the very least, with his direct knowledge and approval.

The policy was simple. Get rid of all the bad payers and give the land to those who were not in arrears with their rent.

Those who were sunk in debt were offered assisted passages to Canada. As much as possible of the arrears was recovered from the sale of their stock, if they had any. The rest was written off.

Sir James made all the arrangements for the emigration. He organised vessels and supplies. He met the cost of taking the emigrants from their homes to the Clyde. From the Clyde to the St Lawrence. And from their point of disembarkation to their final destinations in Quebec or Ontario.

He even contributed towards the cost of a Free Church minister to accompany them, so that they would not feel cut off from their spiritual and cultural background.

In neighbouring islands, at the same time, crofters were compelled to emigrate on much less favourable terms and frequently by the use of physical force.

In Lewis the emigration was peaceful. There was no active resistance. No disorder. Neither the police nor the army was involved.

Many of the emigrants afterwards expressed gratitude for their release from an intractable poverty.

The descendants of some of them have been back to Lewis in recent years and have renewed the affection for the island their ancestors expressed in so many soul-searing songs.

Elisabeth Ogilvie, for instance, an American author, with thirty books to her credit. Her great grandmother was a child when the family emigrated from Carnish. The link with Lewis was broken for over a hundred years, but she has been back more than once to trace her island roots and has recorded her "homesickness" in a novel about Lewis.

Despite these facts, the great emigration of 1851 has left a bitter memory which is not yet completely expunged.

Those who weren't forced to go resented the exodus even more than those who were. For them the emigration was only one incident in a process of oppression which lasted, and indeed intensified, for another thirty years.

The implementation of Sir James's policy was in the hands of his Factor, John Munro Mackenzie, a son of the Sheriff who almost drowned in the seal cave at Gress.

Like his father, he seems to have been a fair-minded man, within the terms of his remit, and measured against the conventions of his time. In any event, there was worse to come when he left.

In the month of January he began to broach the subject of emigration with some of the leading men in the community, such as the ministers and the members of the Parochial Boards.

A great many of them agreed that emigraton was desirable. The island population had increased by nearly 16% in the inter-censal period. That represents an annual rate of increase approaching 2%.

The increase did not arise from an influx of able-bodied workers in a Klondyke boom. It was a Malthusian increase, pressing on the means of subsistence which, even to begin with, had been insufficient.

The effect of the rapidly increasing population was intensified by the natural disaster of the potato blight, by the economic pressure of falling prices for kelp and cattle and by the fiscal policy of the government, which restricted the distillation of whisky, and deprived the crofters of a market for their grain.

The only substantial opposition to emigration, among those not directly involved, came from the merchants of Stornoway to whom the crofters were in debt. They believed the landlord had concocted a scheme for the recovery of his own arrears of rent, while leaving them to whistle for their money.

In the course of the year Sir John McNeill, Chairman of the Board of Supervision for Poor Relief in Scotland, visited Lewis. He took the view that emigration on a large scale was imperative. He saw it as the only remedy.

In that he was profoundly mistaken.

Emigration, even on the scale of 1851, had no effect on the Lewis problem.

It was designed to ease the pressure on a limited amount of arable land. To reduce the number of mouths to feed. But the natural increase in the population, in little more than four years, replaced the 800 who left in 1851.

At the end of the decade, in spite of the exodus of 1851 and subsequent years, the island's population had increased from 19,711 to 21,056.

As well as being ineffective, emigration was unnecessary.

A generation later, another government inspector, also a McNeill, put it succinctly.

Some years after the passing of the first Crofters Act, Malcolm McNeill wrote, in an official report to the government:

"In 1851 it was confidently predicted that, unless the surplus population could be induced to remove, some fearful calamity would ensue ... The prediction ... was not verified in the issue.

"The people did not remove, but remained and multiplied with great rapidity. Neither did they starve. On the contrary they, year by year, increased their expenditure in food and clothing by adding luxuries to the former articles of family use."

The explanation was simple. The people of Lewis did not depend on the produce of the land, but the prodcue of the sea. The remedy for the scarcity in 1851 was a vast expansion of the fishing industry.

John Munro Mackenzie was one of the few men in authority who grasped this basic fact. He tried to persuade Sir James Matheson to build the necessary piers and harbours. Sir James refused.

He said, in effect, "let the industry provide the infrastructure."

In the Lewis situation this was impossible. Sir James owned all the harbours and all the land. Nothing could be done without his say-so.

Even if he had encouraged development, the fishermen and curers alike were desperately short of capital.

Mackenzie pointed out to him that he had more to gain than anyone from the development of the fishing industry: the croft rents would rise with rising prosperity. His diary makes it clear that, even without investment by the estate, the rent roll in the fishing villages was already higher than any farmer, dependent on his earnings from agriculture, could possibly pay.

Unfortunately for the people of Lewis, while Sir James was

determined to collect all the rents that were due to him, he was a wealthy man and felt no urge to invest speculatively in the hope of increasing the rent roll still further.

Faced with his master's refusal to develop safe harbours, John Munro Mackenzie got on with his arrangements for collecting as much of the arrears as was possible in the circumstances.

His plan of campaign reflected his knowledge of the true situation.

In villages wholly dependent on the land there was no hope of recovering the arrears. Those in arrears were marked out for emigration.

In villages dependent mainly on the sea, the debts, he believed, were recoverable. There was no pressure to emigrate, but the screw was applied in other ways.

At first he thought he could organise the emigration by persuasion. At that point he consulted Donald Munro. Munro told him to serve notices of removal on all the people he wanted to go.

We can only speculate whether Munro was acting as a canny lawyer, doing his best for his employer, or whether he had in mind the fees that would accrue to his own firm from several hundred evictions processed through the Sheriff Court.

Nor have we any knowledge whether he attempted to collect from the debt-ridden crofters the expenses awarded against them in all these undefended cases.

From that point on Mackenzie seems to have abandoned the attempt to persuade. He went round the villages, day after day, explaining the terms the landlord offered and putting the finger on those who were to go.

Decisions were dictated almost entirely by the state of the rent book. If the head of the house was physically fit, and two years behind with the rent, the whole family was bound for Canada.

The rent book was not altogether a reliable guide, however.

Mackenzie confides to his diary that the arrears were inflated by debts for the meal supplied during the famine and the records were not immaculate.

He was disturbed to find that in one township some crofters disputed the amount of meal supplied while others claimed to have paid for the meal when they got it.

The only evidence of their indebtedness was the say so of the local ground officers,: two illiterate brothers, who could not possibly have kept in their heads the details of so many petty, but complicated, transactions, spread over several years.

There is no indication that the disputed arrears were written off, but, given the financial plight of those compelled to emigrate, it seems unlikely that they were ever collected.

When Mackenzie went round the villages very few crofters volunteered to go, although some did.

Those who were readiest to emigrate were those who had been moved from their original homes by the estate on a previous occasion. This suggests that the pull of friends and community was the dominant element in the crofters' reluctance to leave. Where ties had already been loosened it was easier to make the final break.

Some also appear to have had second thoughts. A few who at first refused to emigrate, later followed the Factor to another village to say they were willing to go.

Whether willing emigrants or not, in June, when the *Marquis of Stafford* arrived in Loch Roag to take the first party to the Clyde, they were there with their pathetic bundles, ready to go.

The Factor claims that, on board ship, some of them thanked him for having resolved their difficulties and given them a new chance in life.

That may well be true.

Thousands of islanders emigrated voluntarily both before that date and since. The greatest barrier to a voluntary exodus in 1851 was the inertia and despair which the years of famine had brought on normally proud and independent people. The greater the need to escape from a quagmire of debt the more difficult it is to break free.

The departure was emotional. The voyage distressing. The very name of the ship was evocative. To Lewis crofters in the 1850's the name *Marquis of Stafford*, must have reeked of the clearances.

Biscuits were distributed to the emigrants as they came aboard. Tinware was distributed — at a price!

Clothes were provided for those who needed them — also at a price.

In the end, the surplus garments were given free to those who were absolutely destitute.

Most of the emigrants, in spite of their poverty, were, "very respectably" dressed when they came on board. No doubt many of them were helped out by relatives and friends. Before the vessel weighed anchor, Rev Mr Campbell preached and prayed, and the sound of a Gaelic psalm rang over Loch Roag. Four hundred devout men and women, placing themselves in the hands of God as they voyaged into the unknown.

How many, I wonder, saw themselves as the Children of Israel fleeing the bondage of Pharaoh facing, perhaps, forty years in the Wilderness?

Their circumstances were very different from the Israelites of old. They were not escaping — they were being driven out. The bondage, however, had been real enough.

The night was stormy. The women and children were miserably sick. When they got to Port of Ness at 3 a.m. the Factor went ashore at once to get away from the stench of vomit. He walked along the beach in the darkness drinking in the clear night air.

The fishermen at Port of Ness refused, at first, to ferry the emigrants from that area out to the ship. It is not clear whether they were opposed to emigration in principle or had been asked to do the job without pay.

Whatever their objection, a peremptory command from the Factor removed it.

The first boat load of emigrants moved out of the shelter of the harbour into the Minch where the *Marquis* was riding uneasily at anchor.

When the "sgoth" got alongside, the Uig emigrants lining the deck refused to let the Ness emigrants clamber on board.

The vessel, they said, was already overcrowded. For good measure they complained there was small-pox in Ness.

Nothing the Factor could do would move them. The old threat, "I'll take the land from you" had lost its potency. The land had already been taken. For the first time in their lives the people of Uig could say "no!" to the Factor. They had nothing left to lose.

Eventually the vessel sailed without the emigrants from Ness.

Before it reached Tolsta, however, the Factor had talked the recalcitrant passengers round. He had found a new threat.

The vessel waiting for them in the Clyde had to have its full complement before it left for Canada. If sufficient numbers did not travel on the *Marquis* the emigrants would be stranded in Troon, at their own expense, until the Nessfolk caught up with them.

That argument prevailed. The emigrants were realists and they were penniless.

Although there was no problem taking a full complement on board at Tolsta there was trouble looming ahead at Stornoway.

The Factor did not want to go alongside the pier. He was afraid that, if any of his emigrants got ashore, they would not come back, especially after that dreadful night rolling up to Ness with the Atlantic on their beam. He was also afraid that some of the Stornoway merchants might try to arrest them for debt.

He told the Captain to anchor in Glumaig Bay, on the far side of the Harbour from the town.

The Captain said he was going alongside the quay. He was picking up his wife and some furniture. It was all right for four hundred emigrants to be ferried out in small boats and hoisted aboard a heaving ship like bolls of meal but that would not do for the Captain's wife.

Mackenzie reasoned with him but he was adamant. In the end, however, he was baulked. There were so many fishing boats in Stornoway Harbour, he couldn't get near the pier. He had to go ashore by small boat: it was the only way.

The result was that four hundred emigrants were kept waiting for five hours in the rain, many of them without shelter, while the Captain was socialising ashore, and attending to his domestic affairs.

As an additional argument for going alongside the pier, the Captain had urged the need to clean the ship of vomit. He could not possibly sail until that was done.

In the five hours spent at Stornoway, however, nothing was done to clean the ship. She left as she came, except in so far as the drenching Hebridean rain had swabbed the decks.

When she was eventually ready to sail, the engineer overheated the engine, and the *Marquis* limped uneasily out of the harbour, as if she were as reluctant to leave as the passengers had been.

Another group of emigrants left a few days later by the weekly boat to Glasgow.

Another larger group sailed from Loch Roag on another vessel hired by Sir James, the *Barlow*, but not without difficulty.

The Captain of the *Barlow* had failed to take with him the contract tickets for the passengers demanded by Customs House rules. The Factor tried to solve the problem by setting his staff to write out tickets by hand.

The bureaucrats of the Customs House stood by the letter of the law. No printed tickets in the style prescribed: no clearance for the ship.

A clerk in the Factor's office — Murdo Morison by name — was despatched to Glasgow by the quickest route he could devise to get tickets printed.

He seems to have made a speedy journey and been rewarded for it. In the following year Sir James helped pay his fare to Australia, then in the frenzy of the gold rush.

He kept a diary of his voyage from Greenock to Melbourne on the *Hamilton Campbell Kidstone*. A miserable vessel. "Lord take me from this filthy den," prayed one of the passengers. He recorded every incident of an eventful voyage, from the antics of a broken-down Glasgow music hall comic named Bailow, to the attempted rape of one of the ladies.

The diary ends abruptly with the passengers stranded in Melbourne Roads. The crew had stolen the lifeboats and gone to the diggings without them.

Morison emigrated to Australia voluntarily, unencumbered by children or elderly relatives and in the relative comfort of the "Intermediate." These bound for Canada left perforce, whole families together, without even the chimera of a gold mine to beckon them on.

Even after young Morison got back from Glasgow with the tickets, the *Barlow* was delayed. She was eight bolls of meal short of the statutory provision for the number of passengers she carried.

Meal was hurriedly obtained from the nearest mill, and at last she sailed with a following breeze.

Having cleared the Estate books of a large slice of rent arrears — on paper at least — by sending eight hundred men, women and children to Canada, the Factor turned his attention to the other half of his remit — squeezing as much rent as he could out of those who remained.

Pressure was put on them in various ways.

The Grounds Officers were instructed to attend the cattle sales and make a careful note of who sold what. The arrears were to be collected as soon as a beast changed hands.

On the Factor's own visits to the townships, rent was collected in cash, or animals taken in lieu. Not surprisingly he found them very reluctant to part with any cow in milk. It was almost the only food they had for their children.

He made a foray into the village of Borve, and rounded up the cattle on the shore, while the people hid in their homes.

Then, suddenly, as he and his assistants approached the road with their booty, men, women and children darted from all directions, driving off a cow here, or a horse there and generally scattering the herd.

In the pandemonium most of the animals escaped. The few that were driven safely to the road had to be released. The Factor had captured them, but no one would tell him who owned which.

Then some of the men came forward and offered to pay their rent. Clearly there was some substance in the Factor's belief that the habit of non-payment, acquired during the famine years, persisted even when people could pay once more.

The Factor's most effective weapon in the struggle to collect his rents was a ban on the cutting of peats.

The fishermen, in particular, were told that if they couldn't pay in ready cash, or give a beast in lieu, they must borrow from a fish curer against the coming season's catch. Until the rent was paid they could not cut peats.

No family could possibly survive a Hebridean winter without a large supply of fuel. The fishermen dug into the family kist for what little reserve they had, or borrowed as the Factor commanded. Even at the end of June they were still trooping into town to clear their debts and get their permits.

It was long past the normal peat-cutting season. With the rainy months of July and August in prospect, there was little chance of getting them properly dried.

There must have been many sulky fires in Lewis in that grim winter.

The emigration of 1851 may seem peripheral to the story of Donald Munro.

He gave some crucial and, I think, misguided advice, to the Factor at the start.

He was present on the *Marquis* when she took the first batch of emigrants on board, although whether he was there as solicitor for the Estate or as Procurator Fiscal is not made clear.

Apart from that he seems to have done little but issue eviction notices, and, presumably, collect the fees. His role was a subordinate one. John Munro Mackenzie was in charge.

The emigration, however, is highly relevant to an assessment of Donald Munro's position in Lewis history.

John Munro Mackenzie's diary for 1851 is the best evidence there is for the all-pervasive and almost absolute power the Factor in Lewis exercised over twenty thousand people in the middle years of last century.

It was much more extensive than the account of the emigration reveals.

Busy though he was organising the exodus, and drumming up the rents, Mackenzie still had time to attend meetings of the Parochial Boards, striking paupers off the roll, in line with the advice given by Sir John McNeill on behalf of the Government.

To pay the salaries of the Established Church Ministers, and the local schoolmasters. Sometimes even to visit the schools and question the pupils.

To harry the farmers, many of whom were even more deeply in arrears than the crofters but were not subjected to a two year deadline under threat of eviction.

To inspect the houses being erected for widows evicted from the old village of Bayhead to make a Home Farm for the Castle.

Even to hold a Baron Bailie Court to hear appeals against the assessments for road money which he himself had fixed!

The record of the diary shows how the power of the Factor pervaded every corner of island life.

In 1854 John Munro Mackenzie left Lewis and Donald Munro became Factor. He acquired all the power Mackenzie had exercised without giving up any of the power he already had as Procurator Fiscal.

John Munro Mackenzie may strike us today as harsh and oppressive. The crofters in his own day thought him so, and complained to the Napier Commission thirty years after he left the island. It was the first time they had ever been free to criticise a factor without fear of reprisals.

However, if we judge John Munro Mackenzie against his contemporaries on other Highland estates, we must come to the conclusion that, by the standards of his day, he was just, and even, at times, compassionate.

He spontaneously reduced the rents of crofts when he thought them excessive. He was clearly troubled by his doubts over the accuracy of the charges levied for meal money. He wanted some paupers kept on the Roll when the majority of the Parochial Board wanted them off.

When he sat in the Baron Bailie Court, hearing appeals against the road fund levy, he granted all but two although the assessments appealed against were his own.

He also tried to establish a human relationship with the crofters. In particular he used to visit Uig to hear the stories of the survivors of the Napoleonic Wars who had come home after years spent campaigning in Egypt, India and Java.

He discovered that they had never received their campaign medals and persuaded the authorities to remedy the omission thirty years after their discharge.

There was a pathetic little ceremony in Uig Glen when the veterans were asked to parade to receive their decorations. By that time most of them were too frail to attend. But, at least, on the Factor's side, the thought was there.

Donald Munro who succeeded him was very different. His power was even greater, and his rule was unrelieved by humour or restraint, or by any interest in his "subjects" as human beings.

To discover the type of man he was, it is necessary to look at my own family's entanglement with him. There we see the man himself, unmotivated by orders from an employer or instuctions from a client: acting purely as the spirit moved him.

The best place to pick up the thread is in Tunis, at a magnificent Masonic function, attended by the Bey and all the leading potentates of the city, which took place some three years after Donald Munro arrived in Lewis.

6. THE STEPHEN CASE

A high proportion of those who sailed in and out of the port of Stornoway in the 19th century were Freemasons.

Between 1801 and 1880 40% of new entrants on the register of Lodge Fortrose No 108 are clearly identifiable as seafaring men: 310 out of a total of 777. Between 1821 and 1840 more than one in two of the 131 new entrants were seafarers.

A few are described as ordinary seamen or ship's carpenters, one as a ship's cook, and towards the end of the period, when sail was giving way to steam, there is a scattering of ship's engineers, and navymen attached to the Royal Naval Reserve Training Base at Stornoway, which was then reputed to be the largest in the country, but the great majority were shipmasters or master mariners: the men on whose activities the trade and prosperity of the town was based.

A surprising number of those entering Freemasonry through the Stornoway Lodge were shipmasters from English, Welsh, Irish and Channel Island ports, Liverpool in particular, but also including, Newcastle, Hartlepool, Sunderland, North and South Shields, Yarmouth, Workington, Belfast, Port Madoc, Londonderry, Colchester, Dartmouth and Bristol.

There were also many foreign shipmasters, from Dantzig, Archangel, Christiansound, St Petersburg, Drontheim, Bergen, Langesund, Copenhagen, Amsterdam, Stavanger, Hamburg, and other smaller or unidentified ports in Norway, Finland, Denmark and Holland.

For those visiting shipmasters, the Masonic Lodge must have offered a quiet haven in a town where there was no other social meeting place, apart from the little quayside inns frequented by their crews, but the fact that they submitted themselves to the process of initiation suggests a stay of some length in the port, and there is evidence that their attachment to the craft of Freemasonry and to Lodge Fortrose in particular rested on a firmer base than temporary membership of a social club.

In 1812 John Knudtson, a Norwegian, who had sailed from Bergen as Captain on a Danish privateer, appealed to the brethren of Lodge Fortrose, of which he was a member, for help in obtaining his parole when he was taken prisoner by the British navy.

He complained that he had to live on "the scanty allowance of two and a half pounds of beef a week and seven salt herrings." "I have not had a farthing of money since I came to this place, and am sorry to say have very little clothes with me so that I am at present in great distress."

The members of the Lodge immediately sent him a modest gift of three guineas.

At the same time they were supporting the wife and family of a Lewis seaman who had fallen victim to the other side in the Napoleonic blockade and was languishing in a Norwegian gaol.

Early in 1834 the young men of Stornoway applied to the brethren, successfully, for the free use of the Masonic Hall, for a "dramatic entertainment," on behalf of the widows and orphans left when the local brig *Mary Ann* was lost with all hands off the Cornish coast, on a voyage from Cape Breton to Limerick.

Lloyd's list reported, on 1st December 1833, that a vessel had been seen, bottom up, between Cape Cornwall and St Ives. "She was driven on the rocks in the night and went to pieces." Her cargo of timber and staves was washed ashore. On the stern of the wreck was painted *"Mary Ann* of Stornaway. M'Kenzie."

She was also identified by letters washed up on the beach, and no doubt forwarded to the addressees with the news that the sons or husbands who had written them were dead.

The widows assisted by the brethren on this occasion included my great grandmother, Annabella Morison, whose husband, Roderick Morison, had been mate of the *Mary Ann*. She had a daughter and two sons all under the age of seven. A third son was born posthumously, a few months after the disaster. When her sons had grown to manhood, she became one of the principal victims of the legal mafia, whose activities I am investigating.

In addition to the element of informal insurance cover for their families which membership of Lodge Fortrose afforded to local seafaring men it seems probable that they also valued the social contacts opened up to them in foreign ports.

The records of Lodge Fortrose provide ample evidence of the importance of this to foreign seamen visiting Stornoway. Evidence for the reciprocal benefit enjoyed by Stornoway shipmasters, when they went abroad, is more difficult to obtain. In so far as it exists, it is diffused through the records of a hundred lodges, in a score of countries, using a variety of tongues. It did, however, survive in the oral tradition of the port.

One story handed down concerns John Mackenzie — *Iain Mac Iain Mhic Ruaraidh Mhòir* — one of the leading Stornoway shipmasters of his day. It was told me by my uncle, Rev Roderick Morison, who died in 1960 in his hundredth year. As a lad he knew Capt. Mackenzie well and heard the story from him many times.

Captain John has been described by R. M. Stephen, his wife's grand-nephew, and author of a book about Stornoway (*Glimpses of Portrona*) as "a man of antique mould" whose "ideas of civil and ecclesiastical government smacked of the quarter-deck."

On a Sunday afternoon he could be seen in "a frockcoat of fine broadcloth, with a red pocket-handkerchief hanging out of its tail, and an old fashioned collar, with an ample swathing of fine silk stock," marching to the Established Church, with a firm step and head held "stiff as in a socket," while all his relatives and acquaintances made their way in droves to the more popular Free.

He was "a careful and methodical man ... He had acquired what passed among us for a modest fortune; but he often feared that it might not serve him until he got his final discharge. He victualled his house for the winter as he would his ship when putting forth on a voyage ... His young friends, on their occasional visits home, were frequently disconcerted with awkward questions as to the price of beef and potatoes in the great cities. But his conversation was chiefly of the past. He dated events by his voyages; this happened when he was in Marseilles with the *Scottish Thistle*, that when he made his first visit to Bahia with the *Eliza Jermyn* and he could date some incident because he heard of it when lying at Leghorn in the *Pearl*."

These ship's names are fictitious — Stephen wrote about his grand-uncle under the alias of "Captain James" — but the likeness was so complete that no one in Stornoway had any doubt about his identity, and the ship I am concerned with, the *Freeland*, a large Stornoway-owned brig, was real enough.

In 1844 Captain John sailed from Liverpool in the *Freeland*. His mate was George Stephen, a young man from Boddam, who had many reasons to remember an eventful voyage.

Running short of water on the way to Naples, the *Freeland* put into Tunis. Captain John, for many years a member of Lodge Fortrose, went ashore to a glittering Masonic function attended by all the notables of the city, including the Bey.

A few days later the *Freeland* sailed. It was becalmed some distance off the port. By that time the Barbary pirates had nominally been suppressed, but, while official state piracy was at an end, it was still a dangerous coast. As the *Freeland* lay there helplessly waiting for a breeze, a corsair slipped "out of the throat of Tunis" — my uncle's words, and therefore, probably, the Captain's own. The pirates swarmed on board. The crew thought they were doomed to "walk the plank," until Captain John recognised the leader as a brother mason, who had been present at the function patronised by the Bey. Both ship and cargo were spared.

When Captain John returned to Stornoway he took his young mate home with him. George Stephen fell violently in love with his Captain's niece, my grand-aunt Catherine Morison. Two years later, on 1st December 1846, they were married. At the ceremony the impetuous young groom thrust his hand into the bride's declaring, "There's my hand, Kate, and you have my heart along with it."

My uncle has described George Stephen as "slightly built, exceedingly wiry and full of spirit. His hair and beard were jet black and through two piercing, laughing eyes there looked out at you a shrewd, practical man with a keen sense of humour and a kindly affectionate nature."

Catherine, his wife, was "a tall handsome woman, of a quiet and gentle disposition, with a shrewd and intelligent mind, and somewhat reserved manner ... It felt like a benediction to be in her presence, recognised as a relative and addressed in kind and affectionate words."

They had need of these qualities.

They knew when they married that their family life would be subject to the long absences, the fears and uncertainties, inevitable in the life of a sailor before the days of phone or even telegraph: they had experienced that in their courtship and survived. They did not know, although they soon discovered, that greater dangers threatened in their own home port, not from pirates, or the elements, but from the malice of the two officials appointed by the state to protect the peace and safety of the inhabitants.

Soon after their marriage, the young bride and groom — he was 23, she was only 20 — placed themselves in jeopardy by a simple, kindly, innocent act of family loyalty.

In January 1855, when George Stephen was in Australia, his wife learned that her uncle, Colin Morison, was in financial difficulties. Like many businessmen of his time in Stornoway, Colin earned his livelihood by combining a number of somewhat incompatible enterprises: he was simultaneously a fishcurer and a publican.

As a fishcurer he had to tie his capital up for relatively long periods at considerable risk; as a publican he could only profit by turning his

A & G. TAYLOR, *1925* 129 FENCHURCH STREET,
PHOTOGRAPHERS, LONDON. E.C.

George Stephen, the shipmaster from Boddam, whose wife, Catherine Morison, was taken to court in
a cart when heavily pregnant, and whose twin daughters died as a result of
their mother's treatment by Munro and Ross.

capital over quickly. It is probably his fishcuring business which caused him embarrassment but it was his wine merchant in Glasgow who pressed for payment.

Whether Colin approached his niece for help or she volunteered it, is not clear, but she gave him £11 to stave off his creditors. It was probably the repayment of many kindnesses which her mother had from her brother-in-law when she was left destitute with four children, after the wreck of the *Mary Ann.*

When George Stephen arrived home, a few months later, he endorsed his wife's decision and cheerfully gave Colin a second loan of £30, as his difficulties were still continuing.

Apart from Colin, the family were in fairly easy circumstances at the time.

George Stephen had gone to Australia as mate on the *Rival* commanded by another Boddam man, Captain Cordiner. Something must have happened between the two in the course of the voyage: when they got to their destination, George Stephen left the ship. My uncle mentions the incident in a short biography of George Stephen's son, Roderick, the author of *Glimpses of Portrona,* but does not give any details beyond the comment that the circumstances were "entirely honourable."

Australia was in the grip of the gold rush, and George Stephen went to the diggings. He did not prosper, and his health was undermined, but, fortunately — or, perhaps, as it turned out: unfortunately! — for the family, he was not the only member in Australia at the time.

In December 1854, when he was preparing to return home, he met his wife's brother, Angus, in Melbourne. Angus handed him £200, a very considerable sum of money at that time: expressed in terms of house values in Stornoway it was equivalent to well over £20,000 today.

Nine years later, when the transaction in Melbourne came under the scrutiny of the Court of Session, George Stephen stated in evidence that Angus had given him the money "to take home with me and to lodge in a bank for safe keeping, either in my own name, or in that of his mother, Mrs Annabella Morison, but that he would prefer it to be in my name so that, if I saw any remunerating employment for the money, I could draw it and use it for his benefit."

The £200 was used to buy a large double house on the seafront of Stornoway, Number 1 Newton, with a garden behind and a large area beyond which was used for many years as a fishcuring station. The house was demolished a few years ago but I spent many happy hours in it as a child, without any knowledge then of the troubled history which I later unravelled.

For a time the house was recorded in the Register of Sasines in George Stephen's name but, shortly afterwards, it was transferred to Annabella Morison's. It was, in fact, as distinct from legal fiction, the joint home of Annabella Morison, her daughter and son-in-law and was open to any other member of the family who had need of it. When I knew it, the house was occupied by George Stephen's daughter, Mrs Pope, and latterly by his grand-daughter, my second cousin, Mary Pope.

Angus never asked to have the money returned, nor did he ask that the house should be transferred to him or registered in his name, even after his mother's death.

This may seem strange to those brought up in the historical British tradition that family ties are subordinate to the protection and accumulation of property, but I can think of no island family, which I know intimately, in which there is not a similar instance of property being freely transferred to whoever could use it most advantageously at the time, or needed it most and, during my chairmanship of the Crofters Commission, I came across many instances of grave difficulties arising because of the inability of a legal system, based on the supremacy of property, to cope with the "irrational" actions of those whose ethos is based on personal relationships.

It was, no doubt, the same modest affluence, which provided the elderly widow with a home, as had enabled her daughter and her husband to help their uncle in his financial difficulties. Their help, however, was unavailing. In October 1855 Colin Morison's creditors had him declared a bankrupt and the kites descended on the carcase.

The action against Colin Morison was instigated by William Weir Bros & Coy, wine and spirit merchants, Glasgow, and sequestration was granted by Lord Neaves in the Court of Session on 25th October 1856. A meeting of creditors was held in the National Hotel, Dingwall — at that time the County Town for Lewis — on 5th November, at which David M'Cubbin, a Glasgow accountant, was appointed Trustee.

At this point Donald Munro and William Ross decided that they should have the pickings. They began to mobilise the local creditors to out-vote the Glasgow creditors and have M'Cubbin removed in favour of their own nominee.

Among the creditors they drummed up for this purpose was George Stephen, who was persuaded, against his natural instincts, to claim repayment of the loans he and his wife had made in an effort to avert her uncle's bankruptcy.

Munro and Ross later protested in the Court of Session that the local creditors had come to them voluntarily, "as the only law agents in the place, to prepare their claims."

Some may well have done so, but George Stephen maintained that Ross sent a clerk to his house and asked him to call at the office. He then urged Stephen to go to a J.P. and swear an affidavit claiming the repayment of the loans. He had the affidavit ready drafted when Stephen called. It was made clear to Stephen that he would incur no cost. The charge for preparing the affidavit was five shillings, but, when he offered to pay it, Ross waved the money aside, saying the expenses would come out of the bankrupt's estate.

Ross vigorously denied that he had summoned Stephen to his office. He was completely unacquainted with him. He could not possibly have prepared an affidavit unless Stephen had first given him the vouchers on which the claim was based.

Ross's argument is plausible and may well be factually accurate. He and Stephen are not likely to have been acquainted: Stephen had just arrived home from Australia, after an absence of several years, while Ross had not been long established in the town. Stephen himself indirectly confirms the fact that they were unacquainted. He told the Court of Session, at a later stage, that he had fended off Ross's blandishments with the comment that he knew Ross no better than he knew M'Cubbin and had no more reason to trust one than to trust the other.

Ross's partner Munro, however, had been a solicitor in Stornoway for fifteen years. He is bound to have known Stephen and his history. It may well have been Munro who sent the clerk for Stephen, and obtained the information on which the affidavit was prepared. There is evidence that thirty years later the equivocal relationship between the partners was still causing confusion, even among their professional colleagues, and was being deliberately exploited for that purpose.

Whatever the truth of it, George Stephen submitted a claim and signed a mandate authorising Ross to vote on his behalf at any meeting arising out of the bankruptcy.

On 25th March 1856, a meeting of creditors was held in Glasgow. The Stornoway creditors were represented by the third member of the "mafia": William Ross Skinner, W.S., Edinburgh, a cousin of Donald Munro and William Ross, and like them a native of Tain.

It must have been a stormy meeting. Skinner moved that M'Cubbin should be removed from the office of Trustee. M'Cubbin disputed the validity of some of the claims for which Skinner produced mandates. Each side asserted that it had a legal majority of the votes. The Chairman of the meeting decided in favour of M'Cubbin.

Munro, Ross and Skinner took the matter to the Sheriff Court in Stornoway. M'Cubbin did not attend the hearing and, on 7th May 1856, Sheriff-substitute Andrew Lothian MacDonald ruled that he had been removed from the office of Trustee by a lawful majority.

Only those with claims of over £20 had individual votes. The Sheriff's tally was that nine valid votes were cast for Skinner's motion and seven against. The margin was narrow and Stephen's claim for £34.13.4. was one of the ranking nine. It is easy to see why Munro, Ross and Skinner were anxious that he should pursue it.

On Skinner's motion, M'Cubbin was replaced as Trustee by Donald Fowler, described as "an accountant in Stornoway." Later George Stephen alleged that Donald Fowler was an employee of William Ross. Ross denied the allegation. The denial was factually correct but grossly misleading.

Fowler, said Ross, was "a clerk or accountant to the Chamberlain of the Lews whose counting house is in a separate part of the town from the office of Munro and Ross." He neglected to add, as in honesty he should, that the Chamberlain of the Lews was his cousin and partner, Donald Munro. Whoever his legal employer might be, Fowler was a stooge of the "mafia," and his later history, which will be examined in its due place, reveals the extent of their hold over the people of Lewis.

M'Cubbin appealed to the Court of Session against Sheriff MacDonald's decision on the disputed claims. The case turned largely on the question whether M'Cubbin, having lost the action in Stornoway by default, was entitled to appeal, as he would have been if the Sheriff had decided the case on the merits of the various claims.

M'Cubbin pointed out that there was only one firm of law agents in Stornoway and their services had been secured by the opposing creditors. It was inconvenient for him to attend in person "at so great a distance." At that time there was only one steamer a week between Stornoway and the Clyde. By a majority, the Court of Session decided that M'Cubbin should have gone to Stornoway, despite the inconvenience, and dismissed all his appeals — except that defended in the name of George Stephen.

The crucial point in Stephen's claim was whether the documents he held from his wife's uncle, acknowledging the loans, were receipts or promissory notes.

The Court of Session took the view that they were promissory notes, and were invalid because they had not been stamped in accordance with the Stamp Act. Sheriff MacDonald had taken the view that they were simply receipts, and were covered by the exemption under the Stamp Act for drafts, orders or letters of credit for sums of less that £100, which required only to be signed across a penny stamp.

Ross later claimed that the debate in the Court of Session on this relatively simple matter lasted for three days. Was it spun out excessively or was Ross, for reasons of his own, attributing to the Stephen appeal the time which had been consumed in hearing the whole twenty eight Stornoway cases involved in the dispute with M'Cubbin? However long it lasted, George Stephen did not even know that it was taking place: he was on his way to Russia as mate of the *North Briton*.

He returned from Russia, at the beginning of September 1856, and had been at home for some days when he received a letter from Ross, informing him that he had lost his case in the Court of Session, that expenses of £49 had been awarded against him to David M'Cubbin, and that he should pay them immediately.

Stephen was aghast. He went round to Ross's office demanding to know on whose authority counsel had been engaged in his name to defend a case in the Court of Session. He reminded Ross of the undertaking he had been given that he would not be involved in any expenditure. Ross denied that such an undertaking had been given, and neither in the letter nor the interview did he disclose that, in addition to the expenses due to M'Cubbin, he and his partners had chalked up, in their own books, a sum of £74:2:10, which they claimed was due to them by Stephen for "defending" his interests in the Court of Session.

Six years later, the conduct of Ross and his partners came under scrutiny in the Court of Session, in an action raised by George Stephen. Four judges decided that Munro and Ross had fought M'Cubbin's appeal at their own risk. It emerged that, although Munro and Ross knew of M'Cubbin's appeal on 1st June 1856, when Stephen was still in Stornoway, they made no attempt to inform him, or seek instructions, until after he had left for Russia, by which time a considerable proportion of the expenses had already been incurred.

The Lord President said he was quite satisfied that Stephen had given no antecedent authority to Munro and Ross which would cover the defence of a case in the Court of Session.

"Indeed," he added, "that is admitted in the very distinct and candid evidence of Mr Ross himself."

Their argument that they were defending the interests of "an absent party" fell because, on their own admission, they had not bothered to ascertain whether Stephen was absent or not before instructing their cousin, William Ross Skinner, to defend the action.

Lord Deas, supporting the Lord President, said that, if Stephen had been asked for authority, he would most probably have refused it, rather than incur the cost of litigation in the Supreme Court for the sake of a dividend on a claim for less than £40.

The Court's ruling was still well in the future when George Stephen left Stornoway, at the end of September 1856, to join the *Eagle of Liverpool*, as first mate. He sailed for China on 2nd November, leaving behind him a claim from David M'Cubbin for £49, which he rightly repudiated, and a bogus claim from Munro, Ross and Skinner of which he had never been told. It was three years before he returned to Stornoway.

In the interval Munro and Ross dealt fairly expeditiously with Colin Morison's bankruptcy. On the 10th January 1858 he obtained his discharge and was able to resume trading. His creditors received only three shillings and ninepence farthing in the £ although, according to William Ross Skinner, they had been offered a composition of ten shillings in the £ before the sequestration.

Skinner blamed M'Cubbin, and the Glasgow creditors, for rejecting the original offer, thereby ruining Morison, and depriving his Stornoway creditors of an advantageous settlement. That may be true, but whether it is or not, it is clear that their own fees for the administration of the sequestration, which they wrested out of M'Cubbin's hands, consumed nearly two thirds of the bankrupt's estate.

While Colin Morison was now in the clear, the man who had helped him was not.

On October 1st 1856, while Stephen was still at Liverpool, waiting for the *Eagle* to sail, M'Cubbin obtained a warrant for his imprisonment for debt.

On the 10th of November, just a week after he sailed, a Messenger at Arms presented himself at the door of Number 1 Newton, wearing his silver blazon with the King's Arms displayed on it, and carrying his long red baton, curiously known as a "wand of peace." He conducted a "most strict, diligent and minute" search of the house while two terrified women looked on.

The Messenger at Arms did not report to the Court that Stephen was on his way to China, pursuing his normal vocation as a foreign-going mate: he reported that "the debtor had absconded for his own personal safety, and his family and servants denied all knowledge of him."

Nearly three years later, on August 1st 1859, shortly after he returned from China, Stephen was arrested for debt at M'Cubbin's instance. For want of a debtors' prison in Stornoway he was incarcerated in an ordinary cell, as a common criminal, and languished there for six months.

He was, however, liberated, "without being called on to pay any portion of the debt," as soon as M'Cubbin realised that he had not authorised the litigation in the Court of Session out of which the claim had arisen.

Skinner, in later proceedings, accused M'Cubbin of "refusing the bankrupt any aliment for his support" while he was in prison. This must be one of the most hypocritical complaints ever penned by a Solicitor to the Supreme Court. There are numerous letters in the Stornoway Sheriff Court records from debtors in other cases, imprisoned at the instance of Munro and Ross, complaining that they were destitute and pleading for help which they did not get. And, as we shall see, Munro and Ross themselves treated Stephen, while he was M'Cubbin's prisoner, with a degree of malice and contempt which can only be described as evil.

His arrest by M'Cubbin was the least of the troubles which faced George Stephen when he returned from China.

7. NIMIOUS AND OPPRESSIVE

Shortly after the house at Newton was searched by the Messenger at Arms, Munro and Ross, through William Ross Skinner, raised an action against George Stephen in the Court of Session for payment of their bogus account, which by now had risen from £74.7.10 to £85.3.11.

They alleged that Stephen had conveyed away his property, drawn all his funds from the bank, and had left Stornoway, "to evade the diligence of his creditors." The Messenger at Arms, and even David M'Cubbin, might have honestly thought that Stephen was absconding: Munro and Ross, who lived in the same small town with him, knew quite well that he had left home in the ordinary course of his vocation.

He was not evading his creditors. They were exploiting his absence!

The auditor of Court reduced the Munro and Ross account from £85.3.11. to £80.14.5 and, on 17th February 1857, a decree was granted, in absence, against Stephen for that amount.

Two months later a curious transaction took place.

On March 21st, Munro and Ross assigned their claim against Stephen to William Ross Skinner, for a payment of £90.6.6. It is not clear that any payment was made by Skinner, and there is force in Stephen's allegation — when he discovered what had happened while he was in China — that the assignation was merely a device to enable Skinner to apply for sequestration of his estate and thus illegally obtain possession of his funds.

Skinner attempted to rebut this suggestion by pointing out that Munro and Ross could themselves have applied for sequestration of Stephen's estate. That, of course, is true. One can only assume that, thick-skinned though they were, they were anxious to distance themselves from an action which was bound to be widely resented in a small community, where the protagonists and the facts were known.

On 18th June 1857, while Stephen was still abroad, the Court of Session granted Skinner's application for his sequestration. The bogus claim against Stephen had by this time been increased to £93.16.1.

On 13th July, the Sheriff Substitute in Stornoway, Andrew Lothian MacDonald, confirmed William Ross as Trustee in the sequestration and transferred to him Stephen's whole "estates and effects heritable and moveable and real and personal wherever situated ... for behoof of the creditors," in terms of the Bankruptcy (Scotland) Act 1856.

The first statutory meeting of creditors was held in the Caledonian Hotel, Stornoway, on July 28th, and the record shows how the three cousins carved the carcase up between them.

William Ross, the trustee in the sequestration, employed William Ross Skinner as agent. Skinner was also for a couple of months commissioner in the sequestration, but he then resigned in favour of James Milwain Wither, a young law clerk from Stranraer, who had just taken up residence in Stornoway.

Having a good deal of spare time in the Stranraer law office where he trained, Wither read the *Encyclopaedia Britannica* from cover to cover and passed as a man of great erudition among his Stornoway friends. He could frequently be seen going home to his lodgings in *Cailleach a' Ghaiger's* (the gauger's wife's) with a penny candle and a book, which he read through the night. For our purpose, the important point about him is that he was a clerk in the Estate Office under Donald Munro.

All the creditors, the Trustee, the Commissioner and the Agent in George Stephen's bankruptcy were members of the "mafia", or their employees.

On December 16th 1858, George Stephen's wife, my grand-aunt Catherine, was cited to appear before the Sheriff Substitute at Stornoway to be examined in her husband's sequestration.

Donald Fowler, who by that time had left the employment of Donald Munro and was trying to establish himself as a law agent in opposition, appeared for her and submitted a letter from Dr Charles Macrae in the following terms:

"Dear Sir, I have at your request visited Mrs Stephen who is obviously *enciente* and, by her own statement, verging on her *accouchement*. In such a situation I am of opinion that any unusual mental excitement or physical exertion might prove hurtful to her."

Fowler asked that the interrogation of Mrs Stephen should be adjourned *sine die*.

Charles Macrae, the son of the minister at Barvas, Lewis, was a physician of unusual skill and complete integrity. He had studied arts and divinity before deciding to become a doctor. He was gold medallist in his year in Sir James Y. Simpson's class at Edinburgh, then probably the most renowned medical class in Europe, but he turned his back on the opportunity of a remunerative city, or English, practice to labour among the poor in his native island. He came back to Lewis in 1849 and remained in practice until 1906, when he was in his 88th year. He was unquestionably the most highly respected man of his time in Lewis as doctor, theologian and educationist.

Nevertheless, his certificate carried little weight with William Ross.

Ross asked the Court to issue a fresh warrant, citing Mrs Stephen to attend Court two days later, "under certification" that, if she failed to do so, "a warrant would be granted for her apprehension." He supported his demand with what were described, in later proceedings, as "unfounded allegations."

No indication is given in the available records of the nature of these allegations, but I suspect Ross represented to the Court that Mrs Stephen could not be enciente because her husband had been absent from home for more than two years. He might even have hinted at the implications, if she were.

Mrs Stephen was, in fact, pregnant but there was no scandal.

It was a common practice for Stornoway seamen's wives to go to Liverpool to meet their husbands between voyages. There was a little Lewis "colony" there. W. E. Gladstone's mother was born in Stornoway and many Lewismen sailed in her husband's ships, among them the Ryrie brothers, who figure prominently in Basil Lubbock's book *The Opium Clippers*. My mother was in Liverpool while still a baby, because my grandmother had to go to meet my grandfather. We still have some of the crockery bought in the city at that time.

March 1858, when Mrs Stephen's child — twins as it turned out — must have been conceived, was almost exactly half way through George Stephen's long absence from Stornoway, which suggests that he made two consecutive voyages to China returning to Liverpool between them.

She certainly had good reason to go to see her husband then, if only to tell him that he had been made a bankrupt without his knowledge.

Astonishingly, in the face of a duly attested medical certificate, Sheriff MacDonald granted the warrant sought by Ross, which seems to justify the criticism levelled against MacDonald, before the Napier Commission, thirty years later, that he was an "amiable and accomplished gentleman" but quite unable to maintain the "position and dignity" of his office, in the face of the "arbitrary power" exercised by Munro and Ross.

Two days after the rejection of Dr Macrae's medical certificate, my grand-aunt appeared in Court.

She was too far gone in her pregnancy to walk. She was taken in a cart, accompanied by her mother and the midwife. She had to be carried from the cart to the Court room.

Even so Sheriff MacDonald attempted to administer the oath, so that Ross could examine her. She was in an excited condition, quite unfit to plead, and the midwife intervened on her behalf. Unfortunately the records do not reveal what the midwife said to the men around her but I have a suspicion it was pretty salty.

Unmoved, William Ross, — "disgracefully and unfeelingly", it was suggested later — moved the Court "to grant warrant to commit her to the prison of Stornoway until she is prepared to express her readiness to be examined in terms of the Statute founded on in the Petition."

That was too much even for Sheriff MacDonald. He granted an adjournment, at Fowler's request, and my grand-aunt was once more carried down to the cart and conveyed to her home where, ten days later, she gave birth to twin daughters.

Three months later, on 7th March 1859, Mrs Stephen was again summoned to Court at the instance of Munro and Ross. Her mother accompanied her.

She had a difficult labour, because of the emotional stress she was under, and had not fully recovered. Under examination on matters which concerned her husband's affairs rather than her own, she became hysterical and unable to answer the questions.

Ross asked for a warrant for her imprisonment.

Sheriff MacDonald granted it and she was detained in a cold cell from noon until eight o'clock at night, when she became more composed and agreed to try to deal with the questions. Her examination lasted until nearly 11 pm.

In the meantime the twins, whom she was breast feeding, were at home, unfed.

For several days after her ordeal she was "unable to leave her bed or to give suck to her infant children, the milk having left her."

Five days after Mrs Stephen's appearance in Court, one of the twins — Hectorina Mary Stephen — died "of bronchitis". On the following day, the second — Grace Stephen — died "in convulsions." They had both been in normal health when their mother was taken to Court.

The nearest male relative available to register the deaths, make the funeral arrangements and comfort the mother, was their granduncle, Murdo Morison. All the younger members of the family were at sea.

The circumstances in which the twins met their deaths might seem an appropriate subject for investigation by the Crown but the officials of the Crown, on whom the responsibility rested for undertaking such an inquiry, were Donald Munro and William Ross, the Procurators Fiscal, who were later accused before the Court of Session of having themselves caused the deaths, by their "nimious and oppressive proceedings."

While Munro and Ross were harrying Mrs Stephen through the Courts, on the pretext that her husband owed them money, which he refused to pay, they were also developing a new line of attack against her mother, prompted possibly by their failure to poind the furniture in the Morison-Stephen household.

Before he sailed for China, George Stephen consulted a solicitor in Glasgow — Joseph Taylor, Buchanan St. He had to record the transactions concerning the Newton Street House, and there was no solicitor in Stornoway who could do it for him, except the two with whom he was in conflict.

Taylor, presumably in answer to a cry for help after the first visit of the Messenger at Arms, wrote Mrs Stephen in March 1857: "If an officer should come to poind, mother must appear before him and stop the things as hers; and, if the officer requires it, she must take her oath that they are hers, and then he is obliged to desist. I think they may have found out from the record that the property is transferred and perhaps they will not bother you more."

They had found out, but it was a vain hope that they would cease from bothering her.

On the face of things, George Stephen's principal asset was the new and substantial house his family occupied on the seafront of Newton; a large two storey, double house, harled and slated, which stood out conspicuously on a street then almost wholly composed of small thatched cottages.

The house, however, did not belong to him. On 27th September 1856 George Stephen signed a disposition selling the house to his mother-in-law. His own title to the house was formally recorded in the General Register of Sasines on 30th September, and the title of the new owner was similarly recorded on October 1st.

William Ross, in his capacity as Trustee in George Stephen's contrived bankruptcy, raised an action in the Court of Session against Mrs Morison, on August 31st 1857, for the reduction of her title to the house. He argued that the house had been transferred to her, when George Stephen was already bankrupt, that no just price had been paid for it, and that the Disposition from George Stephen to his mother-in-law was "a gratuitous deed granted for the purpose of defeating the just rights of his lawful creditors."

The old lady defended the action.

She said she had paid £200 to George Stephen, which was a fair price. There can be no doubt she had such funds at her command: it was precisely the sum her son Angus had sent her from Melbourne. George Stephen later stated that he sold the house because he needed funds to advance himself in his profession. He was in process of qualifying as a shipmaster and, presumably, had to spend some time, unprofitably, ashore as well as equipping himself with navigational instruments and other gear for his new responsibilities when he got his own command.

The action never came to proof and we have no means of knowing which of the conflicting stories a bench of judges would have believed, after hearing witnesses and evaluating the evidence.

If the sale of the house was just a device to defeat his creditors, George Stephen must have been a far-seeing man of business. He made the move before David M'Cubbin, through John Walls SSC, had taken the first effective step against him by getting a warrant for his imprisonment as a debtor — a warrant that could not be activated until he returned from China nearly three years later — and before Munro and Ross had given any indication that they intended to charge him for "defending" his interests in the Court of Session, and were prepared to destroy his children in their attempts to collect the pretended debt.

There seems little reason, in the circumstances, to doubt his claim that the sale of the house was genuine, but, even if it was not, he was merely trying —unsuccessfully as it happens — to protect his family, in his absence, from a debt which a bench of four judges decided later had never been due.

It seems probable that the interrogation of Mrs Stephen, which led to the death of the twins, was an attempt by Munro and Ross to extract from her admissions bearing on the sale of the house, which would be of assistance when the action for reduction of her mother's title eventually came to trial.

A hearing was arranged for 28th March 1859 but, just before the jury was empannelled, Mr Arthur SSC, for Mrs Morison, asked for an adjournment because of the absence of a material witness "without whose evidence the Defender cannot safely go to trial."

Who the missing witness was does not appear from the surviving records.

Was it Mrs Stephen, who earlier that month had lost her twins and might have been in no condition to travel to Edinburgh? Or was it Angus

Morison, who was in Stornoway from Sept 1857 until January 1858 and possibly longer? His evidence could have been crucial because he was the source of his mother's funds? Or is it possible that George Stephen had been expected home from China by that date, but was delayed?

It signifies little. Without the case ever going to proof, Munro and Ross had achieved their objective.

Because of the adjournment, at the last minute and on Mrs Morison's behalf, expenses of £135.5.10 were awarded against her: an immense bill for an elderly widow to meet at the money values of the day.

It was no longer necessary for Munro, Ross and Skinner to reduce Mrs Morison's title to the Newton House: a process which might have blown up in their faces if it ever came to proof. They could gain control of all her assets, including the house, by pursuing her for a contrived debt, just as they were pursuing her son-in-law.

On 21st December 1859, William Ross brought an action of adjudication against her, in respect of the £135.5.10 which, not surprisingly, she had not paid. She defended the action, but the Court decided against her. The whole property at No 1 Newton effectively passed under the control of William Ross.

Three years later, in October 1862, he brought a second action of adjudication against her, in respect of the expenses awarded against her in the first. This increased still further the mass of debt which had to be cleared before she could regain a legal title to her own home.

For the next 25 years, until October 1884, the whole property, which had been bought with so much pride and hope, was in the hands of strangers. The rent of the front house (which had always been let out with the family) and of the curing station at the rear was now paid to William Ross, or his accomplices and their successors.

The family do not seem to have been evicted from their own part of the property but they had to pay rent for it, and when eventually they recovered the legal ownership, it was by purchasing it — for a second time!

It is surprising, perhaps, in view of the harshness of their other actions, that the "mafia" did not evict the Morisons and the Stephens, even when, as appears to have been the case from time to time, they were behind with the rent. The explanation may perhaps be found in the public reaction in Stornoway to the death of the twins.

Rev N. C. Macfarlane, recalling in the *Stornoway Gazette*, in 1929, the ship's captains of his youth, wrote 'There was the story of the captain whose wife gave birth to twins on board ship. The mother's supply of milk failed, and the infants sucked the ship's milk through the shaft of a clay pipe. Then there was the captain who put his apprentice ashore in an Indian port without wage or recommendation. Strange to say both captain and apprentice were Stornowegians. In those far off days men were sent to prison for debt. There was a Stornoway captain who incurred debt, but he was abroad, and, in his absence, his wife was imprisoned. She had twins and, while they were only a few days old, the mother and the babes were lodged in a prison cell. The shock may have poisoned the mother's milk. In any case, one of the babes died in prison and Stornoway blazed with anger."

The last reference is clearly to the imprisonment of Mrs Stephen. Macfarlane got some of his facts wrong, which is not surprising: he was writing about an incident which happened before he was born. But, significantly, it had left such a mark on local opinion it was still being talked about with anger when he was old enough to be interested.

The ultimate irony arose with Donald Fowler's bankruptcy.

Napier Campbell, a Glasgow solicitor who settled in Stornoway in 1863, breaking the Mafia monopoly, although only in appearance, as we shall see, told the Napier Commission in 1882 that, before he came to Stornoway, six or seven agents had failed to establish a footing, owing to all appointments of profit going one way.

Donald Fowler was one of the six or seven.

Not long after he appeared for Mrs Stephen in the Sheriff Court, and produced Dr Macrae's medical certificate about her pregnancy, he left Stornoway for Dingwall, frozen out by Munro and Ross. By August 1861 he was bankrupt and the Trustee in the bankruptcy was William Ross Skinner.

In his capacity as Trustee, Skinner raised an action against my great-grandmother and her brother-in-law, Colin Morison, for £40.4.6, which he claimed was due to the estate of Donald Fowler, for professional services and disbursements made on their behalf.

The list of more than 75 separate items runs from 14th Sept 1857 to 25th June 1859. Many of the charges refer to the writing of letters — at 3/4 a time — to Joseph Taylor, solicitor, in Glasgow but more than half the total is accounted for by travelling expenses and subsistence for a trip to Glasgow and Edinburgh, allegedly to attend, on their behalf, the trial in the action of reduction brought against Annabella Morison by William Ross to gain possession of her home.

Both Colin Morison and Annabella Morison denied that they had ever employed Donald Fowler "to do law business" on their behalf, or authorised him to act for them in any way. In particular they denied authorising him to go to Edinburgh. They also both asserted that no account for these alleged services had ever been rendered to them by Donald Fowler.

Colin Morison went even further. So far from being indebted to Donald Fowler, he said, Donald Fowler was indebted to him, for articles supplied from his shop.

"When I saw him in Dingwall last year, he admitted this and promised to pay me something to account. Mr Fowler was Trustee in my estate and was often in the spirit shop kept by me and sometimes spoke of the law business as a mere matter of conversation."

The references to Colin Morison in the account seem to relate to occasions when — having obtained his discharge from bankruptcy, resumed business and prospered moderately — he was advancing money to his sister-in-law to pay Mr Taylor in Glasgow.

There is no indication that Fowler ever transacted business on Colin Morison's own behalf, and it is difficult to understand why Colin was being pursued by Skinner.

With Mrs Morison it is different. There seems no reason to doubt that she was frequently in Fowler's office in regard to correspondence with Taylor. Being illiterate, she needed the services of a penman, quite apart from any legal advice involved.

The mystery is why Fowler, when he was teetering on the verge of bankruptcy, did not himself take action against Mrs Morison or even render an account.

A possible explanation is that Fowler was not acting on Mrs Morison's instructions or on her behalf, but was Taylor's Stornoway correspondent and looked to him for remuneration.

If so, did Taylor fail or refuse to settle with him, (perhaps because his charges were excessive) or was Skinner pursuing Mrs Morison for a bill that had already been paid by someone else?

Perhaps the most significant fact is that Skinner made no claim against Mrs Stephen, for whom Fowler had undoubtedly transacted law business when he appeared for her in court. That bill, presumably, had been rendered and paid, which in itself casts some doubt on the authenticity of the bill presented to Annabella Morison and Colin Morison.

Whatever the truth of the matter, Mrs Morison was now being asked to pay her pursuers for the protection she had sought, unavailingly, from their own harassment!

8. THE FIGHT BACK

As soon as George Stephen got home from China he was imprisoned for debt, and remained incarcerated like a common criminal for six months. In prison, however, he began to fight back, although not without difficulty.

Around that time another young law agent tried to establish himself in the territory so jealously guarded by Munro and Ross.

His name — Morrison — suggests that he may have had some local connection, although most of his Lewis clansmen at that time spelt their name with one r, emphasising that they were not descended from any Morris but from "Mores sone of Kennanus whom the Irish historiance call Makurich," in the phrase of one of the best remembered of the name, John Morison of Bragar, who was one of Martin Martin's principal informants, and wrote his own brief account of his native island.

Whether he had any local influence or not, Morrison's sojourn in Lewis seems to have been brief. The vigour with which he prepared George Stephen's counter-offensive suggests that Munro and Ross would have been even more anxious to squeeze him out than they had been to get rid of his predecessor, Donald Fowler.

On the 19th July 1859, Morrison wrote William Ross, as Trustee in Stephen's bankruptcy, asking for access to the Sederunt Book, which he wished to consult on his client's behalf.

Ross refused to let him see it, saying tartly that "very probably" he would "have to take criminal proceedings" against the bankrupt.

Morrison wrote a second time, asking for a copy of the document, if he could not have access to the original. "The most important and material interests" of his client were involved and his right to access, or copies, was evident. His client was threatened with criminal proceedings and a copy of his Deposition on Oath, in the bankruptcy proceedings, was indispensible for his defence.

He also warned that Stephen might raise an action against Ross, "for count and reckoning or even for neglect of duty" and that he was contemplating an application to the Court of Session for a recall of the Sequestration. Again Ross refused.

On the 25th August, Morrison raised an action in the Sheriff Court on behalf of "George Stephen, mariner, now prisoner in the gaol at Stornoway," asking for access to the proceedings in the Sequestration.

Ross tried to stall by arguing that Stephen should be obliged to lodge a bond of caution, to protect his opponents from the risk of loss, before the action was allowed to proceed. Sheriff MacDonald agreed.

Morrison appealed. Sheriff Principal Cook reversed Sheriff MacDonald's decision, pointing out that there was no absolute rule requiring a bankrupt to find caution for expenses. Stephen had not yet got access to the papers he needed but, at least, his agent was now free to try to convince the Court that he should.

In his Condescendence, Morrison pointed out that "Mr Donald Munro, Chamberlain of the Lews, acted as agent in the Sequestration, his partner, the Respondent (William Ross) as Trustee, and James Milwain Wither (an employee of Munro) as Commissioner" while the only creditor was William Ross Skinner, "as assignee of Munro and Ross."

Ross replied that Stephen had undergone his examination in Bankruptcy "under the fostering care and protection of two solicitors;" that he showed no assets except a claim for £36 against another bankrupt, which claim had already been judicially rejected, while on the other hand there was a debt of £94 ranked on the estate (their own claim for legal expenses) and Stephen was at present in jail for non-payment of another sum of considerable amount not hitherto ranked on the Estate (M'Cubbin's). He alleged that Stephen wanted access to the Sederunt Book, not for himself, but to assist his mother-in-law in resisting their attempt to reduce what they regarded as her bogus claim to the Newton house.

On 23rd September, Sheriff MacDonald decided that Stephen was entitled to copies of the Sederunt Book but, as if he could not give a decisive no to Munro and Ross, he ruled that each side should bear its own expenses. The result was that both sides appealed to the Sheriff Principal: Ross against the decision; Stephen against the award of expenses.

Morrison, in asking for the decision on expenses to be altered in Stephen's favour, argued that the action had been undertaken through absolute necessity, to vindicate a right which was oppressively and illegally withheld.

"Throughout the whole course of the proceedings it will also become evident to your Lordship that every opposition which an action could admit of, both dilatory and on the merits, was given by the Respondent to the claim now properly recognised by his Lordship the Sheriff Substitute."

He also argued that the Court should not "impose upon one who has already suffered so much, and whose present position can so ill afford it, the additional hardship of paying for the vindication of a right to which he was admittedly all along entitled, and which was only withheld from him by the determined, illegal and utterly captious opposition of the Respondent."

The normal rule was that expenses should be awarded against the unsuccessful litigant and the reason why the rule should be departed from in this instance was not easily discernible in law or in justice, he argued.

"The Sheriff Substitute himself with characteristic truthfulness and feeling supplies full testimony of the fact that 'the *unfortunate position* of the Petitioner but too well testifies his interest in making the limited demand to which his application is confined.'

"The Petitioner, when he left this country and went abroad, in the exercise of his lawful calling, did so under the conviction that he owed no one a debt of any description. He had all his lifetime earned as much as served, with honesty and independence, to support him and his family, in their own frugal and humble walk in life; and he was due no debt whatever. But, on his return home, this dream of independence and security was to him mysteriously, but too surely and speedily, dispelled.

"He found that in his absence, without his knowledge, most certainly without his consent, and entirely against his desires, he had been involved in a *mare magnum* of litigation. Large accounts of law expenses had been incurred or fabricated against him; he was rendered a Notour Bankrupt; his estates had been sequestrated; his family and relatives had been oppressed and persecuted in a manner and by proceedings more akin to those which might be supposed to take place in a Despotic country and at the hands of irresponsible agents than in this free and enlightened Kingdom, and under its just and benign laws; and ultimately he was himself immured within the walls of a criminal cell, though only a civil debtor, where he has since been kept in close confinement, and from the depths of which this *limited demand* to your Lordship was made ...

"How is this poor persecuted man, whose industry has been thus arrested, and whose personal liberty has been thus abridged, able to pay the expenses of a protracted process for securing a 'limited' right which is declared to have been his, in terms of law, *ab initio?*

"By the kindness and sympathy of several friends, who are aware of his sufferings and those of his family, he may manage to pay the Respondent for the copy of his Examination and Oath, to which he is now found entitled; but it would be unreasonable to expect that the same humane persons should enable him to pay the expenses of the present case also."

Ross replied that it was not the bankrupt who was unfortunate but those to whom he owed money.

"Reckless bankrupts with unscrupulous agents may involve honest and industrious people in ruinous expenses by actions, however groundless, without any means of redress; not only so but parties in that position frequently ... indulge in invective and scandal which solvent litigants would not dare to adopt."

He denied that he was in any position to interfere with Stephen's personal liberty because Stephen was already in jail. It was "most incongruous to raise an action for the defence of the personal liberty of one who designs himself 'presently prisoner in the Prison of Stornoway'." "This is a fair specimen of his miserable shifts and shuffling throughout the whole proceedings," added Ross.

In a legal argument running to forty foolscap pages, Ross argued that the Bankruptcy Acts gave no warrant for a bankrupt to see the Sederunt Book in his own Bankruptcy. In the whole history of jurisprudence there was no precedent for Stephen's demand. Once a Sequestration had been granted a bankrupt was no longer a party to the case and had no more interest in his own affairs than he would have if all his property had been sold.

Ross argued further that the language used by Morrison in Stephen's name was "a libel upon the just and benign laws of this free and enlightened Kingdom." No one but a bankrupt, shielding himself under his sequestration, in his "criminal cell," would indulge in it.

He protested against the idea that the Commissioner in a Bankruptcy should be called on to copy long papers, at the expense of a Bankrupt who had just sworn that he was not the master of a penny.

As for the alternative that he should have access to the documents, "how could he leave the cell wherein he is immured to avail himself of what he asks?" Nor could he (Ross) be expected to wait on the prisoner with the Sederunt Book and immure himself in his cell while copies were being made.

To this Morrison replied by raising once again the question, who were the creditors and agents and commissioners on whom the great and exclusive privilege of access to the Sederunt Book devolved, a privilege withheld from all other mortals?

"Why, simply and solely, (Ross) himself ... aided by his Edinburgh agent ... and his clerk ... No other creditors did, or could, appear, for during the whole course of his life, the Respondent (Stephen) had incurred no debt whatever and was due no one even to the extent of a shilling.

"The Petitioner (Ross) has been the Alpha and the Omega of the whole of the proceedings. By a system of Agency as unscrupulous as it was unauthorised ... he set up ... a large amount of law expenses as due to himself ... (He) is virtually creditor, agent, trustee and commissioner all at once."

On 25th October 1859, Sheriff Principal Cook confirmed Sheriff MacDonald's view that George Stephen should have access to the documents in his own Sequestration, but reversed Sheriff MacDonald's decision on expenses.

If Ross's view of the law was accepted, he pointed out, George Stephen would have been reduced to the position of an outlaw.

Although a bankrupt was divested of his estate, he still remained a party to the process and had certain important privileges, such as applying for his liberation if, as in this case, he had been incarcerated by his creditors, said the Sheriff. He added that he could find no sound principle for refusing to a party, access to the proceedings, in a process for the payment of his own debts, by means of funds adjudged from himself. Nor should he be put to expense in vindicating a privilege which should have been at once conceded to him.

After a long legal process, Stephen's agents had at last succeeded in gaining access to the documents they needed, to prepare a case for the Court of Session, for the Suspension of the award of legal expenses against him, out of which all his troubles arose.

At that point, as I mentioned earlier, four judges unanimously decided in his favour on the major issue, but before he reached that stage, his opponents, for the third time, tried to thwart him, by asking the Court of Session to rule that he must find caution, before he was permitted to move in his own defence.

On 9th March 1860, the Lord Ordinary, Lord Mackenzie, ruled that Stephen need not find caution, pointing out that it would be impossible for an undischarged bankrupt to do so, and the practical effect of such an order would be to enable William Ross Skinner obtain a decree by default, whereby he would pocket the expenses, and escape from any investigation into the merits of a claim, for which a decree had only been granted, in the first place, because Stephen was on the high seas, and could not appear in court to resist it.

He also commented on "an important speciality of the case," namely that the Trustee, William Ross, had a personal interest in the outcome, adverse to the bankrupt's.

Skinner appealed from the Lord Ordinary's judgment but a bench of three judges upheld it.

The Lord President commented that the fact that William Ross had refused to sist himself as a party to the action was an indication that it was not well founded.

Lord Ivory, concurring, said Stephen was really in the position of a defender, and added (one suspects with some acerbity) that Skinner "seems to be the whole corporation of creditors in his own single person."

Lord Curriehill also concurred but with an ominous caveat: he doubted whether a sequestration once granted could ever be recalled.

So it proved.

Although four judges decided, on 17th December 1863, that Stephen had never owed the legal expenses for which both M'Cubbin and the others pursued him, the family home was still in the hands of the "mafia", and he was still a sequestrated bankrupt.

Three years later, on 28th April 1866, he raised an action in the Court of Session against Munro, Ross and Skinner, for £2000 damages — an immense sum in the values of the time — on account of the loss and injury sustained in consequence of their "unjust, nimious, oppressive, illegal, malicious and unwarrantable acts."

The Condescendence alleged that his imprisonment, at the instance of John Walls SSC (acting on behalf of M'Cubbin), was caused by the acts of Munro, Ross and Skinner, and that Stephen had sustained both bodily injury and much pecuniary loss as a result; that the death of the twins and the precarious state of Mrs Stephen's health were caused by their oppressive actions; and that Stephen himself had suffered severe loss and injury in his feelings, character and position; had incurred heavy law expenses and other real damage; and had been much disappointed in his prospects in life.

Two days later, a parallel action was begun in the Court of Session on behalf of Annabella Morison, seeking damages for all she had suffered at the hands of Munro, Ross and Skinner.

Before she could commence the action, however, she came up against the difficulty that there was no Messenger at Arms in Stornoway to serve the summonses on the two principal offenders.

The nearest Messenger at Arms was in Portree, and the passage boats called at Ullapool, Lochinver and other intermediate ports, so that a round trip took a week at the very least. She had to apply to the Court in

Edinburgh for permission to have the summonses served by the local Sheriff Officer.

That was as far as either of them got in their quest for redress.

The nature of George Stephen's profession, which exposed him to the machinations of Munro Ross and Skinner in the first place, also made it difficult for him to bring the offenders to trial. He had to choose between continuing his career, or remaining ashore for a prolonged period, without earnings, to pursue his law suit.

Before he had resolved this difficulty, death intervened.

Annabella Morison died in 1868, aged 75. Four years later, in January 1872, George Stephen died at sea, on the Gold Coast. He was only 49, but was worn out by repeated bouts of malaria contracted in West Africa, to which he sailed for a number of years, in the palm oil trade. Three years later, in June 1875, his wife died of a broken heart. She was also only 49.

All the members of the family directly involved with the mafia were now dead, but William Ross was still Trustee of the sequestrated estate of George Stephen.

Shortly before Stephen's death, in answer to a query from the official Accountant in Bankruptcy, he wrote rather peevishly: "No funds belonging to the estate came into my hands ... but I have been called on from time to time to make payments out of my own pocket."

Twenty-three years later — nearly forty years after George Stephen made the ill-starred loan to his wife's uncle — Ross, replying to a similar query from the same official — or his successor — wrote: "I beg to state that the funds were all exhausted years ago and there are no further assets to be recovered ... The bankrupt is dead."

By that time George Stephen's family were once more in full legal possession of No 1 Newton. The explanation of how they came to recover it must be sought, strangely enough, in papers relating to an action "for maills and duties" raised by a grocer in Stockbridge, Edinburgh, against a Lieut. Colonel in Hamilton, Ontario.

In May 1861, the Court of Session granted an adjudication, at the instance of Willian Ross Skinner, transferring the title of No 1 Newton to William Ross, "heritably, for payment and satisfaction to him" of £147.17, alleged to be due by Annabella Morison, in respect of legal expenses with interest. A second adjudication in 1863 added a further sum of £61.1.3 which had to be cleared before she could recover the ownership of the family home.

In December 1874, William Ross disposed of his interest in the house to James Hogarth Balgarnie C.A., Edinburgh, for £180, assigning to him "the rents and arrears of rents now due."

The record in the Register of Sasines states that the £180 had actually been paid, but subsequent events raise a doubt whether any money actually changed hands: it looks rather like a device to distance Ross from the ownership of the house, and bring into action someone who could apply pressure on the Stephens, to pay rent for their own home, with less embarrassment than a neighbour in the same small town, who must have been in almost daily contact with members of the family.

Six years later, the widow and trustees of James Hogarth Balgarnie raised an action in the Court of Session against "William Morison, mariner, residing in Inaclete or Newton, Stornoway, eldest surviving son and nearest lawful heir," of Annabella Morison, as a result of which the Court ruled that the house No 1 Newton had not been redeemed by the payment of the debts, within the legal period, and was now irredeemable.

The application was made by John James Galletly SSC, but the papers lodged with the Register of Sasines, recording the final transfer of ownership out of the Stephen family, were written by Thomas Harron Manson, a clerk in the office of William Ross Skinner, and were witnessed by Skinner, who also effected the registration in the Register of Sasines. The "mafia" was still in control, but a little more discreetly.

William Morison, as it happens, was not the "eldest surviving son and nearest lawful heir" of Annabella Morison. My grandfather, Roderick Morison, was seven years older than William, and survived him by 31 years.

William Ross could not have been unaware of my grandfather's existence, nor his relationship to Annabella Morison, because he was involved, around that time, in another protracted law suit against the family which will be examined later. William, however, was more accessible, having come home to Stornoway in ill-health, while Roderick, and Angus, the older brothers, were still at sea.

On the same day, and at the same time — "between the hours of one and two afternoon" — a disposition of No 1 Newton was lodged, transferring the property from Mrs Balgarnie (who had just become irredeemably the owner) to William Ross Skinner, for "certain good causes and considerations, but without any price having been paid therefore."

This transaction was carried out "with consent of William Ross,

Rev R.M. Stephen, son of George Stephen, who bought back the family home after William Ross Skinner's death. His attitude to the persecution of the family by Munro and his associates is well summed up in a poem about the clearance of the village of Dalmore in his book,
'Glimpses of Portrona':
"I complain not, nor condemn, nor cherish anger.
Was a wrong done? Those that did it, those that bore —
All have stood before the Judge and the Avenger
Where the humble are not hustled from the door."

writer in Stornoway, Trustee on the sequestrated estate of George Stephen."

Even more interesting is the fact that, "notwithstanding the date hereof," the transfer to Skinner was effective "at the term of Martinmas 1874" — six years before the bargain was struck with the widow Balgarnie, and the very date on which her husband was supposed to have acquired the property from William Ross for £180.

On October 1st 1881, a year after he acquired the property, William Ross Skinner used it as security for £150, which he borrowed from the Trustees of a deceased fellow lawyer, James Paris. In the following month, on 8th November, he borrowed another £100 from the same source, on the same security.

These debts were still unpaid when Skinner died in November 1883, and the Trustees of James Paris raised an action against his heir — his cousin, Col James Aitchison Skinner, Woodstock, Glenelg, Hamilton, Ontario and the tenants of the Stornoway property, namely Mrs Annabella Stephen or Pope (George Stephen's daughter) and her husband, Peter Pope, a shipmaster, who occupied the main house; Donald MacNeill, who occupied the smaller house; and James Geddes, a fish curer from Macduff, who tenanted the curing station at the back, and who was himself bankrupt.

The action was not defended and decree was given to the Trustees, who promptly offered No 1 Newton for sale.

Three unsuccessful attempts were made to sell the property.

At the fourth attempt — a public roup in October 1884 — Roderick Morison Stephen, youngest son of George Stephen, (already mentioned as the author of *Glimpses of Portrona*) bought the family home back for £295. With it he acquired the two bonds signed by Skinner for £250, with accumulated interest.

The bonds were worthless.

9. WHIFF OF AN ANCIENT SCANDAL

In the Stephen case Munro and Ross were pursuing their own personal interests. In most other cases they appeared as agents for the estate, or private litigants, which makes it much more difficult to assess their influence and their motivation.

There is, however, plenty evidence of Munro's growing stranglehold on the community.

In 1849, taking a year more or less at random, the Estate served 64 summonses of removing on crofters in Lewis. All of these were multiple summonses, affecting a number of crofters. Each crofter evicted was the head of a family. At a modest estimate, the 1849 evictions must have affected fully 10% of the population in rural Lewis.

All of these summonses were taken out in Munro's name as the legal agent for the estate.

That does not mean that he was responsible for the policy behind the evictions, nor does it mean that families were being left completely destitute, as they were during the Sutherland clearances.

The removals of 1849 were part of an on-going process of re-lotting the land, to put an end to runrig.   Each family was being allocated an individual area of arable instead of a series of isolated strips which, in some districts, changed hands from year to year. The old system was supposed to give everyone a fair turn of the good and the bad but it made improvements in husbandry impossible.

It was around that time, in the late forties and early fifties, many of the Lewis villages were given the shape they still have today.

Although Munro's responsibility for the policy behind the notices of removal was subordinate to that of the Proprietor and the Factor, the question remains whether the re-lotting of the land could have been carried out by agreement, if the regime had been less dictatorial and less legalistic.

There is some evidence that the Factor at that time, John Munro Mackenzie, did try to carry the crofters with him. We have no clear knowledge whether the eventual decision to proceed by legal "diktat" rather than persuasion, arose because Munro Mackenzie's attempt had failed, or because Donald Munro advised against it.

A clearer indication of Donald Munro's growing power in the community is given by an examination of the removals taking place that year within the town of Stornoway.

In the Record Office in Edinburgh, among the Processes for 1849 relating to Stornoway Sheriff Court, there is one bundle of seven summonses affecting sixteen tenants of property. Donald Munro was involved in every one, and in four different capacities.

In some he appeared for the Estate, in others for local property-owners, but he also appeared as a heritable proprietor in his own right, and as Procurator Fiscal, representing the Crown as the ultimate heir in an intestate estate.

A fair-minded and genial solicitor could have acted for the pursuer in all these cases, both in town and country, without raising any resentment against himself personally. Right from the moment of his arrival in Lewis, however, Donald Munro seems to have been a focus for resentment, and not from the crofters only.

Six months after Munro came to Lewis, even before the evictions at Loch Shell, the minister of Stornoway, Rev John Cameron, openly accused him of manufacturing legal business and exceeding his authority.

Munro had written Colin Leitch, the Session Clerk, who was also the Sheriff Clerk, demanding the right to supervise the administration of the Poor Funds, then under the control of the Established Church.

He was acting in the name of the Factor, Thomas Knox, and claimed the right to attend all meetings of the Kirk Session at which the Poor Funds were dealt with, and to see all relevant documents.

When Leitch refused to accede to the request, Munro wrote direct to the Minister, who replied, with surprising acerbity, "I have seen your correspondence with Mr Leitch and I have heard of your tendering your services to Mr Knox, at two guineas per day, to force the Session Records. Trade must be slack with you when you have no other Butt than the Poor Funds and the members of Session."

He promised, however, to place the letter before the first meeting of the Kirk Session and let Munro know the outcome. The meetings, he explained, were held on the first Wednesday of each month. He was clearly signalling to Munro that he was not going to be hustled into calling a special meeting.

Munro kept up the pressure and, in June, Cameron wrote again. He said the Records would be produced in due time, and assured Munro that there would be "neither fraud, deceit or extravagance found in the distribution to 200 paupers in a population of more than 5000."

Then came the warning, "Should you press the case, I shall sooner go to gaol than submit to Mr Knox till I have his special mandate from

Seaforth for making such a demand."

Cameron clearly believed that either Knox or Munro, or both of them, were acting without authority from their employer.

It would have been difficult for Munro to produce a mandate from Seaforth. At that time he was Lord Chief Commissioner of the Ionian Islands, and no doubt had other things to think about than the Poor Roll in Stornoway. Munro did the next best thing, however: he got a mandate from the Trustees of the Seaforth Estate in Edinburgh, authorising Thomas Knox to inspect the Kirk Session's books and attend all meetings.

Armed with this, Knox issued his own mandate transferring the power of inspection to Munro.

When the Session met, on the 1st of August, they declined to accept the mandate in Munro's name. They explained that they were prepared to accept the Trustees' mandate in favour of Knox. They had always been ready to give access to the Heritors, or anyone holding a mandate from the Heritors, but they did not accept that Knox had any authority from the Heritors to transfer his mandate to Munro.

Even at that early stage, the Kirk Session had marked out Munro as a man with an appetite for power. They did not succeed in stopping his progress, but it should be on the record that the very first group to resist his rise was the Kirk Session of the Established Church of Scotland.

The members of the Session were the Minister, the Sheriff Clerk Depute and the Comptroller of Customs. Hardly a triumvirate of anarchists.

What makes their resistance even more remarkable is that Rev John Cameron was one of only three ministers in Lewis who, in the following year, did not "come out" at the Disruption. The resistance to Munro came from the very heart of the Establishment.

By this time Munro had raised an action, in Knox's name, against the Kirk Session in the Sheriff Court. The Kirk Session was faced with the usual difficulty that they could not get legal help in defending it.

They were not as badly placed as most litigants because their Session Clerk was an official of the Sheriff Court. Even so, the Sheriff ordered the withdrawal of their Answers to Munro's case because they showed "so wide a deviation from the accustomed and prescribed form of pleading."

In his submission to the Court, Munro claimed that Knox was acting in the name of the Trustees in Edinburgh, and also on behalf of the Honourable Mrs Mary Elizabeth Stewart Mackenzie of Seaforth and His

Excellency the Right Honourable James Alexander Stewart Mackenzie of Seaforth, Lord Chief Commissioner to the Ionian Isles.

He asserted that various applications had been made to the Kirk Session but these applications had been refused. He asked for expenses against the Session.

The Kirk Session's Answers do not seem to have survived but it is clear, from other sources, that the Kirk Session thought a demand to inspect the books, "by those who contribute nothing to the funds, a most ungracious and invidious request."

Does this, I wonder, imply that Munro and Knox were not Church goers, and made no contribution to the relief of the poor of the parish?

Although the Sheriff rejected the Kirk Session's original Answers, he must have accepted their amended submission because they won their case.

Sheriff Substitute R. S. Taylor decided, in January 1843, that the Factor had no authority to transfer to Munro the mandate he had received, in his own name, from the Seaforth Trustees.

It was also proved that Munro had raised the action before he informed the Kirk Session of the existence of the mandate, and that the Kirk Session had made it quite clear that, if a proper mandate had been produced, it would have been acceded to.

The inference is that Munro, as later in the Stephen case, was manufacturing litigation for his own personal profit.

He appealed and lost the appeal.

In this way he suffered his first defeat before he had won his first victory.

The significant point, however, is that an organisation like the Kirk Session was able to stand up to him: the crofters and private individuals could not.

There were occasions, however — rare occasions — when Munro appeared on the side of the angels. These suggest that he was an able and diligent lawyer, who might have presented a very different face to the public, if he had to contend with adversaries in court of his own calibre, instead of being placed in a position of almost unlimited power.

One of the cases in which Munro defended the oppressed involved the litigious Dr Macaulay.

In September 1837, Dr Macaulay, who at that time was tenant of the island of Ensay in the Sound of Harris and tacksman of "Pennydonald and other lands in Lewis," set off for the Falkirk Tryst on the *Maid of Morvern*, which plied between Glasgow and the Isles.

At Portree, Ann Macaskill, a young woman from Dunvegan, joined the vessel. She was going to visit friends in Fort William.

Dr Macaulay "made up to Ann, who was a stranger to him, and paid marked attention to her during the passage." He was "in close and secret conversation with her," in various parts of the ship, to an extent which aroused comment among the crew and passengers. He also plied her with spiritous liquor.

When the vessel berthed at Tobermory, he offered to take her to "a house where she could find lodgings," while they remained in port. She was a stranger to Tobermory, and the night was dark, so she accepted his guidance. He took her hand and led her from the ship — to a plantation on the outskirts of the town, where he seduced her.

He then asked her to accompany him to the Inn. She refused to go, and hurried back to the ship.

Dr Macaulay went to the Inn, but at 4 a.m. he returned to the ship in search of her. She was sleeping, wrapped in a cape he had given her when they were in the wood. He wakened her and began to ply her with drink again.

When they came to the parting of the ways in Oban, he tried to persuade her to come to Glasgow with him, and then return to Ensay as his servant.

At first she seemed tempted by the offer, but, when she asked what her duties would be, she discovered there was already a servant at Ensay, "whom he could not dismiss, as she had lost her reputation in his employment."

In the following year, when Macaulay went to the cattle sales in Skye, Ann accosted him in Sligachan Inn and presented his son to him.

He took the child in his arms, apparently with affection, and said it was his perfect image. He promised to provide for its keep, but did nothing to redeem the promise. He once more invited her to come to Ensay as his servant and she once more refused.

Next year again she waylaid him, in Uig, Skye, where he was joining the packet boat for Harris. On this occasion he gave her five shillings. Later he gave her £2 through an intermediary, Dr Macaskill, Claggan. That was all the help she got from him.

Dr Macaulay, still ambivalent in his attitude, arranged with Rev William Oldfield, Episcopalian Minister at Drynoch, to baptise the child. Ann refused because she was a Presbyterian.

The Kirk Session at Duirinish took the matter up, presumably on Ann's initiative. They asked Rev John Cameron, the Church of Scotland Minister in Stornoway, to interrogate Dr Macaulay.

He seems to have admitted paternity, but Rev John Cameron did not pass the information to the Kirk Session in Duirinish, because Macaulay was not one of his parishioners!

When the child was five years old, Ann went to Stornoway and demanded the arrears of aliment due to her.

Dr Macaulay asked her not to go about the town, and, if anyone asked why she had come to Stornoway, to say she was seeking the price of some cattle her father had sold him.

He warned her not to take him to court, "because I generally come off victorious." Which raises the question: how many bastards had he got?

Ann continued to pursue him in his lodgings, demanding payment of the aliment, which by this time amounted to £43. 10/- In modern money perhaps a couple of thousand pounds. Eventually Dr Macaulay threw her out.

She then raised an action in court and won the case, both before the Sheriff-substitute and the Sheriff Principal, which cost Dr Macaulay a good deal more than the £43. 10/- he had refused to pay.

During the court proceedings, Dr Macaulay showed all the viciousness of a cornered rat.

He denied that he had ever been on the vessel with Ann. Then contradicted himself by saying the friend she was going to see in Fort William, when they met, "was a baker whose paramour she was and to whom she already had an illegitimate child." He produced no evidence in support of this allegation.

He declared that the woman, whom he had just said had not been on the vessel, had drunk, during the voyage, "spirituous and other liquors so as to have made her utterly regardless of every vestige of decency and virtue."

"The use of these liquors to excess accounts for the notorious aberrations of mind and sense which alone would make her transfer to the Defender, under their delusive influence, the obscene entertainment which she admits herself to have indulged in with some other person very different from the Defender."

Having tried to argue that he was not the philanderer involved, he then went a stage further and suggested that the child he was supposed to have fathered did not, in fact, exist. At the same time he admitted that he had paid a certain amount of aliment to the mother of the non-existent child.

As a last resort, he argued that the case against him was fatally flawed because, in the pleadings, the Pursuer was sometimes named Macaskill and sometimes McAskill and her address was incomplete.

This last argument would be of no avail even in a criminal trial, said the Sheriff. Macaskill and McAskill were pronounced in precisely the same way.

In desperation Macaulay put up the plea that there was no solicitor in Stornoway to represent him. He asked for time to get help from the mainland.

It was a plea frequently heard in the Stornoway Court and it was generally a valid plea. In this case, however, it was, to borrow Dr Johnson's phrase, "the last refuge of a scoundrel." The Court dismissed it as such.

"Although in particular cases, and on sufficient cause shown, a party may be permitted to have time allowed for communicating with a professional agent, it is impossible, consistently with the administration of justice, to grant such delay as a matter of course," commented the Sheriff Principal, when Macaulay's appeal came before him.

"It is a simple case, not depending upon points of law, and the Record must be adjusted upon matters of fact known to the Appellant himself without requiring any professional assistance."

So Ann triumphed in the end, in so far as money could right the wrong which had been done her.

Her success was largely due to her own determination, but not entirely. Behind her in the final stages of the fight was the formidable figure of her solicitor, Donald Munro.

If Dr Macaulay had foreseen that Ann would eventually go to court, and had engaged the services of Donald Munro before she got to him, the chances are there would have been no case; no redress for the victim; and no record of the affair.

The true history of the legal services in Lewis, in the period I am dealing with, is not to be found in the records of the courts, revealing though these are. It lies in the numerous instances of oppression, which reverberate through the oral tradition of the island, but have no written memorial because they never came before the courts. The only legal adviser who could have pursued them was already engaged on the other side.

The triumph of Ann Macaskill is one of the rare exceptions which prove the rule.

Dr Macaulay certainly realised that he had lost the case, as soon as he knew that Ann had found a solicitor. He tried to persuade Munro to pull out. It was his only hope.

In a private letter, he alleged that Ann had agreed to settle for £3 a year, and give him custody of the child, but now refused "to deliver up the creature, expecting, no doubt, to make it a source of extortion."

He repeats his previous attack on Ann's character, and taunts Munro with the question, "Is it possible that you have turned whore agent?"

A few year's later, Munro appeared on behalf of an elderly widow who had been supported from the Poor Fund while it was administered by the Church but was struck off when the new Parochial Board was established, after the "reform" of the Poor Law in 1845.

The oppressor in this case was the state, through the new legislation. Colin Leitch, who as Session Clerk, had supported the widow for 16 years, now refused her relief as Inspector of Poor for the Parochial Board. The Session's liberality had gone beyond what the new law permitted.

The widow, Christina Murray or Macaulay, might not have found anyone to fight her case but for the chance that Colin Leitch, as I mentioned earlier in another connection, was Sheriff Clerk as well as Inspector of Poor. He conducted the Board's case himself, leaving Donald Munro free. The Sheriff appointed Donald Munro to act as agent for the widow.

Leitch argued that the widow could not be supported by the Parochial Board because she had a house and land, and had children who could support her.

Donald Munro argued that two of her sons and one daughter were married, with large families and had heavy responsibilities of their own. The daughter who lived with her could not go out to work because the old lady was in ill-health and needed constant care. Mother and daughter had no means apart from the charity of neighbours.

The Sheriff agreed with Munro. It could not be argued that she was able to maintain herself simply because she had a little plot of ground. In her old age such a holding might be considered a burden rather than a benefit.

"No explanation is given why this applicant, having been a recipient from the old Board, has been cut off by the present, when her infirmities must in the course of nature be increasing."

It is ironic that Donald Munro should have successfully defended the widow against a harsh interpretation of the law. He was for many years both chairman and legal adviser to all the Parochial Boards in the Island, in which dual capacity, he devoted his not inconsiderable talents to the saving of public funds. And, as we have already seen, one of his first acts on coming to Lewis had been to seek access to the books of the Kirk Session, to ensure they were not squandering money on the poor.

The reason that he found himself in the unlikely role of champion of the widow and the oppressed lies deep in Scottish history.

In 1424, in his very first Parliament, at Perth, James I decreed "Gif thar be ony pur creatur that for defalte of cunnyng (meaning knowledge) or dispens (meaning wealth) can nocht or may nocht follow his caus, the king, for the lufe of God, sall ordane that the juge before quhame the causs suld be determyt purway and get a lele and wyss advocate to follow sic creaturis caus."

As a result, Scotland had a legal aid system — primitive, but, within its limits, effective — centuries before England, the cost of sustaining it being borne, in part, by the legal profession and, in part, by the unsuccessful litigant in each case.

To carry out James's great principle, which is basic to any true system of justice, each Scottish court appointed a solicitor to be "Poors' agent" either for a year, or in a particular case.

Clearly this important part of the Scottish legal system was inoperative in Lewis, over the hundred years or so I am reviewing, except on the rare occasions when there were two independent solicitors in the island, or the one solicitor practising in the court was free to be "drafted" in by the Sheriff, as Munro was in the case I have just referred to.

The situation deteriorated when William Ross joined his cousin as partner. There were then two solicitors in Stornoway but they were as inseparable as the Siamese twins. It would have required a third, thereafter, to protect the poor.

Moreover, Ross was appointed Inspector of Poor for the Parish of Stornoway almost as soon as he arrived.. From this point on, especially after Donald Munro became chairman and legal adviser to the four Parochial Boards, the partners were involved almost exclusively in attempts to have people in need excluded from the roll.

We can only speculate how and why Colin Leitch ceased to be Inspector, but there is at least a presumption that he was levered out to make way for William Ross.

The effect of Ross's arrival is well illustrated by the case of John

Urquhart, a mason from Dingwall, who came to Lewis with his wife, Ann, and established a small contractor's business.

In his latter years, Urquhart, who had been a much respected business man and a prominent member of the Free Church, fell on hard times.

His trouble began when the Factor, at that time a Mr Scobie, refused to pay him for work he had carried out for the estate. After a good deal of bickering over Urquhart's account, Scobie engaged an architect, named Gair, to go over all his work in town and country and measure it up.

Gair was paid at the rate of £1 for every day he spent in the country and 10/- for every day he spent in town. His bill came to £31, which means that it took him between 31 and 62 days to measure up the contracts. That suggests Urquhart must have been standing out of a considerable sum of money.

It is not clear from the records whether Urquhart's bill was paid in full or whether it was reduced as a result of Gair's report. It is clear, however, that the Factor would pay only half of Gair's account. He told him to collect the other half from Urquhart.

Urquhart refused to pay. By that time he was probably unable to pay. Colin Leitch, the Inspector of Poor, was quietly supplying him with meal to keep body and soul together, although he was not formally on the Parochial Roll.

Gair consulted Donald Munro, who promptly raised an action against Urquhart. The action was undefended and Urquhart's indebtedness of £15. 10/- was increased by £2. 3/- of legal expenses.

At this stage Urquhart applied formally to the Parochial Board to put him on the Poor Roll. It must have been a bitter blow to the pride of an independent craftsman.

Worse still, his application to the Board was refused.

Urquhart took the only course open to him. He appealed to the Sheriff to over-rule the Parochial Board. He was able to get legal advice in drafting his application, but there was no lawyer in town who could represent him in Court.

William Ross, as Inspector of Poor, was denying him aid. Donald Munro, as a private solicitor, was pursuing him for the debt which had driven him to seek aid in the first place.

Unexpectedly, however, Donald Munro came back to the Court with a most unusual application. He wanted the decree against Urquhart recalled.

Gair had come to know of Urquhart's circumstances, and no longer wished to pursue him for a debt he could not pay.

Gair was not the only one to change his mind when he got to know the true circumstances.

Two local merchants, who were on the Parochial Board, voted against Urquhart's admission to the Roll, but then came to Court as witnesses in his favour. They had learned the truth. William Ross was unimpressed. If Urquhart was indebted to them for large sums, he told the Court, that merely proved that his circumstances were better than they had previously appeared to be. Not being pursued for the debts he could not pay, was "the same as if he had received a legacy of the amount of their claims."

I dont think either the merchants, who were not paid, or the debtor, who could not pay them, would have found it easy to follow the logic of that argument.

Ross also dismissed the evidence of the local doctor, Alexander Maciver, as "novel and Jesuitical," because he said Urquhart was now unable to do a day's labour although he knew that, for more than fifteen years, Urquhart had not earned his living by labouring, but "occupied the higher and more remunerative position of contractor for and superintendent of buildings."

The Inspector of Poor was on somewhat firmer ground when he pointed out that Urquhart had a lodger, but the lodger could not have been much of a payer: he was himself a pauper, being supported by the Parochial Board in Edinburgh.

Urquhart's problem, said Ross, was not incapacity but unemployment, "and the Poor Law Act does not recognise such."

He also argued that, even if Urquhart was destitute, it was for his children, not for the parish, to support him.

When he made that suggestion, William Ross already knew that one of Urquhart's sons was "believed to be in the Canadian west" and the family had lost contact with him, the second was unemployed, and the third — an itinerant painter — was being pursued by the Inspector of Poor's own partner, Donald Munro, on behalf of a Glasgow firm, for debts he could not pay.

The Sheriff Substitute, Andrew Lothian MacDonald, rejected Ross's arguments and admitted Urquhart and his wife to the Parochial Roll.

William Ross appealed, and the Sheriff Principal struck them off again.

The Sheriff Principal said he could find no evidence that Urquhart, in his own right, or as the husband of an aged wife, was a proper subject for Parochial Relief.

"However much the Sheriff may regret the privations to which the applicants may be exposed, he conceives he has no choice in administering the law but to refuse the application."

The form applicants had to fill in shows what the Sheriff was talking about.

There were 23 different questions, or rather 23 different categories of question. They covered, not only the financial circumstances of the applicant, but such irrelevant matters as their degree of literacy, where they worshipped and whether they were communicants.

They were asked for the name of the parish they were born in, and their reasons for leaving it, if they had. They had to list all the parishes they had ever lived in, and state how long they spent in each.

They had to give the names, ages, residences, occupations and earnings of all their children and their children's children.

At the top of the form was the warning: "OBSERVE. Those only are entitled to permanent Relief who by reason of physical imbecility or incurable disease, idiotcy (sic) or insanity are incapable of earning subsistence by labour, have no relative bound in law to support them and who continue destitute of the means of subsistence otherwise than by Parochial Relief...

"Parents and Children are reciprocally bound according to their circumstances or means — which the Parish is entitled to enquire into — to maintain or contribute towards the support of such Pauper relatives; and such Parents and Children, and their ascendants and descendants ... who refuse to do so, will be prosecuted to compel them to discharge their natural and legal duty."

Every last crumb a pauper had was bequeathed to the parish before he got relief.

In many of the activities which repel us most, as we read of them today, William Ross and Donald Munro were merely applying, with efficiency and zeal, the laws by which the richest nation in the world, at the height of its power, ground down the poor.

10. THE VULTURES AND THE DOVE

In 1851, John Munro Mackenzie, the Factor, was so busy, collecting rents and organising the mass emigration, he worked late into the night, every day of the week from Monday to Saturday, sometimes on Sunday, and even on Xmas day. He had only two half-days off in the course of the year.

On one of these, he took his wife and some friends by gig to Callanish, "to see the Druid stones."

For centuries, one of Britain's archaeological treasures had been half concealed by the accumulation of peat, growing year by year in the damp Lewis air. By the 1850's, when the stones were around 4,000 years old, the peat had reached a depth of five feet, reducing the great megaliths to unimpressive pygmies. Then Sir James Matheson employed the crofters to remove the peat and the Callanish Stones were once more revealed in all their majesty.

The Factor's other day off was of a different nature. He attended the sale of James Robertson MacIver's furniture.

MacIver, who had represented his father so effectively in defence of the fishermen of Loch Shell, had himself fallen on hard times.

Lewis MacIver died shortly after the Loch Shell evictions, from a chill he caught travelling on business into England. James Robertson MacIver, who succeeded to his empire as farmer, fishcurer, shipowner, merchant, money-lender, and general public figure, lacked his father's drive and acumen.

Shortly after he took over his father's estate, James lost his vesse,l the *Peggy*, with a cargo of salt fish, worth £1000, and uninsured.

The family rallied round him, and he limped on. Even when his furniture was sold, in 1851, he was still a sufficient figure in the community to be one of the guests at Lews Castle when Sir John McNeill was entertained to dinner.

It was quite a splendid occasion. Sir James and Lady Matheson were not at home, but the Factor went over early in the day to hand out the silver and the wine. In the evening he did the honours in his master's name.

It was nearly ten years later the MacIver saga ended, when a Glasgow merchant, Robert Coltart, had James Robertson MacIver's estate finally sequestrated.

The MacIvers had been a power in Lewis for several centuries.

Evander MacIver in *Reminiscences of a Highland Gentleman* — a title which tells a good deal about the family's view of their own importance — claims that, when Lewis became the property of Lord Kintail, afterwards Lord Seaforth, in 1610, "the MacIvers assisted him powerfully in establishing his authority, by the sword, over the lawless inhabitants."

Among the many MacIvers sent to Lewis, in that troubled period, were two sons of the minister of Fodderty, who had studied at Aberdeen, one training for the ministry, the other for the law.

One was instructed to promote religion in the island, the other to administer justice. Their descendants became known respectively as *Clann a' Mhinistear* and *Clann a' Bhaillidh*. Children of the Minister and Children of the Bailiff. Like hereditary dynasts, they continued to hold sway from generation to generation, although their role changed with the passing years.

Principal MacIver Campbell of Aberdeen, who wrote a history of Clan Iver, reckoned, in 1861, that there were eleven hundred MacIvers in Lewis out of a population of twenty thousand.

The descendants of the Vicar of Fodderty were undoubtedly men of high ability.

Before they reached the twilight of the family power in Lewis, the MacIvers of Uig, who were shipowners, had moved from Loch Roag to the Clyde, and from the Clyde to Liverpool where, with Samuel Cunard, they established the Cunard Line.

The MacIvers of Gress also moved from the local to the national stage.

John MacIver, a younger brother of James Robertson MacIver, became agent for the Caledonian Bank in Dingwall. It was the first modest step on a prosperous career, and had a rather inauspicious beginning.

When he staged a dinner party in his Dingwall home, the maid prepared a sauce for the roast with monkshood root in mistake for horseradish. Everyone who ate it was poisoned. John MacIver survived, despite a serious illness, but three of his guests died.

Two of the victims were Roman Catholic priests., and Lord Lovat came post haste from Beauly, suspecting a plot against his co-religionists. He quickly realised it was all the result of the maid's ghastly blunder.

Not long afterwards, John MacIver moved to India, where he became prominent in banking circles. His son, Sir Lewis M'Iver, Bart., was M.P. for Edinburgh for many years, and a noted orator in his day.

The family interest in the Highlands was maintained. Sir Lewis M'Iver, in the years just before the First World War, encouraged John

Perceval Day, of St Andrew's University, to complete a comprehensive study of Public Administration in the Highlands and Islands. It was this study which first identified the true nature of the Highland problem, one aspect of which is illustrated by the career of Donald Munro.

The Highlands and Islands, Day pointed out, were a remote area, alien in sentiment to the middle class, urban communities which dominated government thinking. The full exercise of State adminstration came belatedly, and with difficulty, to the Highlands, and, when it did come, the system imposed was quite unsuited to local conditions.

At the same time he identified the importance of the Highlands as a laboratory — his phrase — for administrative and legislative experiments. The faults in the national system, he pointed out, were most quickly and clearly identified at the periphery, and, at the periphery, it was possible to try experimental remedies without the risk of far reaching disaster.

The fall of the House of Iver is very relevant to the story of Donald Munro. in several respects.

In the first place it points a contrast. When Munro himself fell from power, some twelve years later, no one else was hurt by his personal calamity. In fact the whole island rejoiced. A notable tyranny was at an end with no loss to the community.

When James Robertson MacIver became bankrupt, small businesses fell around him like a house of cards. He had been one of the keystones of the local economy. However inefficiently, he had contributed to the general wellbeing.

Among the first to suffer were the crofter fishermen whose enterprises he had financed. They lost everything they had, when his creditors called in the advances MacIver had made to them.

At this point Munro and his partner became directly involved in the bankruptcy.

There is no indication that they helped to precipitate it, but, when it occurred, Donald Munro moved very quickly, as, perhaps, in duty, he should, to eject MacIver from all the lands he held in Gress and Little Bernera, and to file a claim for his outstanding rents.

More importantly, most of the pickings in the bankruptcy went to Munro and his cousin, as the only solicitors whom the Trustee in Glasgow, William Copland, could conveniently engage to pursue those in Lewis who owed money to the bankrupt.

In this way, the odium of harassing the local debtors was

transferred from the Glasgow creditors and the Glasgow Trustee to the two men on the spot.

Munro and Ross were merely the agents of other people, but, to the fishermen, they were the front line troops in an army of predators.

In 1861, 43 civil cases came before the Sheriff Court in Stornoway. In all bar one either Munro, or his cousin William Ross, appeared for the Pursuer.

In one or two actions James Morison appeared for the Defender, but, as we saw in the Stephen case, his residence in Stornoway was of short duration. Most of the actions were undefended.

Twenty-six of the cases were for the recovery of debt, and in twenty of these the partners acted for a creditor resident outside Lewis. Eight of them, at least, arose directly out of James Robertson MacIver's bankruptcy.

On two occasions, in the course of the year, debtors, imprisoned by William Ross, appealed to the Court for aliment, because they were wholly destitute.

On 17th September, 1861, John Henderson, Sheriff Officer, in Stornoway, set off for the village of Back, to seize the property of a group of fishermen, owners of a vessel named the *Dove*.

The *Dove*, and the nets that went with it, were being sold, at the instance of William Ross, acting on behalf of William Copland, as Trustee of the sequestrated estate of James Robertson MacIver.

The nets and other gear were to be taken from the homes of the crofters, and auctioned, along with the boat itself, on the sea beach where the boat was lying.

According to Henderson's account, a crowd collected when he read the warrant. He was threatened with violence. He explained the consequences for anyone who obstructed him in the execution of his duty.

In spite of that the crowd took possession of his horse and cart, turned them round and drove them a considerable distance along the road towards Stornoway.

He and his assistant were also driven back, "by threats of the most violent kind, repeatedly threatening to take my life, and throwing turf and stones with which I and my assistant were repeatedly struck."

At that point William Ross arrived on the scene, in his capacity as Judge of the Roup. Or was it as a solicitor representing the Trustee in James Robertson MacIver's sequestration? Or was it as Joint Procurator Fiscal concerned with the maintenance of law and order? Or was it as legal agent for the Lews Estate, which was also a creditor in MacIver's sequestration, and of which all the debtors were tenants at will, with no security whatever?

The crowd did not wait to enquire which of his many hats the Procurator Fiscal was wearing. They turned and ran.

The Sheriff Officer then returned to the village and read the warrant once more, in the presence of the Procurator Fiscal, and the auctioneer, Thomas Clark.

He repeated the warning of the consequences of obstructing him, and Ross explained the warning in Gaelic.

The Sheriff Officer then approached the home of George Morrison, skipper of the *Dove*, accompanied by Roderick Campbell, a Stornoway blacksmith, as his witness.

In the intense darkness of the black house, the Sheriff Officer and his witness were ambushed.

"Whilst removing the poinded effects," he reported, "we were jostled and buffeted with turf and manure by men who were concealed in corners ... and by Morrison's wife throwing water about us until our clothes were entirely covered with filth."

The water, one assumes from that, was not fresh and sparkling from the village well.

Undaunted, according to himself, the Sheriff Officer made his way to the house of Donald Maciver, a member of the crew, where there was no resistance and he took what he wanted.

By the time he reached the house of the next crewman, Neil Maclennan, the tiny windows had been blacked out so that the darkness in the house was more profound than ever.

"Men concealed in all corners immediately attacked me. One gave me a blow in the face which discoloured my left eye. Another, in the opposite corner, gave me a severe blow on the right side. I then forced my way out to the open air as I considered my life in danger.

"On looking at the entrance to the house possessed by Murdo Macleod, I observed, in the dim light, that the place was full of men, some of whom had stones or peats in their hands, evidently bent on using violence.

"I considered it dangerous to proceed further. I ordered the cart to proceed to the place of sale with such effects as had been collected, when some hundreds of the population, chiefly grown men, followed the party, yelling and hooting and throwing peats and stones.

"Two or three came over and endeavoured to push me into a pool of water on the roadside, and one of them took off my cap and threw it into the water.

"About the same time I got a severe hit with a stone on the left wrist, and another on the right shoulder, both of which have caused me a considerable amount of pain.

"They then followed the cart and, on overtaking it, took out the lynch pins which caused the wheels to come off and upset the contents.

"I then declared myself deforced and protested that the said Deforcers had incurred the penalties of law provided and accustomed in like cases."

There is no doubt whatever that the Sheriff Officer was deforced. There is equally no doubt that, if a crowd of some hundreds of grown men in a Lewis village had seriously attacked him with stones, he would have been martyred, just as surely as St Stephen. Whatever stone throwing there was, must have been sporadic, and the work of youngsters.

On his return to Stornoway, William Ross, in his capacity as a solicitor, acting for the Trustee in Glasgow, went back to Court for authority to arrange another date for the sale.

The sale was advertised by handbills attached to the Parish Church door in accordance with the law. As the Parish Church was five miles away, in Stornoway, and no one from Back belonged to the congregation, a notice was also posted on the door of the village school.

The Sheriff Officer also went with a notice to the home of each of the fishermen. The doors were locked against him. Probably the first time, and the last time, in their whole history, they had ever been closed in the face of a visitor. He gave six loud knocks to each, but no one paid any attention. So he rolled up the notices, stuck them into the lock holes, and went home.

On the due date, the boat and nets were exposed for sale on the sea beach at Back.

The Judge of the Roup was there. The Auctioneer was there. The Accountant was there. The Sheriff Officer was there. But no one else. The boat and its contents had to be carted away, with all the additional expense that that entailed.

Even if they did eventually find a buyer, no one would have been a penny the richer, except William Ross and the officials he had employed.

The value of the poinded goods was set at £41.15/-. Even if they fetched that sum, there would have been nothing left for the creditors of

James Robertson MacIver, once the legal expenses had been met.

There was no unwillingness on the part of the fishermen to meet their debt. As soon as Ross, on behalf of the Trustees, raised an action against them, they scraped around and paid him £19 to account. The balance would almost certainly have been forthcoming, if they had been permitted to continue in business, and pursue their calling.

Having discharged his duty as a solicitor in private practice, to his own pecuniary advantage, although not to that of his client, William Ross, remembered his responsibilities as Joint Procurator Fiscal. Discreetly, however: he did not act himself, nor appear as a witness, although he had seen the deforcement. He passed the papers to his partner and cousin, Donald Munro, and retired into the shadows.

Five men, four in their very early twenties, one in his thirties, were charged with resisting, obstructing and deforcing the Sheriff Officer. They appeared before a jury in an elaborate show trial for which no fewer than forty witnesses were called.

In the absence of any solicitor who could appear for the defence, the accused were represented by the Free Church Minister, Rev Donald MacMaster.

Two were acquitted. Three were convicted and sentenced to a month in gaol.

The most interesting part of the proceedings, however, was the preliminary examination of the five accused before Sheriff Andrew Lothian Macdonald, in chambers.

The statements confirm much of the Sheriff Officer's story. The accused all admitted seeing clods being thrown at him, his cap being flung in the water, his horse and cart being turned around. Some of them even admitted their own participation, up to a point.

Angus Morison, aged 20, said "I threw a clod myself at the officer but it did not hit him."

The evidence of Roderick Morison, aged 21, shows that the fishermen drew a distinction in their minds, which was logical to them, although the law did not recognise it. They accepted the right of the Sheriff Officer to take the nets they had bought with the money advanced by MacIver, but they refused to part with the nets they had bought "at Wick", out of their earnings at the fishing there.

Donald Mackenzie, a married man, said he saw a man he knew to be an officer of the law come out of Donald Maciver's house carrying some nets which he placed in a cart.

As he came out of the house, he knocked down Mackenzie's child.

Mackenzie went to William Ross, who was sitting in a gig, and asked how he would like to see his own child treated in that way. Ross made no reply.

Roderick Morison, who gave his age as 21, said Henderson had broken down a door to get at the nets in George Morison's house. Later he saw Donald Mackenzie with his fist over the Sheriff Officer's head, threatening to strike him because of some injury done to a child.

Morison said he was lame and could not keep up with the others. He missed some of the action, but he did see people on the tops of two houses near the schoolhouse, throwing clods or stones.

When the Sheriff Officer came out of George Morison's house, he was covered with chaff. "I cried out 'hurray' as I was amused at his appearance."

Norman Macdonald, aged 23, admitted quite freely that he had gone up to the Sheriff Officer's horse, seized it by the bridle and turned it around in the direction of Stornoway.

He advised Roderick Campbell, the Sheriff Officer's assistant, to go back to town because "the people were gathering and might do him harm."

He gave a new twist to the story, when he said he saw the auctioneer, Thomas Clark, standing in the gig "holding a pistol."

"This excited the people and we followed them. They collected about the machine Clark was in, to take the pistol from him."

Later he corrected this to say that Clark was standing in the road when he brandished the pistol.

He admitted that it was he who pulled off the Sheriff Officer's cap and threw it into a puddle of water. And that, later, he took the lynch pins out of the cart wheels.

He claimed, however, that, when the horse became restive, he assisted Campbell in getting it unyoked. He also assisted Campbell to reload the nets, when the vehicle was on its way back to Stornoway.

The oldest of the accused, Donald Murray, aged 33, said he knew the *Dove* had been poinded for a debt due to James Robertson MacIver for whom they used to fish. The boat was lying near the outlet of the Gress River about a quarter of a mile from the houses. He knew of the sale because of the notices, but he did not hear of any determination to resist it.

He was not very well on the day fixed for the sale, and merely looked out of the door to see what was happening. Eventually, however, he went out of the house, when the officials were on their way back towards Stornoway, but he threw no missiles, "although I might have said some words with my tongue."

Even more interesting than the content of the declarations is the manner in which they were obtained.

The accused, of course, were completely unrepresented. Not even the minister was there.

The declarations are set out as if they were given quite straightforwardly, there is, however, evidence that the information was elicited by pretty close questioning. At one point, for instance, one of the accused is quoted as saying "I did not see him with his hand to his face as if he had been struck."

That suggests the witness was repudiating a suggestion being foisted on him.

The fact that they were not all questioned on the same day, and that two of them were called back a second time, shows that the examinations were protracted, although the declarations are short.

The declarations are recorded in English but none of the accused could speak English. They were interrogated by the Sheriff, Andrew Lothian Macdonald, in Gaelic, and the declarations were explained to them in Gaelic.

The declarations were witnessed by Donald Munro, described neither as Fiscal nor Factor, but simply as "writer in Stornoway." They were also witnessed by two clerks in Munro's office and by the Sergeant of Police.

There is no indication that the Sheriff was anything but fair in his examination of the accused. At the same time it must have been very difficult for them to stand up to the sustained pressure of a vigorous interrogation, each of them alone, in the presence of a formidable array of officials, including the Factor, who held the fate of all their families in his hands, and who did not scruple at any time to use his power, as we shall see when we examine the events which brought an end to his reign.

As well as losing their fishing boat, and the nets on which the livelihood of five families depended, the crew of the *Dove* had to pay the expenses of their own dispossession, including the additional expenses incurred by the deforcement, in which none of the debtors participated.

In that year there were 12 cases of deforcement in Lewis, and none anywhere else in the county of Ross and Cromarty. If, however, we set the general police statistics for Lewis against those for Wester Ross—the most directly comparable area — we find there were fewer crimes of violence, despite the larger population.

The difference in the number of deforcements must lie in the provocation rather than the response.

Most of the deforcements at that period arose out of arbitrary evictions by the Estate. Some from warrant sales, as in the case of the *Dove*. Occasionally, however, they arose from the harshness with which the state, at that time, treated the mentally disturbed, especially in remote areas.

The committal of lunatics involved a legal process initiated by the Procurator Fiscal, so that, even in this element of the community's life, Donald Munro and William Ross had an intrusive role to play.

To protect the civil liberty of the patient, the fact that committal proceedings had been embarked on had to be advertised in the public press. So far as Lewis was concerned, the nearest newspaper was published on the other side of Scotland, and was seen by comparatively few people in the Gaelic-speaking areas. The advertisement served no practical purpose whatever.

There was no mental hospital in the island, so the patient was confined in Stornoway gaol, while the Court went through the motions of conforming with this irrelevant procedure.

So far as the patient's family was concerned, the stigma of gaol was added to the stigma which then attached to mental illness itself. The patient was immediately removed ten, twenty, thirty, perhaps even forty miles from home, with the prospect of being sent, eventually, to a mainland institution, where any link with the family was almost irretrievably broken.

In January 1851, Donald Munro applied to the court for an order committing a crofter from Garrabost "to the jail of Stornoway *ad interim*" because he was "in a state of Lunaticy (sic) Furious or Fatuous and threatening danger to the lieges."

The Sheriff Officer, with two assistants, was sent to Garrabost to seize the patient, but his wife refused to admit them. They went to get "two farm constables" to help them force their way in, but, by the time they returned to the house, the neighbours had surrounded it and they couldn't get near.

That incident appears in the criminal statistics as a serious breach of public order.

In the perception of the local community it was a victory — a rare event! — over a remote, alien, autocracy personified by Donald Munro.

11. THE BATTLE FOR STORNOWAY BAY

The relationship between Sir James Matheson, his Factor, and his legal advisers in Edinburgh, comes over very clearly in the struggle of the people of Stornoway, in the early 1860's, to gain democratic control of their town and harbour.

The Stornowegians wanted to take advantage of the legislation of 1862, as soon as it became operative, to obtain for their lively little town the status of a Police Burgh.

Even more urgently they wished to obtain powers from Parliament, for the regulation of the harbour, so that the fishing industry could develop uninhibited.

As far back as 1816, the business community of Stornoway raised funds for the building of a public pier — in replacement or improvement of an earlier pier, which had existed from time immemorial. Townsfolk who could not afford to contribute in cash gave free labour.

The proprietrix, Lady Hood, afterwards Mrs Stewart Mackenzie of Seaforth, supported the project and contributed a hundred guineas: nearly a quarter of the total cost. She also agreed to the setting up of a Quay Committee to manage the harbour.

In 1825, she went a stage further. She granted the town a charter, containing provision for its government by elected councillors, as a Burgh of Barony. The Council took over control of the pier.

In 1834, as we have seen in an earlier chapter, the business community of Stornoway appealed to Mrs Stewart Mackenzie and her husband — then a Member of Parliament, and a junior Minister in the Government — to get Parliamentary powers for the proper regulation of the harbour.

Some of those using the quay were refusing to pay dues, and the Council found there was some doubt about their legal power to compel payment.

Before he had an opportunity of promoting a private bill for Stornoway — if he ever intended to do it — James A. Stewart Mackenzie accepted a government appointment as Governor of Ceylon. As a result the management of the Island of Lewis passed into the hands of Trustees in Edinburgh.

The canny city lawyers had a close look at the charter which Mrs Stewart Mackenzie had given the townsfolk, to help them regulate their affairs. They decided it was invalid because, in their view, she had no legal power to grant it.

In that sentence lies the key to Lewis history.

The island lagged behind the rest of the country, not because the people were lazy or ignorant, but because, in the tightly structured, over centralised British system, the inhabitants could do nothing to help themselves, unless a remote, uncaring, ill-informed and sometimes hostile Parliament first gave them leave.

The problem was compounded by the efficiency of the Scottish legal profession, in keeping their clients out of trouble, by discovering the reasons why something essential to the life of the community could not, in law, be done.

There have been times when the island almost died of *ultra vires*.

Elections for the Stornoway Council ceased in 1838, but a Committee of those who subscribed to the public appeal in 1817, still tried to manage the affairs of the harbour, although it had no legal right to exist.

The Committee succeeded up to a point. By 1860 it had accumulated some funds, and the question of a Private Bill was once more being actively discussed.

At this stage, Donald Munro induced them to enlist the services of Sir James Matheson, as their proprietor and Member of Parliament. On the Factor's advice, they offered to make over to Sir James the funds which stood to their credit in the bank, as a contribution to the cost of the legislation.

All the surviving members of the Committee signed the petition to Sir James. A number of the leading feuars and shipowners signed along with them.

The majority of the ordinary townsfolk refused to sign, but whether from apathy, or distrust of Donald Munro, does not appear.

If it was the latter, they were quickly justified.

Instead of going for a Private Bill, Sir James approached the Lords Commissioners of the Treasury, behind the Committee's back, seeking to purchase the whole foreshore of Stornoway, right out to the harbour entrance, and even beyond, giving him absolute personal control over the destiny of the port, the town, and indeed the island.

The Treasury referred the matter to James K. Howard, one of Her Majesty's Commissioners of Woods and Forests — the forerunners of what we now know as the Crown Estate Commission.

Without consulting, or informing, those whose livelihood might be affected by the transaction, the Commissioners agreed to the sale, in principle. Their one difficulty was that, as Sir James made it clear he was concerned with protecting amenity, rather than developing commerce, they had no yardstick by which to fix a price. They asked Sir James to make an offer.

Sir James suggested £400. After the usual period of bureaucratic gestation, the Commissioners accepted the offer, and, early in 1863, the foreshore of Stornoway harbour became the personal possession of the proprietor.

It is not clear whether this had been Donald Munro's intention from the start, or whether the Factor was over-ruled by his master.

My guess is that the advice to purchase the foreshore came from Sir James's Edinburgh agents, anxious, as lawyers always are, to prevent their client from surrendering power unnecessarily. Especially when there is a chance to increase it.

Sir James was not averse to having the harbour regulated, but he wanted it regulated to suit his purpose, not the Stornowegians'.

They saw the harbour as an area ripe for industrial development: a key to the prosperity of the whole island. And they were right.

Sir James saw the harbour as the gateway to the magnificent castle he had built over-looking it. Industrial development was an intrusion on his amenity.

He wanted South Beach to be a grand esplanade along the sea front, leading in a sweep through James Street and Matheson Road — both named after himself! — to the Castle entrance.

He could do little to change the appearance of South Beach Street. It was already built up. He could control the development of James Street and Matheson Road because the land had not yet been feud.

The charters he granted there carried an obligation to plant trees along the frontage, creating, at no cost to him, a wooded avenue leading to the massive gates at the Porter's Lodge which barred the ordinary citizens' entrance to the thousand acres of wooded grounds he had created round the Castle.

Stornoway today derives great benefit from the Castle Grounds, which, thanks to the generosity of the first Lord Leverhulme, are now a public park, while the Castle itself is a technical college.

It was different in the 1860s, when Stornoway was involved in a classic conflict between industry for the many and amenity for the few. The conflict was all the more bitter because many families in Stornoway, and the surrounding villages, had been evicted from their homes, or their grazing land, to make possible the creation of the Castle Grounds, and the

Manor Farm adjoining. The battle for the harbour was a new phase in an old campaign.

In his Memorial to the Treasury, seeking to purchase the foreshore from the Crown, Sir James expatiated at length on the benefits he had conferred on Lewis over the preceeding 18 years.

He made roads, drained lands, built warehouses, encouraged trade and the fisheries, established steam communication with Glasgow, erected schools, created employment, and endeavoured to raise the moral and social position of the people.

All that was true up to a point. But the question must be asked whether an autocrat, however benevolent, has ever succeeded in raising the morale, or liberating the human potential of a community, by pumping money into it, at his own whim and pleasure.

The question must also be asked why, in the face of so much benevolence, his agent on the ground — his Factor, Donald Munro — was seen as a tyrant, rather than the distributor of his master's largesse.

Sir James's reasons for wishing to purchase the foreshore were set out at length.

On the west side of the Bay, the Memorial explained, the foreshore "bounds his private pleasure ground and policies." It was occasionally taken possession of by fishermen for purposes "which were offensive in themselves, and attended, in some instances, with risk of injury" to the shrubberies and plantations.

The risk of injury arose from the lighting of furnaces on the beach for the "barking" of nets — an essential operation for herring fishermen in the days before nylon.

To prevent the nets from rotting in the sea, they had to be immersed from time to time in a hot bath of cutch or catechu, — popularly referred to as bark — a water-soluble, resinous substance obtained from tropical plants.

The smell of hot cutch, with which I was very familiar in my youth, was distinctive, and pervasive, but not unpleasant. I can, however, imagine the offence it gave to the ladies at the Castle, signalling, as it did, an invasion of their privacy by common tradesmen or fishermen.

Sir James made it clear to the Treasury that, under the Royal Charter creating the Barony of the Lews, he already owned the foreshore, although he was prepared to buy it a second time, to save the cost of a legal action to establish his existing right.

From the terms of the Memorial, it would appear that there had

This modern view over the roof tops in Point Street illustrates the close relationship between the area which had been the busy fishing port in the great days of the herring industry and the Castle. Between the two can be seen the line of foreshore just beneath the lawn where the barking of nets by the fishermen offended the ladies of the Castle. (Photograph by courtesy of the 'Stornoway Gazette'.)

been an on-going argument, in which the fishermen contended that their furnaces were erected below high-water mark at spring tides, on parts of the foreshore from which only the Crown had power to exclude them.

On the east side of the bay, Sir James wanted to deal with areas where the sea was encroaching because of the removal of shingle from the beach as ships' ballast.

He also complained that he was in a difficulty. Mrs Stewart-Mackenzie had given grants of the foreshore to private individuals who had then erected quays and piers. Sir James was bound, by the terms of his purchase of the island, to confirm these grants, but he could not do so because he did not know whether he owned the foreshore or not.

The only interpretation one can put on that is that Sir James was distressed that he could not confirm his predecessor's charters, as he wanted to do, and was in honour bound to do. The situation, however, was very different.

The Disposition of the Foreshore by the Crown to Sir James is dated 14th January 1863. Fifteen days later, Donald Munro intimated the completion of the deal to the people of Stornoway in his own inimitable way.

He sent peremptory letters to all those feuars, who had built piers which encroached on the foreshore, warning them that they could no longer use them for fish-curing or boat-building, and that they could not let them to others during the herring fishing season, as they had done in the past, in exercise of their rights under their feu charters.

When one considers that the Disposition was signed in the office of the Commissioners of Woods and Forests in London, and had to pass through the hands of Sir James's Edinburgh agents, and perhaps of Sir James himself, before it filtered down to his Factor in Stornoway, Donald Munro must have acted with considerable alacrity.

From the terms of the letters he also seems to have acted with a certain amount of glee.

In the specimen letter which survives, he told Mrs Mackenzie of the Lewis Hotel that "neither she nor her late husband had a vestige of right" to the pier opposite the hotel, despite the fact that it had been erected, at their own expense, with the consent of the previous proprietors, and had been tolerated for upwards of twenty years by Sir James himself.

It concluded, "I am, Dear Madam, Yours Truly, Don. Munro."

No one in Stornoway called him "Don." It was strictly a business-like abbreviation, distancing himself from the recipient of the letter. It was certainly not an affectionate diminutive used among friends.

The letters made it clear Sir James was taking all the piers into his own hands, to regulate as he thought proper, both as regards the prevention of nuisances and the accumulation of a fund for their improvement, and other purposes connected with the town.

To many families this meant the loss of a significant source of income which they had enjoyed for many years. It was a savage and unexpected blow.

The townsfolk responded quickly, but moderately.

On 11th February, they held a meeting in the Masonic Hall. It was presided over by Kenneth Smith, known locally as "California" because he had spent some years in business in the States. Three resolutions were passed.

The meeting first appointed a Provisional Committee of eight: to "confer with Sir James Matheson, in order to secure his powerful co-operation in promoting the commercial prosperity" "and regulating the sanitary condition of the town."

They included Donald Munro in their Committee. Clearly they were not challenging Sir James's authority. They were seeking an effective compromise.

The other seven members of the Committee were prominent businessmen whose names occur frequently in the local history of the time.

In the second resolution they welcomed any steps to secure additional quay accommodation, and promote the sanitary improvement of the town, but suggested improvements should be carried out "under public management."

The third expressed the "greatest solicitude for meeting the views of Sir James Matheson, in everything that tends to the prosperity of this community."

The Provisional Committee met Sir James the very next day, but he appears to have given them something of a brush off.

The Committee held a meeting on the 17th and decided that, as Sir James "did not enter into the views expressed in the resolutions," another public meeting should be held.

Sir James in the meantime appears to have had second thoughts.

While the Committee was still in session, Kenneth Smith, received a letter from him, offering to consult with the Committee, provided Capt Donald Mackenzie was added to their number, and stipulating that any future members must be feuars.

The letter, at the same time, demanded that the funds, collected by the old Quay Committee, should be "at once transferred to my name, as trustee and superior of the burgh, and, as such, the only legally-constituted authority vested with any right of property in the quay, for the public benefit, as was explained to you by the opinion of eminent counsel read at our meeting."

Instead of spending the money on setting up a statutory harbour commission, backed by an Act of Parliament, he wanted to use it to fill up a hole near the Lewis Hotel, "notoriously a great nuisance, polluting the atmosphere, during and after the herring season, especially in warm weather."

Sir James's interest in sanitation and amenity is to be applauded, but there was rather more to it than a hole in the foreshore. A hundred years later, when the waterfront was faced with solid concrete, that area was known as "the Lazy Corner", because the set of the tide still created a stagnant pool, where "the moving waters" stubbornly refused to perform "their priestlike task of pure ablution."

If the Stornowegians had acceded to Sir James's demand, their money, metaphorically as well as literally, would have been poured into a hole in the ground.

Sir James no longer considered an Act of Parliament necessary. It had only been required because the Crown, by claiming the foreshore, was preventing development. Now that he had purchased the foreshore, at considerable pecuniary sacrifice, for the public benefit, the obstruction no long existed.

It was superfluous for him to add, he continued, that "any proceedings adopted by me will be for the public good, in consultation with the Committee."

While "hailing" the Committee's assurance that they supported him in everything he did, he added, a little sourly, that he hoped the assurance would be followed "with better results than the plans I propounded as far back as 1846 for the improvement of the town and the comfort of its inhabitants—at my own cost but in which nothing was done owing to their supineness and indifference."

He also blamed the people of the town for the failure of some subsequent, unspecified, attempt to carry out improvements through the Chamberlain.

With Sir James's letter was another, from Donald Munro, authorising the Committee to read it at the public meeting, but insisting that any objections they might have to its terms must be discussed with him beforehand.

Sir James's approach to the matter was no doubt influenced by the fact that he made his fortune as an eastern potentate and was used to getting his own way.

The townsfolk of Stornoway would have none of it.

The Committee replied immediately that they had been set up to act "in co-operation with Sir James" and they objected to being treated as "merely a committee of consultation."

For good measure they added that they were in no position to anticipate the objections that might be made to Sir James's letter by those attending a public meeting.

The public meeting was postponed until February 20th, to give people time to digest Sir James's reply. When it was held, the general public of the town unanimously endorsed the Committee's reply and reinforced the Committee by appointing eleven additional members.

Malcolm Mackenzie, a member of the original Committee, criticised Sir James's claim "as arbitrary and likely to operate against the welfare of the community."

Next day, Kenneth Smith, as Convener of the Committee, sent a letter across to the Castle, expressing the disappointment and alarm of the business community at the position Sir James had taken up.

The claim that Sir James was the only legally constituted authority vested with the right of property in the Public Quay deprived the Committee of Management of rights which they had exercised for forty years.

The offer they had made, in 1860, to transfer their funds to Sir James, was on the understanding that an Act of Parliament would be obtained, and the Committee consulted on its terms, but, under the "peculiar circumstances" which had now arisen, "the Committee cannot consent to have the public money transferred to Sir James's name, nor avail themselves of the pleasure of acting as a Committee of Consultation in giving effect to the claims put forward by Sir James."

The letter concluded by offering that, if Sir James helped them to get the Act of Parliament they wished, the community would relieve him of the trouble and expense of providing additional harbour accommodation.

In what looks like a veiled threat at the end, Kenneth Smith asked Sir James to obviate the agitation that might ensue, if he insisted on the views expressed in his letter.

The Committee then made arrangements, in defiance of Sir James, to "expose the dues to public roup according to use and wont."

It had been their custom for many years to let the dues annually to a tacksman, and the tack went to the highest bidder. It was not an efficient method, but it meant the Committee got their money immediately and did not have to employ staff for day to day collections.

At the same meeting they considered how to obtain "the written sanction of the inhabitants," for their plans to make the harbour more efficient for trade and fishing.

The roup of the dues took place on February 23rd. On the same day the purchaser, Andrew Gibson, a fish-curer, received a letter from Donald Munro, telling him that Sir James repudiated the pretended sale as illegal and incompetent. He was warned that, if he collected dues, or let any of the quays for curing purposes, he would be held legally liable.

The prohibition on the collection of dues would have hurt no one but Gibson. The ban on curing threatened the trade of the town.

Donald Munro no doubt realised this. Almost as soon as he prohibited Gibson from letting the quays, he tried to let them himself.

The Committee protested to Sir James.

He responded by raising an action in the Court of Session against sixty-three separate owners of property in the burgh.

Not surprisingly merchants and fish-curers figure prominently in the list. But it also includes the two local doctors, a bank accountant, a retired naval captain, the Inspector of Poor, the light-house keeper, and Donald Munro's own cousin and partner, William Ross.

Many of those on the list still have descendants in Stornoway. One of them, Matthew Russell, a merchant, was the great grandfather of Sir Russell Johnston M.P.

Sir James asked the Court of Session to declare that he had the sole and exclusive right to enlarge the pier, without interference from the Defenders; to order them to hand over to him the funds held by the old Quay Committee, and to account to him for any dues they had collected.

He raised a separate action against those who had built piers, asking the Court to declare that they had no right to have done so, despite the fact that their charters (or some of them anyway) obliged them to build a pier, at their own expense, "conform to the rest of the piers and quays on the street where the said houses are built, and in a line with them."

The Committee engaged a W.S. to fight the case for them but they were in a dilemma.

They were faced with a legal action by a Pursuer with a bottomless purse and an autocratic disposition, who had just fought a dispute about the boundary between Lewis and Harris, all the way to the House of Lords.

Many of those named in the summons would not, or could not, contribute to the expenses.

No doubt, too, their Edinburgh agents advised them they were on pretty treacherous ground. The Court would almost certainly decide in Sir James's favour, in view of his purchase of the foreshore from the Crown.

The Committee changed their tactics. They called another meeting, asking for a mandate to take the matter to the House of Commons.

Kenneth Smith was once more in the chair and went straight to the point.

"These proceedings of Sir James are so much at variance with common justice, and so much opposed to all late legislation upon harbours, the subject demands the attention of Parliament.

"It is not usual, I believe, to alienate from the Crown the shore of public harbours, in favour of private individuals.

"The grant does not in any way meet the requirements of this harbour; it does not provide for any legitimate improvement, and it is proper that we should know the pretext on which the grant was applied for, and the object for which it was given."

He poured scorn on Sir James's claims of all that he had done for the town. None of the great promises had been fulfilled. Instead an embargo had been laid on the trade of the port, and an attempt had been made to stop the fisheries.

"He threatens parties here for making use of private piers, built at their own expense, on their own property. He tells them they have no right to use them! That he is to take them for his own private use — for the public benefit!"

"Are we tamely to allow ourselves to be deprived of our public rights? Those who went before us kept their ground nobly. Posterity would brand us with infamy, if we surrendered ours."

Significantly the next speaker was Captain Donald Mackenzie, Sir James's own nominee on the Committee. He was equally forthright.

He had built a pier on his own property on South Beach Street but agreed to give up the use of it, because Sir James wished to make the street a public promenade. Later, Sir James built a pier of his own immediately beside it, and let it for fish-curing.

"A piece of gross injustice," thundered the irate Captain.

Malcolm Mackenzie, one of the leading merchants, condemned "the hole and corner job with the Woods and Forests," analysed at length what he called "the superfine sophistry" of Sir James's case, and accused him of "legal spoliation."

A view which the huge crowd present at the meeting endorsed unanimously.

Within a few days, 292 people signed a petition to Parliament, calling for a public inquiry into the circumstances in which Sir James Matheson purchased the foreshore from the Crown. That number represented well over 50% of the adult males in the burgh.

About fifty described themselves simply as feuars or householders, but 16 were fishcurers, 30 were shipowners, master mariners or shipmasters, 36 were fishermen, 13 coopers, 13 ship's carpenters, 2 sail-makers and 3 rope-makers.

Twenty-three merchants also signed, along with 18 shop assistants, the banker, the Sheriff Clerk Depute, an architect, a druggist, an accountant, a cabinet maker, a blacksmith, two porters, a pensioner and a tinsmith. Even Sir James's own gamekeeper signed.

The shoe-makers were particularly active. Thirty three put their names to the petition. This is not surprising. Down even to my own boyhood, the shoe-makers' shops were the great academies for theological and political debate. In fact the tradition is not yet wholly dead, although theology does not figure so frequently on the agenda.

It must have been a great embarrassment for Sir James. The people who arraigned him before Parliament were not only his tenants but his constituents.

He was not one of the old aristocracy who could brush a matter of that sort aside. He was one of the *nouveaux riches* who had to struggle for his place in Society, despite his great wealth, and his city home — Stornoway House — little more than a stone's throw from Buckingham Palace.

In fact he had been lampooned by Disraeli in one of his novels, because his wealth derived in large part from the opium trade. Disraeli did not name him, but there were few others the cap would fit.

As they could not call on their own MP to present their petition, the Committee sent a deputation to London and secured the services of Sir James Ferguson.

Donald Munro reacted immediately in a characteristic way. He obtained a lithograph of the petition, and hung it on his office wall. Those who had signed it were invited to call.

"Is that your signature?" they were asked.

If they admitted the offence, they were commanded to sign a counter-petition, withdrawing their names.

Those who refused — and they were many — were told they would get no more contracts or employment from the Estate, which for some was almost a sentence of bankruptcy.

In spite of the bullying, the people of Stornoway had played a winning card.

Sir James's Edinburgh agents published a twelve page statement, rebutting the charges made at the public meeting, and setting forth once more all his benefactions, including the building of an Industrial Seminary, a ship building yard, and the only quay, north of Oban, which vessels could approach at all states of the tide.

The quay was in fact an old sailing vessel, the *Amity*, and there was a notice posted on it warning the public that it wasn't entirely safe and they used it at their own risk.

The long list of benefactions ended with something of an anti-climax. "Sir James has given an enclosed Bleaching Green for the use of the town."

It does not seem like a great piece of philanthropy, but it was an essential amenity before the arrival of washing machines or even soap powder, in a crowded town, where many poor families had no garden or clothes line of their own. It was still in use in my childhood.

Whatever sympathy for Sir James the statement might have aroused outwith the Island of Lewis, it certainly infuriated the natives.

The Edinburgh agents, who no doubt shared the general prejudice of their day against Gaelic-speaking crofters, quoted a statement by Sir John M'Neill.

"It is remarkable that conduct so liberal should have failed to gain as its reward the gratitude of the population. The people of Lewis appear to have no feeling of obligation or of thankfulness for the aid that has been extended to them by the proprietor but, on the contrary, regard the exaction of labour for wages as oppression.

"The best informed persons believed that there were able bodied men in Lewis who would starve, and allow their families to starve, rather than earn their subsistence by ordinary labour."

Sir John M'Neill's comment on the crofters of the rural areas was completely irrelevant to a petition to Parliament by the merchants, fish-curers and shipowners of Stornoway.

Moreover, and more importantly, it was completely untrue.

In the same document, Sir James's Edinburgh agents boasted that during the famine, in the middle forties, he had offered free passage on his boat — named *Mary Jane* in honour of his wife — to anyone prepared to go to the low country in search of work. In seven months in 1847, they claimed, nearly 2300 people availed themselves of the offer.

Two thousand three hundred people represents more than one in eight of the total population of Lewis in 1847, including women, children, the ill, and the aged. The *Mary Jane* no doubt picked up emigrants from other islands on the way to Glasgow, but, even allowing for that, there must have been a quite remarkable exodus, in search of jobs, from the island where, according to the Government's official adviser, heads of households would rather see their families starve than work for wages.

It is a pity the contradiction, implicit in their own document, did not inspire Sir James's agents to seek out the real reason why his undoubted generosity was not as widely appreciated by the people of Lewis as he would have liked.

If they had, this book might never have been written.

The Edinburgh document denied that Sir James had agreed to apply for an Act of Parliament to regulate the harbour. It denied that he had acquired any new rights when he purchased the foreshore. It asserted that he alone had the power to levy dues, and that he had taken over the piers (which other people had built!) merely to prevent the appropriation by private individuals, for their own exclusive benefit, of what should be left common or public.

In other words, Sir James was the public. Louis XIV could not have put it better.

In spite of the bluster, however, Sir James did not relish the publicity.

On 4th February 1864, his Edinburgh agents informed the Commissioners for Woods and Forests that "the big Quay case, as they call it in Stornoway" had been amicably settled.

Sir James had agreed that the harbour should be run by a properly established Harbour Commission, with seven members, three elected by the townsfolk, three appointed by himself, and the seventh nominated by the Sheriff.

On the same day, the Quay Committee wrote Sir James Ferguson telling him, in effect, to call off the dogs.

12.   A £1000 SILENCER

In May 1863, when the dispute over Stornoway Harbour was still raging, a group of businessmen invited Napier Campbell, then practising as a solicitor in Edinburgh, to set up business in Stornoway. They wanted to break the monopoly maintained by Donald Munro and William Ross.

In the previous December, Gordon Macleod of Lochbay, Isle of Skye, applied for permission to practice in the Sheriff Court at Stornoway.

The Sheriff Substitute, Andrew Lothian Macdonald, referred his application to the two men who had a vested interest in keeping him out — Donald Munro and William Ross — as "examinators" to consider his qualifications.

They objected that Macleod produced no evidence that he had served a formal apprenticeship and completed his indentures. The examination was deferred to give him a chance to produce the evidence they wished.

Gordon Macleod replied that in Lanark, Argyll, Forfar and other counties, a certificate of having served five years as Clerk in the office of a Writer to the Signet, or Solicitor before the Supreme Court, was accepted in place of discharged indentures.

He met that criterion. He had worked as a Clerk for ten years in the office of Horne and Rose W.S. in Edinburgh and, in addition, had attended, for one session, the Scots Law class at the University.

Horne and Rose, in a letter to the Court, confirmed that he had ample opportunity to make himself acquainted with the forms and practices of the profession while in their office, and had conducted himself with propriety. They had heard nothing against his respectability since he left.

Munro and Ross maintained their objection, and Sheriff Macdonald upheld it, refusing Macleod permission to practice in the Stornoway Court.

The monopoly was still intact, but not for long.

Napier Campbell, possibly on local advice, did not apply to the Sheriff Substitute in Stornoway for permission to practice in his court.

He applied to Sheriff Principal Cook, in Edinburgh, for permission to practice in all the Courts in Ross and Cromarty.

His application was granted, and he promptly set up his office in Stornoway.

One of his first tasks was "to get Stornoway created a police burgh, so as to give the people a status to defend their public rights."

He succeeded, according to his own account, despite Estate opposition.

The townsfolk were in a much stronger position than they had been in regard to the harbour. They did not need the assistance of Sir James, in his dual role of proprietor and M.P., to promote a Private Bill. They were acting under general legislation, already on the Statute Book.

Realising that fact, Donald Munro, with or without the consent of his employer, changed his tack. His name appears first among the signatories of the application asking the Sheriff to determine the boundaries of the Police Burgh. And the Town Council was not long in existence before he was Chief Magistrate, presiding over its affairs.

He was unable to stop the runaway horse, so he got on its back!

Whether the townsfolk would have got Police Burgh status at all, if they had not imported a solicitor from the south, is something one can only speculate about.

Napier Campbell's influence was certainly felt in the Sheriff Court, although, unfortunately, as we shall see, his enthusiasm was greater than his judgment.

Early in August he defended a crofter, John Beaton, three of whose cows had strayed on to Goathill Farm and been poinded.

The farmer, Alexander Gerrie, demanded 7/6 before he would release them. Beaton could not raise that amount on the spot.

He consulted a friend, who advised him to offer 3/3, which was approximately double the amount specified in the Winter Herding Act of 1686, which still regulates these matters.

The farmer refused to accept 3/3, and raised his demand to 15/-.

When Beaton refused to pay, Gerrie consulted William Ross.

Ross advised him to release two of the animals, and raise an action in the Sheriff Court asking authority for the sale of the remaining animal, to cover his claim for damages, plus the cost of the legal proceedings.

When the case came before the Court, Napier Campbell raised a number of trivial objections which added nothing to his case, but he also made a number of substantial points.

He argued that the poindfold, in which the farmer kept the animals, did not conform with the law, because not enough fodder and drinking water was provided. That an offer of compensation, in excess of what the law demanded, had already been made in the presence of witnesses. That the damage, the cattle were alleged to have done, had not been independently assessed. And that the sum claimed was so small the action should have been raised in the Small Debt Court, where the legal expenses would have been very much less, even if the crofter lost the case.

Sheriff Andrew Lothian Macdonald turned down all Campbell's arguments in language which suggests that he resented his presence, disturbing the peace of the Court, or that some personal animosity had developed between them.

One of Campbell's defences is dismissed as "utterly valueless", another as "pure nonsense," a third as "a wretched quibble", and a fourth as "the height of absurdity."

In conclusion the Sheriff accused Campbell of an "apparently inordinate desire to make a display of his legal knowledge and acumen."

Fortunately for Beaton, as well as defending the case in Court, Campbell sent a personal letter to William Ross, in which he said some pretty hard things.

"This is the second time I have been consulted to defend poor people against claims arising out of the arbitrary, illegal, unwarrantable and oppressive exactions of the same Pursuer," he wrote.

"I have passed the first but feel disposed to make a stand on the second, in defence of the poor people of this island who, I understand, positively groan under such excessive exactions, to which the badly fenced and enclosed farms seem improperly to expose them.

"Unfortunately too the summary procedure, countenanced by the practice of this Court, seems to make the matter ten times worse."

The fifteen shillings demanded precluded Beaton, because of his poverty, from redeeming his cattle. Yet the difference between Beaton's offer and the farmer's exorbitant demand was only 11/9. "It is absurd to say that a valuable beast was required for security of such a sum, and to apply for sale on such a miserable pretext seems to me to be done with no other object than the cruel and inconsiderate one of depriving a poor man of his property — nearly a third of his free estate — and to saddle him with a debt for the balance of law expenses which might be used to wrest the remainder from him.

"Were my client not so very poor as not to justify me, in the proverbial uncertainty of the law, risking his too easily accomplished ruin, I may state confidently that I could interpose such obstacles to the present proceeding as would either prevent its being carried into execution, or entitle him, if proceeded with, to heavy damages."

Campbell, on behalf of his client, offered to pay a reasonable sum "under protest," but suggested that it might be prudent for the farmer to make no demand at all.

William Ross replied with some heavy sarcasm.

"Your magnanimity in coming forward in defence of 'the poor people of this island who you understand positively groan under excessive exactions' cannot be too highly commended, and I only hope you will continue to use your influence on behalf of these sufferers, but you must excuse me stating that, in my humble opinion, you might with great propriety have avoided applying the expressions 'arbitrary, illegal, unwarrantable and excessive exactions' to my client in taking steps to protect his own property, and that of others whom he represents, from being wilfully eaten up by his neighbours."

In spite of the terms of his letter, and the Court's decision in his favour, Ross advised his client to accept 13/3 in full settlement and waived all claim for legal expenses.

Why?

The records give no clue, but the answer might lie in the Court of Session in Edinburgh where, around that time, George Stephen had begun his fight back, and the activities of the little mafia in Stornoway were, for the first time, coming under the scrutiny of the higher courts.

Unfortunately that initial success seems to have given Napier Campbell a taste for letter writing, and that was his undoing.

A few years later he was consulted by the farmer at Aignish, James Alexander, who found himself bogged down in a morass of litigation.

He would appear to have been quite a good farmer in his early years, but he was now around eighty, suffering from loss of memory, and drinking heavily.

As early as 1851, the then Factor, John Munro Mackenzie, confided to his diary that Alexander was drinking, and the Estate might be better rid of him. In spite of that, his lease had been renewed for nineteen years. The trouble in which he was now involved arose on the very last lap, after he had actually left the farm and was living in the neighbouring village of Knock, although his lease had some months still to run.

The Estate was clearly anxious to get Alexander out as quickly as possible. A new tenant had been selected. Munro, as Factor, pressed Alexander to leave two fields — the two best on the farm — uncultivated in the last year of his tenancy, so that the incoming tenant could have the use of them. He was offered neither compensation nor remission of rent, for this reduction in his earning power.

When Alexander tried to crop the disputed fields, Munro, in the name of the proprietor, applied to the Court for an Interdict.

Munro maintained that Alexander had agreed to give up the two fields. Alexander denied this.

Munro suggested Alexander was so frequently under the influence of drink he didn't know what he had agreed to or not agreed to. Napier Campbell, for Alexander, retorted that Alexander had been called to meetings in the Factor's Office, and induced to sign documents to his prejudice, when he was too drunk to know what they contained.

He also alleged that documents were altered after the terms had been agreed, and that, when Alexander was short of funds for his defence, his difficulties were increased by actions in the names of creditors for whom Munro and Ross were agents.

This last point was certainly true. When Munro was pursuing his Interdict, Alexander's difficulties were compounded by an action raised in the name of the Dingwall and Skye Railway Co. for the payment of the final call on some shares Alexander had bought. The local representative of the Railway was William Ross.

At the same time, Donald Munro raised an action for Multiple poinding against Alexander, in the name of the proprietor, for arrears of rent. While William Ross raised an action, on his own behalf, for the immediate payment of a bill for legal expenses amounting to £9.16.6, some of the items in which were for services said to have been provided thirteen years before!

William Ross's bill covers a variety of items such as making inquiries at the Post office about a missing Postal Order, preparing a summons of removing against a sub-tenant, arranging for the sale of sheep Alexander had poindfolded, raising an action for trespass against the crofters in Garrabost, and advising Alexander in a dispute about a faulty horse.

All these items, and the charges, seem reasonable enough, and there is evidence that Alexander was of a litigious disposition. But, if the bill was completely genuine, why was collection so long delayed?

The relationship between Ross and his client was rather more than anomalous.

Ross was law agent for the Estate, and business partner of the Factor. In some of the cases in the Alexander series, William Ross was acting as legal agent for Donald Munro, as Factor for Sir James.

Alexander, as a tenant of Sir James, would have had many occasions for visiting either Ross or Munro on matters which affected his interests but were not private legal consultations.

It is not common, I would also suspect, for a solicitor to act as a client's legal adviser for many years, then suddenly appear for other people in a series of actions against him. That, of course, was an inevitable consequence of the monopoly Munro and Ross had maintained over legal services in Lewis for many a year.

In the event, Ross dropped the claim, "in consequence of an error made by the Sheriff Officer in citing the Defender." He also paid Alexander's expenses of 16/-. A turnabout which raises questions of its own.

In his Defences to the Interdict action, Napier Campbell made some sweeping charges against Munro and Ross, in particular he alleged that "there was a secret and collusive agreement or understanding" between Munro, "or his doers," and the incoming tenant of Aignish Farm for the purpose of enabling Munro to enrich himself at Alexander's expense and evade legal consequences.

It was a serious charge but Sheriff Andrew Lothian Macdonald would have none of it.

He struck out a great deal of Napier Campbell's Defences. The document is scored and scribbled over in a confusion of red and blue pencil marks. Eventually, he instructed Napier Campbell to withdraw the whole document because it contained "various diffuse statements altogether foreign to the question at issue."

As in the Beaton case, Napier Campbell began a correspondence with William Ross in regard to the matters under dispute.

On August 5th 1870, he wrote complaining that he had been denied an opportunity of paying his client's accounts, before legal expenses became payable, "clearly showing a most determined purpose on your part, as well as your so-called 'client', Mr Donald Munro, to ruin my poor client or take advantage of his necessities."

Four days later he wrote again, apparently in a fury. Alexander had come to him complaining that he was still being dunned for the various bills against him, although Napier Campbell had assured him they would be paid before legal expenses were incurred. He had difficulty in getting his client to believe that the payment offered had been refused by Ross, for unspecified technical reasons.

In this second letter to Ross, Napier Campbell repeated the offer to pay in full, provided Alexander was "afforded reasonable time to do so."

Alexander's money, he complained to Ross, was "tied up in the hands of a confederate of yours whom you call 'client'."

This may be a reference to an agreement Munro had induced Alexander to sign, making over the cattle on the farm as surety for his rent, but, more likely, it refers to the Multiple poinding under which Munro had frozen Alexander's assets until his creditors were satisfied.

Unjudiciously, Campbell went on to declare his intention of getting at Alexander's "true enemy face to face, and bringing the blush of shame to his cheeks, if he has such a commodity about him." He appealed to Ross to assist him in this, "as you take credit occasionally for compassion for my client and a desire to save him expenses."

In this Napier Campbell was clearly drawing a distinction between Munro, as the true oppressor, and William Ross as his more compassionate associate.

Having, not very convincingly, tried to soft-soap Ross, Campbell went on to threaten him.

"I have shown no special eagerness to embroil you *personally* but upon my word I think you have *taken up a wholly mistaken position* ... If you beggar my client so much the worse for you in the end."

In a P.S. Campbell said one of Alexander's minor creditors had just called to see him. He offered to give the poor man his money, but he refused to take it. It had to be paid through his solicitor, William Ross. Ross was away from home and neither the senior partner, Donald Munro, nor the office clerk, Mr Anderson, "had power to accept a prescribed account" in Ross's absence.

"You are a precious lot," Campbell concluded, with a flourish.

In Ross's absence, Campbell's letter was opened by his assistant, John Norrie Anderson, who later became provost of Stornoway, and one of the outstanding public men in the island's history. Forty years later he was one of those marked out for a seat in the House of Lords, if new peers had to be created to ensure the passage of the Parliament Act.

Anderson replied, in a letter which does not survive, but which appears to have been *a tu quoque*, accusing Napier Campbell of milking his client by "the multiplying of sheets." On the face of it there is some substance in the charge, judging by the length and irrelevance of Campbell's defences.

As soon as he got home, William Ross wrote a further letter to Napier Campbell repudiating Anderson's reply. It was not the answer he would have made, it did not represent his views, and he was in no way responsible for it.

Ross was probably annoyed with his assistant for replying to

Napier Campbell in kind because he had quite another line of attack in view.

"In your said letter of 12th curt you charge me with being a leading conspirator against your client's *property, means, life and reason*. A charge so grave that I feel bound to call upon you to retract it immediately and make an ample apology for having used such unfounded expressions towards me."

Napier Campbell did not retract. He repeated the view that all the proceedings against Alexander were linked together, in an attempt to deprive his client of his property, or a considerable part of it, and that William Ross was more openly and prominently involved in the proceedings than anyone else.

"Holding these views conscientiously I cannot, I am sorry to say, retract the charge made by me on behalf of my client till satisfied that it is unfounded. That must be a question of time and investigation, and certainly circumstances appear to me to justify the opinion ... which, in due time, I will probably consider it my imperative duty to press."

At that point William Ross sent the correspondence to his cousin, William Ross Skinner, who promptly sued Napier Campbell for £1000 damages for libel. In modern money probably in excess of £50,000.

Napier Campbell was aghast. He couldn't afford to fight an action in the Court of Session, even if he was sure of winning, which, in the circumstances, he could not possible be.

Many years later he gave a brief account of the incident: "In defending a tenant (Alexander) from vexatious litigation, and a net-work of complications of a very peculiar character, I used words which were so far indiscreet that I did not see my way to defend an action of damages for £1000 in the Court of Session. I preferred to retract and pay £30 of expenses."

That is somewhat misleading. It implies that Napier Campbell apologised, paid the legal expenses, and the action was dropped.

The truth is that, although he retracted, the action against him was pursued but not defended, and decree was given in favour of William Ross.

In view of the retraction, however, Ross did not exact his £1000, or bankrupt Campbell in attempting to recover it.

He was quite content to have a Court of Session decree for £1000, waiting to be extracted, if ever again Napier Campbell became difficult.

He held his peace for thirteen years.

In 1883, under the immunity from harassment promised to witnesses appearing before the Royal Commission of Inquiry into the Condition of the Crofters and Cottars in the Highlands and Islands of Scotland, he was able to unburden himself.

He wrote at length of the abuse of the legal system in Lewis.

"The crofters complain that there is no law for their redress; but in any view they dare not resort to law with their laird or anyone under the shelter of his ample wing...

"The rental does not, I think, show all or anything like all, the various exactions imposed on the crofters. It will not, in particular, show *the law costs recovered* — one very severe method of punishment, and *not an uncommon one* ....

"I have met the factor Munro in seven different capacities in one case. I also heard him boast of appearing in sixteen different capacities at one time. He could thus cut himself up into sixteen different personages in law, or he could, at pleasure, unite all these parts or personages into one great person under the powerful name of the sole proprietor of Lews....

"To follow the intricate windings of a Lewis legal labyrinth, in the hope of obtaining justice, required great independence, some means, considerable nerve, and resolute steadiness of purpose. Above all, it required a reliable tribunal within the compass of the person's purse. How seldom could all these elements be united in Lewis ... It was like fighting with some hydra-headed monster.

"Nor was it free from risk to an agent — as I experienced ...

"The wielders of this terrible complex legal machinery could almost be 'a law unto themselves'. Silence resulted from *sheer dread*."

Napier Campbell clearly wrote that with some passion, but he must also have written it with some satisfaction.

By that time Munro had been discredited. He had been sacked both as Fiscal and as Factor, in circumstances which will be examined in the next chapter.

13. THE RIOT THAT NEVER WAS

Donald Munro finally over-reached himself when, on 19th March 1874, he served summonses on nearly sixty families, evicting them from their "acres, gardens, grass and houses," in the Island of Bernera, and from their summer sheiling ground, on the main island of Lewis.

He had no intention of evicting them from their homes. He wanted to take away their summer grazings and give them something less acceptable instead. He knew they wouldn't like it. His method of ensuring obedience was to hit them over the head first, and then present his commands as if they were concessions.

He served the summonses without the consent, or even knowledge, of his employer. When questioned about it, later, in the Sheriff Court, he replied "I am not in the habit of consulting Sir James about every little detail connected with the management of the estate."

It was such a little detail in fact, he couldn't be sure how many summonses he issued. "Possibly fifty-six, but I don't remember!"

The number tossed off carelessly like this has been accepted by most writers as correct, but Dr I. M. M. MacPhail points out, in his recent book *The Crofters' War*, that a private police report puts the total at fifty-eight.

The original documents, preserved in the Scottish Record Office, confirm the police report. Eleven summonses were issued. Nine of them bore six names each. The tenth had three names. One favoured individual got a summons all to himself.

Fifty-six or fifty-eight, the summonses of eviction were not a "little detail" to the people of Bernera. The progress of the Sheriff Officer through the island, handing them out, created panic.

The panic was not allayed by the behaviour of the Sheriff Officer, Colin Maclennan, a despicable bully who relished his mission. Nor by the attitude of the Ground Officer, James Macrae, who seems to have been infected by the general high-handedness of the regime.

Macrae sent messengers ahead commanding the crofters to collect at certain points.

The messengers were unnecessary. The news, travelling more quickly than the Factor's agents, brought the people out.

When the official party got to the village of Tobson, there was a crowd already collected, but not in the spot Macrae had designated. He sat on a hillock eighty or a hundred yards away and commanded them to come to him.

In this autocratic approach Macrae may have been apeing his superiors. Donald Munro later declared in Court, "the people come to me. I don't go to them!"

On the other hand Macrae's attitude may have reflected his personal unease at the dirty work he had been given to do.

The people at first refused to come nearer, muttering sourly, "If it was for any good to us, you would not have called us here like this."

Eventually they came, and Macrae told them they had to give up the hill grazings at Earshader and take instead the hill grazings at Hacklet.

The crofters objected that the area offered them was too small.

They also objected that they had already been moved, just three years before, from the hill grazings they held from time immemorial, and had been compelled to enclose their new grazings at Earshader with a dyke seven miles long — entirely at their own expense!

The dyke was of no benefit to the crofters. It was not erected to protect their land. It was to keep their stock out of the deer forest established on the land they had lost.

When questioned about it later in Court, Munro said it had cost the crofters nothing to build it. They had merely given their labour free.

When asked if the labour of a Lewis crofter had no money value, he replied contemptuously, "It is not worth much."

Reluctantly, the crofters had accepted that exchange, but only because the Factor gave them an undertaking, which they maintained was embodied in a written document, assuring them they would hold the new sheiling ground as long as they held their crofts, and they would hold their crofts as long as they paid their rent and generally behaved themselves.

The document was left in the hands of Donald Munro but, when it came to the crunch, he denied all knowledge of it.

No compensation was offered to the crofters for the dyke they were now being asked to abandon. They were offered no reduction in rent to compensate for the smaller grazings. In fact they were given no guarantee that their rent would not be increased, on the pretext that the new area was more convenient for them, because it was nearer their in-bye land.

When Macrae had completed his explanation of the change being imposed on them, the Sheriff Officer gave the crofters their summonses of removing.

Whatever the Ground Officer said about a change only of summer grazings, the documents handed out were quite specific. They included everything the crofters had.

Donald Munro's flamboyant signature on the bundle of Summonses of Removing which caused the so-called Bernera Riot still gives us an idea of the untroubled confidence he felt when the affair began. (Photograph by courtesy of the Scottish Record Office.)

Which were they to believe? The verbal assurances, given by a minor official, or the written summonses of removing, bearing the Factor's signature and the authority of the Court?

The sequel was almost inevitable.

In the gloaming, as he crossed the moor between Valasay and Tobson, the Sheriff Officer was attacked with clods and stones.

He was in no danger. He was not alone. He was accompanied by James Macrae, the ground officer, and by Malcolm Macaulay, the farm constable, a local man. Also with them was Peter Bain, an exciseman, visiting Bernera on business of his own. He had shared a boat with Maclennan, when they sailed across from Callanish.

All of them were hit but no one suffered anything that could be called an injury. The attack seems to have been the work of youths, carried away by the wave of excitement which swept the island.

Peter Bain, an independent witness, put the number of assailants at only five or six.

Maclennan, however, took it seriously. He commanded Macaulay to give him the names, so that he could have the culprits punished.

Macaulay said it was impossible to identify the culprits in the dark.

Maclennan declared that, if he had a gun, some of the Bernera women would be mourning the loss of their sons.

Macrae told him he was lucky he hadn't a gun. If he had, he would be a dead man himself.

Despite the warning to moderate his language, the Sheriff Officer repeated the threat on several occasions, in houses where Bernera crofters heard him.

Peter Bain believed the threat was intended seriously.

In the morning, as the party made their way back to the ferry, a party of thirteen fishermen blocked the path, and demanded to know from Maclennan what he had said about using a gun.

Maclennan refused to answer and made for the boat. One of the men caught his jacket to detain him. There was a minor scuffle and the jacket was torn. His overcoat was also slightly damaged.

This delighted Maclennan. He believed he now had evidence which would stand up in Court. According to Bain, he tore the overcoat again himself, on the journey back to Stornoway, to make the evidence more impressive.

During the scuffle Bain heard someone shout, "Whatever you do don't hurt him!"

He also heard the man Maclennan was grappling with assure him he would not be injured in any way.

So far from being upset, the Sheriff Officer was in great glee. As soon as they landed from the ferry boat, he borrowed Peter Bain's bagpipes and entertained his companions with lively airs all the way to Garynahine. He talked at great length about his right to use a gun, if people interfered with him in the execution of his duties.

It was not just the exuberance of a petty bully. There is evidence, which I will look at later, that Maclennan had been sent to Bernera deliberately to provoke the crofters into some rash act, to justify Donald Munro in breaking the promise he had given them about their summer grazings and their crofts.

As soon as Maclennan reported back to his superiors, warrants were issued for the arrest of three of the men who accosted him — Angus Macdonald, Tobson; Norman Macaulay, Tobson and John Macleod, Breaclet.

They were charged on indictment, before a jury, with assaulting an officer of the law, "in revenge for having executed his duty, and to the injury of his person," "a crime of an heinous nature and severely punishable."

Before the three Bernera men were arrested — in fact before they knew they were being charged — Donald Munro went across to the village of Earshader, on the mainland side of the channel, and summoned the crofters to meet him. About fifty attended.

He explained that he was offering them the farm of Hacklet instead of the farm of Earshader, because all their land would then be within the island of Bernera. They would be spared the necessity of swimming their cattle, twice a year, across the Sound to the summer grazings, which, in his view, was dangerous. He was really doing them a favour, he said. The new arrangement was safer for themselves, their families and their cattle.

He couldn't have been convinced by his own argument, however. He considered it necessary to add that, if they did attempt to swim their cattle across the sound, he would bring the Volunteers from Stornoway to stop them.

Later he pretended the threat to use the Volunteers was a joke, and the people knew it was a joke. He had been Commander of the Volunteers for many years but he had given up that "unpaid honour." Under cross-examination, however, he admitted that the threat might well influence simple-minded people to accept his terms.

Whether or not the crofters were scared by the threat, they were certainly unimpressed by Munro's concern for their safety. He had been the Factor for twenty years, but this was the first occasion on which he had spoken of the danger of swimming their cattle across the Sound.

Simple-minded the crofters might have been, in the eyes of the worldy wise, but they knew enough of human nature to realise that Munro's real aim was to deprive them of any legitimate excuse for being on the mainland of Lewis, in the vicinity of Morsgail deer forest, or the Grimersta River, which is one of the best angling rivers in Europe.

As a great concession, Munro told the crofters he was prepared to have the rent and souming for the new grazings fixed by three arbitrators. All the arbitrators would be chosen by him. If the crofters didn't trust any of them, they could have a fourth arbitrator. He, too, would be chosen by Munro.

Although he admitted his threat to use the Volunteers when he was reminded of it in Court, Munro was very vague about what was said at the meeting, either by himself or the crofters. Clearly there was no mileage for him in remembering.

In Court he couldn't say whether he had offered the crofters compensation for the dyke they had built round Earshader. He couldn't say whether they grumbled or accused him of breaking faith. He couldn't even remember the date of the meeting.

With a little prodding, however, he did remember that, despite their anger over the dyke they had built, many of the crofters agreed to the exchange he proposed, provided the lands of Strome were added to Hacklet, which was too small to replace Earshader. The crofters, although annoyed, were not being obstructive.

More importantly, he admitted that, although he had gone to Earshader as Factor, to discuss a point of estate management with the crofters, he carried in his pocket the precognition taken from the Sheriff Officer, by his cousin and partner, William Ross, as joint Procurator Fiscal, on the basis of which three Bernera men were to be charged with a very serious offence.

He gave the crofters no hint at the meeting that three of their sons were to face charges, which might lead to terms of imprisonment, but, combining Court business with Estate business, or perhaps even combining business with pleasure, he discussed the Sheriff Officer's precognition, privately, with James Macrae.

It was unusual, and wholly improper, for Munro to disclose the

This sheiling was built on the Bernera Moor during Donald Munro's long reign in Lewis. It was only a summer, not a permanent, dwelling but it illustrates the difference in life style between croft and Castle. It also underlines the importance to the people of Bernera of their summer grazing ground.

evidence of one potential witness to another, but he went further than that. He altered the Sheriff Officer's precognition to accord with the information given him by Macrae.

The nature of the changes he made is not recorded, but one can only assume it was his intention to instruct the Sheriff Officer to amend his evidence to accord with Macrae's, so that there would be no conflict, when the case against the three Bernera men came before the Court.

When cross-examined about the changes, Munro made the astonishing admission that he thought he was acting in his two capacities as Fiscal and Factor simultaneously.

He could not remember what the changes were, and protested — as if it were an adequate excuse — that he had never altered a signed precognition before.

Whether that is true or not, it is certainly true that he never altered a signed precognition again.

Before the admission was forced out of him in Court, Sheriff Principal George Dingwall Fordyce sacked him from the post of Procurator Fiscal, which he had held for more than thirty years.

The Sheriff Principal's action was precipitated by a report from his Substitute, Charles Grey Spittal, on the events in Bernera and Stornoway which followed Munro's visit to Earshader.

On the 7th April, William Ross, as Joint Procurator Fiscal, set off from Stornoway with Supt Donald Cameron, who was in charge of the Police in Lewis. They travelled to Callanish together. Their purpose was to arrest the three Bernera men accused of assaulting the Sheriff Officer.

At Callanish they were told it was unsafe for them to venture into Bernera, the people were in such an angry mood.

Cameron pooh-poohed these fears, and went across to Bernera alone. Ross, discreetly, stayed in Callanish.

On Bernera, Supt Cameron got a friendly welcome. He knew the people. He spoke their language. He sympathised with their predicament. His own parents had been evicted, when he was a child, from a croft in Inverlael, on Little Loch Broom. But he was still a policeman prepared to enforce the law.

He went first to Breaclet, where he was told Macleod was away from home but would be back in the evening. He was also told there was to be a Prayer Meeting in Tobson that evening and it was very likely the other two accused would attend it.

He went then to see the minister, Rev Mr Campbell, and explained the purpose of his visit. He told the Minister he would attend the Prayer Meeting himself, and asked the Minister's help in explaining the position to the people.

Only one of the accused — Norman Macaulay — was at the Prayer Meeting. Angus Macdonald had gone to Stornoway on business.

At the end of the service, Cameron spoke to Macaulay, who raised no difficulty about giving himself up to the police. He explained, however, that he would prefer to wait until he was joined by the others. Cameron accepted his promise that he would attend the Court, and in due course it was redeemed.

When Cameron got back to Callanish, William Ross was gone. He too had learned that Angus Macdonald was in Stornoway, and had set off post haste to have him forcibly detained.

As soon as he got to Stornoway, Ross sent the Sheriff Officer scouring the streets to find Macdonald. When he was spotted — in front of the Fiscal's own house, as it happened! — two constables seized him.

Macdonald had no idea why he was being arrested and stoutly resisted. The passers-by came to his assistance. The police sent for Munro and Ross, who arrived with all the clerks from their office. The tug of war became intense, as more and more of the townsfolk joined in to hold the prisoner back, while Munro and his henchmen tried to drag him towards the gaol.

Munro then sent for the Sheriff Substitute, who read the Riot Act and called on the crowd to disperse. They paid no attention.

The Sheriff then called by name on some of the men in the crowd whom he knew, asking them to assist the police. They did so, no doubt reluctantly, and finally the prisoner was secured behind bars.

The gaol was only a hundred yards from the place where Macdonald was first apprehended, but it took four hours to get him there.

The struggle, however, was not continuous. An independent eye-witness, writing later in the *Inverness Courier*, reckoned the real struggle lasted less than half an hour. The rest of the time was taken up in summoning reinforcements and general palaver.

"The only circumstance which can in any way justify the appellation of a riot to a disturbance of no extraordinary character is the fact that the Sheriff read the Riot Act," commented the eye-witness.

This is borne out by police evidence to the effect that Macdonald repeatedly called out, "If you summon me to Court, I will attend." The Sheriff and the Joint Procurators Fiscal ignored the offer. They had their man and were determined to gaol him.

At the time of the arrest they did not even have a warrant. Supt Cameron had it with him in Bernera. They promptly wrote a duplicate, and had Macdonald judicially examined and committed the same evening.

At that stage, the Sheriff took a serious view of the situation and the mainland press carried alarmist reports.

It was rumoured in Inverness that Sheriff Principal Fordyce had asked the authorities in Edinburgh to have a detachment of military standing by for despatch to Lewis which, according to the editor of the *Courier* is "usually one of the most peaceably disposed parts of Her Majesty's dominions."

There might well have been need for the military if Munro and Ross had their way.

When Ross hurried to Stornoway in pursuit of Macdonald, he left instructions for Cameron to remain in Callanish until he got back. One can only assume it was his intention to secure Macdonald by force in Stornoway, and then return to Bernera to secure the others in the same way.

Cameron sensed the situation, disregarded the Fiscal's instructions, and hurried to Stornoway.

By this time Sheriff Spittal himself was becoming uneasy. He was so anxious to consult the Supt he called in person at his house, and left a message with Mrs Cameron asking her husband to see him as early as possible the following morning.

The Supt bluntly advised the Sheriff to release the prisoner immediately. The charges against him did not warrant holding him. The Sheriff took his advice. Which was fortunate for all concerned.

Although Cameron did not know it at the time, a hundred and thirty men from Bernera, and the villages along Loch Roag, were already marching on Stornoway, with a piper at their head, playing 'The Campbells are Coming."

They were normally peaceable, as the *Courier* asserted, and as Supt Cameron himself had proved, but he was quite convinced that, in the face of the action taken by Munro and Ross, the men marching on the town would take the gaol to pieces, stone by stone, to set the prisoner free. They would then seek revenge on everyone who had a hand in his imprisonment.

As it was, the prisoner met them half way between Stornoway and Bernera, and turned back with them to town, to demand a meeting with Sir

James Matheson and lay their grievances before him personally.

After the long march from Bernera, the little army rested for the night at Marybank. In the morning they marched into town and camped on the slopes of Goathill.

As soon as he heard of their arrival, Supt Cameron hurried to meet them. They greeted him warmly and gave him a dram. They even got the piper to play what the Supt afterwards described as, "an appropriate tune complimentary to me," although he does not tell us what it was.

The Superintendent's first task was to persuade the three Bernera accused to submit themselves to a judicial examination by the Sheriff. They refused to go to Court for this purpose, but he was able to persuade the Sheriff to take their declarations on the field.

After the al fresco examination, the Bernera men marched to the Castle accompanied by the Supt.

They demanded an audience with Sir James. When they had made their complaint, they were ushered into the Conservatory — a huge glass structure demolished in the 1930's by the Stornoway Trustees. There they were served with bread, beef, coffee and milk, under the supervision of Lady Matheson.

Lady Matheson asked the men not to go back into Stornoway. She was afraid they would get drunk and create a disturbance. The men were in a dilemma. Many of them had friends they wanted to see or business to transact. In any event, they had to go into town to pay for the whisky they had already bought and with which they had treated the Supt of Police.

The problem was resolved when the Supt said he would be personally responsible for their behaviour. Again his faith was justified. The men marched into town, spent an hour or two there, and left again in good order, without molesting anyone.

The Supt had taken the precaution of advising the police, and all who had helped them, to stay indoors until the Bernera men had gone!

Three months later, on 17th July, 1874, a memorable date in Highland history, the three men from Bernera stood trial for their alleged assault on the Sheriff Officer.

The case was heard before Sheriff Principal Fordyce and a jury of tacksmen, merchants, fish-curers and tradesmen, of whom only one could be suspected of any bias towards the crofters' cause. Descendants of several of them are still prominent in the business and public life of the community, including Sandy Matheson, for many years Convenor of Comhairle nan Eilean.

CONSERVATORY, STORNOWAY CASTLE. 11,980. G.W.W.

The Conservatory at Lews Castle where Sir James and Lady Matheson entertained the Bernera marchers. Some of the plants were so rare photographs appeared in the scientific press when they flowered. The contrast with the conditions under which the Bernera crofters then lived could hardly have been greater. (Photograph from the George Washington Wilson Collection, Aberdeen University Library.)

After a hearing which lasted all day, and well into the night, the jury unanimously found the three Bernera men not guilty of any assault.

On the following day, Colin Maclennan, the sheriff officer and complainant, was tried before Sheriff-substitute Spittal and another jury. He was found guilty of assaulting Angus Macdonald by kicking him, when he was a prisoner in Stornoway gaol and unable to defend himself.

The jury unanimously recommended him to the leniency of the Court. He was fined £1, with the alternative of ten days' imprisonment. The fine was paid at the bar.

As for the great "riot" in Stornoway, nothing came out of it but a charge of obstructing the police against one poor baker named John Smith. He was tried before a jury, who unanimously found the charge not proven.

Supt Cameron, in a report to his Chief Constable, a few days after the "riot" in Stornoway said quite unequivocally that it was "created by the Fiscal, who ought to be the last official to raise such."

He went even further. He wrote, "I have no doubt whatever in my own mind the Sheriff Officer was put up to say something to aggravate the people when serving the writs, in order to get them to commit an offence, which the Fiscal would make a handle for to cause the police to interfere, in order to strike terror into the people so that they will submit to the Factor's arrangements."

It may not be good grammar, but it bears the stamp of truth.

By that time Ross and Munro were trying to cover their tracks.

Ross, the Supt complains, was interrogating the Stornoway policemen closely about their past service, presumably with the intention of trying to blame their inexperience for the commotion he and his partner had precipitated.

Munro went further. On Sunday morning, on the way to church, he tried to nobble the Supt. The Supt curtly replied that he did not discuss business "on the Sabbath."

There was a good reason for the Supt's reticence. He was in process of writing his Chief Constable to say the police could get on with the people and maintain peace, in both town and country, but for the fact that the Fiscal was also the Factor. As long as Munro continued to interfere with them, however, the position of the police in Lewis would be untenable.

The Chief Constable read the letter to Sheriff Principal Fordyce. The Sheriff's only comment was that Sheriff Substitute Spittal's report "was expressed in much stronger language."

Sheriff Fordyce immediately suspended Munro from acting as

Fiscal. When the full facts came out, at the trial of the three Bernera men, he dismissed him altogether.

With remarkable foresight, Supt Cameron made two predictions. First he said the mishandling of the Bernera affair had created a precedent in Lewis and, in future, if anyone was thought to be unjustly imprisoned, he would be released by force.

The prediction was not fulfilled precisely in that way, but there can be little doubt that the actions of Munro and Ross, as Fiscals in 1874, had a good deal more to do with the Park Deer Raid of 1887 and the Aignish Riot of 1888, than the so-called Fenian agitators who were blamed at the time. Injustice casts a long shadow.

The Supt's second prediction was that, if the charge against the Bernera three ever came to trial, Munro would sink in a bog of his own creating.

That was fulfilled to the letter.

The trial of the Bernera Three, as we shall discover, was transformed into the trial of Donald Munro.

14. THE TRIAL OF DONALD MUNRO

It was Charles Innes, an Inverness solicitor, one of the founders of the firm of Innes and Mackay, who transformed the trial of the so-called Bernera Rioters into the "trial" of Donald Munro. His name is still remembered with respect in Lewis and a street in Stornoway was recently named in his honour.

There is a tradition in Bernera that Sir James Matheson paid Innes's fee. This is not quite as absurd as it looks.

Sir James knew it was because of his Chamberlain's provocative actions the Bernera men were in trouble, but he could not halt, or abort, a criminal trial. It was quite in keeping with his aloof, autocratic, but paternalistic, regime to buy himself out of the difficulty by ensuring the victims didn't have a grudge against him, personally.

Alternatively it has been suggested that Innes defended the Bernera Rioters for political motives. Innes was a Tory. Sir James was a Liberal. It was a good opportunity to attack a political opponent.

This theory is quite untenable. Solicitors do not go round the country offering their services to those who have fallen foul of their political opponents. Besides, Sir James was no longer in Parliament. There was no need to discredit him.

In his handling of the case, Innes was very careful to direct his fire at the Chamberlain, distancing his employer from all his wrong-doing. This is much more consistent with the first theory than with the second.

I. M. M. MacPhail in *The Crofters' War* puts forward still another possibility. He suggests that Innes might have been engaged by Daniel MacKinlay, a native of Lewis, who had made a fortune in Calcutta. MacKinlay took a let of the shootings at Gress in 1874, not long after the Bernera Riots, and in 1878 he published a pamphlet of his own, attacking the whole system of administration in Lewis.

There is a long tradition of wealthy Lewismen over-seas taking an active interest in the welfare of their fellow islanders, but I wonder whether it is necessary to look so far afield for the crofters' champion or champions?

When Angus Macdonald was arrested, he was in Stornoway to do business with Kenneth Smith, the fish-curer for whom he worked. When the Bernera men marched on Stornoway to release Macdonald, they sent their representatives on in advance, to consult Kenneth Smith and get him to arrange a meeting with Sir James.

Kenneth Smith was the leading man in Stornoway at that time. It was he who led the townsfolk in their fight with the estate over the development of Stornoway Harbour, and organised the Petition to Parliament which brought Sir James to the negotiating table.

The action of Lewis MacIver, in support of the evicted crofters of Loch Shell, provides a precedent for a fish-curer coming to the assistance of fishermen in trouble with the estate.

Smith had a more direct interest in the fate of the Bernera men than MacIver had in the fate of the people of Loch Shell. If three of his fishermen were sent to gaol, during the fishing season, the loss would have been his as much as theirs. He, and many other businessmen in Stornoway, were anxious to end the Chamberlain's tyranny, even if it didn't bear as heavily on them as on the crofters.

Whoever paid the legal fees there can be no doubt Innes earned them.

Donald Munro was called as the first witness for the prosecution. No doubt he would have avoided the witness box if he could, but it was essential for the prosecution to establish the reason for the Sheriff Officer's visit to Bernera.

Munro's examination took only a few minutes. His cross-examination took many hours.

Innes went straight to the heart of the matter. "I should like his Lordship and the gentlemen of the jury to know exactly who you are, Mr Munro."

He took Munro painstakingly through his long list of public offices, jogging his memory whenever he professed to forget. Then at the end came the barb.

"Oh! by the way, I was almost forgetting a very important appointment. Are you procurator fiscal of this district?"

"I was."

"You were! Have you ceased to act?"

"I have."

"Did you resign?"

"No."

"Were you removed from office?"

"Sheriff Fordyce, from whom I derived the appointment, withdrew my commission."

"Did he give any reason?"

"None satisfactory to me."

*Charles Innes, Inverness, who defended the Bernera "rioters" and exposed the tyranny of Donald Munro.
(Photograph by courtesy of Mr John Barron of Innes & Mackay, solicitors, Inverness,
and Ken Macpherson, Photographer.)*

"That I don't wonder at. Tell us the reason that was not satisfactory."

"The Sheriff stated he considered I should not hold the two offices of factor and fiscal, but I know there are other factors in the country who act as fiscals."

"Will you kindly tell us who they are?"

"The fiscal at Inverness."

"For whom does he act as factor?"

"I cannot say."

"I take it the difference between you and the gentleman to whom you have referred is this — you have ceased to be a fiscal, while he has ceased to be a factor."

Special piquancy is given to this exchange by the fact that the case was being heard by Sheriff Fordyce, the man who had sacked Munro. That probably also explains why Innes was given so much latitude by the Court, despite Munro's frequent complaints that questions put to him had nothing to do with the case.

Munro said the inclusion of all the crofters' possessions in the summonses of removal was merely a matter of form. It had to be done that way, because the sheiling ground was merely a pertinent of the holdings.

"In the summonses did you describe the sheilings as mere pertinents?" asked Innes.

"The document speaks for itself," growled Munro.

The document did indeed speak for itself and, after it had been read to the Court by Innes, Munro admitted it gave him power to remove all the tenants from their crofts and houses, if he wished.

When he failed to get protection from the Court against the barrage of questions, Munro feigned loss of memory.

He could not remember whether he had made an agreement with the crofters when he gave them Earshader. He could not remember if the agreement had been embodied in a document. He had been told such a document was lodged with him, but he couldn't remember if he ever saw it. He looked for it, but couldn't find it.

"You must remember there are 22,000 people in Lewis and I have the management of all," he protested.

He couldn't be sure whether he had told the people they would be compensated for the seven mile dyke they had built round Earshader. He thought he told them when he met them. Or told the ground officer to tell them. Or put it in a letter.

"Have you a copy of the letter?" asked Innes.

"I think it is in my letter book."

"Well, send for the letter book."

"I am not sure it is in the letter book. I don't see that its being sent for will do any good."

"Will you swear that you wrote to any of the Bernera tenants, promising them compensation for the dyke, or that you wrote to them at all, before they were served with the summonses of removal?"

"I can't swear. I don't remember."

He couldn't even remember whether the crofters were displeased when he finally did meet them. He thought they were quite jocular. Under pressure he admitted they were excited, "the most of them talking to me at the same time."

"What!" exclaimed Innes. "The whole fifty? Did they dare to behave in such a rude manner to you, the Great Chamberlain?"

Having exposed the manner in which Munro had tampered with the Sheriff Officer's precognition, and discussed it with another key witness, Innes turned his attention to the people of Bernera.

"What is the character of the Bernera people? Are they, as a rule, decent, quiet and well behaved?"

"I decline to answer the question," replied Munro. "I came here to give evidence as a witness in what I believe to be a criminal charge. I have nothing to do with the people's character."

Innes submitted to the Court he was entitled to ask Munro about the character of the people in general, and the three accused in particular.

The Sheriff agreed.

When the question was repeated, Munro replied, sourly, "I can't say as to the character of the people."

"I hope you may never have to go to Bernera for a character," was the riposte.

Grudgingly, Munro finally answered, "Looking at the matter in a Christian spirit, I may say they are decent but I cannot say if they are quiet."

"You almost persuade me to bow to such a representative Christian," said Innes.

Munro denied he had made any special arrangement with the Sheriff Officer before he went to Bernera, but admitted that he had not paid him the full fee "because there were so many summonses."

He also admitted he was in the habit of evicting Bernera crofters if their rent was in arrears.

He refused to reply, when asked if he compelled the new tenant, in such a case, to pay the arrears left behind by the old.

On this point the Sheriff supported him.

"It is quite immaterial whether he answers or not," commented Innes. "If he refuses to reply, the inference is that that iniquitous practice is carried out in Lewis." As it undoubtedly was.

It was ten o'clock before the hearing of evidence ended, and even then it was curtailed on the initiative of the jury. Innes had all the Bernera men, who confronted the Sheriff Officer, waiting to give evidence, but, when the three accused had been heard, the foreman of the jury intervened to say it was unnecessary to call any further witnesses to establish what had happened at the ferry.

If the Fiscal had dropped the charges at that point, he might have saved his cousin and partner from a good deal of further bruising. Instead he elected not to address the jury, because of the lateness of the hour, but still to ask for a conviction, on the strength of the evidence led.

Innes took the opportunity. He told the Sheriff that, despite the lateness of the hour, he had a great many things to say.

Having examined in detail the history of the grazings he turned briefly to the character of the people of Bernera.

"From the way these poor people have been treated, one would be naturally led to suppose that they were undesirable tenants, but, though repeatedly asked by me, the Chamberlain, who was also for many years the Procurator Fiscal — an office from which the Sheriff has now very properly removed him — could not give one single instance in which anyone from Bernera was accused, during the last twenty years, of having committed any crime."

"It used to be said that the slave who breathed the air of Britain immediately became free. But from what one hears, and from what has come out in evidence in this case, I very much fear that that could not be said of this island, at the present moment ... It may be well to enquire who is responsible for this sad and unfortunate state of matters?"

Having put the question, Innes pointed the finger unequivocally at Munro.

"The proprietor of this and the neighbouring islands might be a little king. He lives and entertains, I hear, in princely style. But it appears to me he has, so far as the management of his realm is concerned, absolutely abdicated in favour of the great man we had before us today

"The latter told you himself (with my assistance, being modest, as great men always are) the number and the nature of the various appointments held by him ...

"It occurred to me, when the long list was closed, that Mr Donald Munro was vested with the whole power, both civil and military, if not entirely of the state, at any rate of the estate...

"In this court, looking to the nature of his multifarious offices, I can almost fancy it possible for him to appear at one and the same time in the capacity of prosecutor, judge and jury.

"It is a matter of great difficulty, if not impossibility, to think in the singular about so great a pluralist.

"Today and here, he appeared in a new capacity — one in which it is doubtful if he ever appeared before, namely that of a witness ...

"You must have observed how often Mr Munro, in answer to my questions, — especially when they were calculated to tell in favour of my clients — replied 'I don't remember', 'I can't remember'. From this it would appear that even his brain and his memory have at last begun to be affected.

"Had this island never been united to the neighbouring islands of Great Britain and Ireland, and had Munro been king de jure, he really would not be the great man he is, occupying as he does, the position merely *de facto*.

"Then he would have Houses of Parliament and Cabinet Ministers to control him, but now there is no man to say him nay.

"His power seems to be absolute. His word seems to be law. The people seem to quake and tremble at his approach ...

"You can imagine how helpless the men of Bernera are, in dealing with such a person, armed with so much power.

"Oppressed as they are I, as a stranger, cannot but admire them. Had Mr Munro, instead of being Chamberlain of Lewis, been an agent in either Connaught or Munster, he would long ago have licked the dust he has for years made the poor men of this island swallow."

Having dealt with Munro, Innes turned his attention to the minor officials. He criticised the manner in which the people had been gathered together, then asked to step forward when their names were called. As each man stepped forward, a summons of removing was placed in his hands. Insult was thus added to injury.

Perhaps the most significant part of Innes's address to the jury was the conclusion. He considered it necessary to exhort the jury to be guided only by their own good consciences, without regard to what might be pleasing or otherwise to the powers that ruled the island.

The manner in which they ruled the island was explained by an anonyomous writer in the introduction to a pamphlet printed by Blackwoods, giving a full report of the trial.

"If a tenant enters the official room of the Chamberlain with his head covered, his hands in his pockets, or with an apparently unwashed face, he is fined.

"If offence is given (to the Chamberlain) — though it appears to be more frequently taken than intended — or if his behests are not obeyed with becoming meekness," the offender is "invariably threatened with ejection" from his lands.

The jury, however, were not crofters. They were men who held feus, or at any rate valid leases. They were safe from the most effective weapon of the now discredited Chamberlain — eviction. They were, moreover, subjected to an even more formidable pressure than the Factor's frown. The pressure of public opinion in an island clamouring for freedom.

The Sheriff Court in Stornoway had never been so crowded before, and I doubt if it has ever been so crowded since.

Those present were not idle spectators. They were protagonists. They were there, they believed, to see a tyrant destroyed.

There were so many of them, it was physically impossible for the jurors to get to the jury room. They spoke to each other in whispers, for a few moments, where they sat, before pronouncing their unanimous verdict.

The comments in the introduction to the pamphlet printed by Blackwoods may be set aside, because we have no means of assessing the status of the unknown author. Even the comments of Charles Innes may be discounted, as the allegations of a hired lawyer making the best case for his clients.

There are, however, other published pamphlets of the period, whose authors are known and whose authority is unimpeachable.

These show that, if anything, Charles Innes understated the truth.

15. ALL MANNER OF JUSTICE

In February 1875, six months after the exposure of Donald Munro by Charles Innes, William Donald Ryrie sat down in the Colonial Club, in London, to write a report on "The Administration of the Charity called Ness Widows and Orphans Fund from 1863 to 1874."

The background to the charity is simple, and stark.

On the 18th December, 1862, thirty-one fishermen set out from Port of Ness, in five open boats, to shoot their long lines. They were caught by a sudden gale. All of them perished.

They left behind in Port of Ness, twenty-four widows, seventy-one orphans, and thirty-one dependent relatives. Seven of the widows were pregnant when the disaster occurred.

One old woman, whose husband, a son and a son-in-law had been drowned in an earlier disaster, lost her only surviving son and her only surviving son-in-law, leaving three widows and five orphans in one house, "with scarcely a potato to eat."

In the view of the local minister, Rev Donald Macrae, other families were even worse off. "The backbone of our fishermen is broken," he wrote.

On the 19th of January, a public meeting was held in Stornoway, presided over by Sir James Matheson. Two committees were set up. A Central Committee in Stornoway, mainly of merchants, bankers and fish-curers, to raise funds, and a Local Committee in Ness, consisting mainly of the ministers, to advise on their distribution.

Donald Munro was appointed Convenor and Treasurer.

William Donald Ryrie, a wealthy Lewisman resident in London, set up a committee there and obtained contributions from a number of prominent people, including the Queen and Prince of Wales. Of a total of £1,488.2.4 contributed to the Fund, Ryrie's committee collected almost one third.

In 1874, Daniel Mackinlay, an old school friend of Ryrie, told him that, while he was tenant of the Gress Shootings, he heard rumours that the Fund had not been well administered.

Ryrie carried out an investigation.

He found there was still nearly £600 lying in a Stornoway Bank, while many of the widows lacked the basic necessities of life.

The money was lodged in Donald Munro's name and operated on his sole signature.

There had never been an audit.

After the initial distribution to the widows and orphans, supervised by the Local Committee, the Fund was administered at the unfettered discretion of Donald Munro.

Between 14th February, 1866, and 21st February, 1871, no meeting of the Central Committee was called by Munro, as convenor.

The duties of the Local Committee were restricted to informing Munro, as treasurer, of any change in the family circumstances of claimants.

Payments were made on rent day. Each widow, who was tenant of a croft, was given a sum equivalent to the croft rent. When the money was laid on the table, the widow touched the pen to acknowledge receipt.

The money was then swept back across the table, into the Factor's rent bag. The "recipient" never handled a penny.

No receipt was issued for the rent so paid.

Whether a widow had one dependant child or six, the sum she was credited with related to the croft rent, not to the family's need.

If a widow remarried, as many of them eventually did, she was removed from the list. Munro relied on the new husband to pay the rent. He had to, or he would lose the croft.

There was no suggestion of fraud or embezzlement. No evidence that Munro had applied any of the money improperly to his own use.

He seems to have believed he was looking after the real interests of the widows. He doubted whether the widows themselves could have applied the money "more profitably."

The thralldom in which the people of Lewis then lived is vividly illustrated by the fact that, according to the local catechist, many of the widows agreed with Munro.

The whole community lived, from day to day, under the perpetual threat of eviction. They adapted their lives and their attitudes to accommodate that fact, just as they adapted to the wind and the weather. Insecurity was a rule of life: an act of God before which you could only bow your head. The most important duty was to have sufficient money in your hand, on rent day, to meet the demands of the Factor.

Ryrie's inquiries were directed mainly to Donald Munro, but he was also in communication with others, including Kenneth Smith, the fishcurer and merchant. Stornoway was buzzing with rumours that something was afoot.

Munro took action to protect himself. After the Bernera Riot, he did not wish another public exposure. He also had to protect his master.

The "honour" of Sir James would be impugned, if it came to public notice that a fund, gathered under his chairmanship, to relieve the distress of widows and orphans, had been used, in effect, to guarantee his own rents.

The members of the two Committees were also in a delicate situation. They had been less than vigilant, in leaving so much to the discretion of the Factor, although, in fairness to them, it must be said that they began to ask questions, in a desultory sort of way, long before Ryrie raised the matter in public.

At a meeting of the Central Committee in 1871 — the first for five years — they ordered Munro to submit his accounts, for audit, to John Ross, the Sheriff Clerk Depute.

The audit, however, never took place. Munro ignored the Committee's instructions, and called no further meetings.

In any event, it was not an audit that was required: it was an examination of the principles on which the funds were being distributed.

An audit would, probably, have confirmed that the moneys Munro purported to have paid had, in fact, been paid. It would not have revealed the manner in which the whole purpose of the fund had been perverted.

In September 1874, after the Bernera trial, and after Ryrie had begun his enquiries, Munro panicked. On his own initiative, he submitted the accounts for audit to Walter Rose. The Committee were not impressed. Rose was a relative of Munro, in his own employment, and, moreover, was clerk to the very fund he was being called on to audit.

When the so-called audit by Rose was questioned, Munro instructed a further audit by R. G. Mackenzie, described as a shipbroker, who had no qualification of any sort as an accountant, and produced a very superficial report, concluding with an encomium on Munro for the trouble he had taken, over a period of eleven years, without remuneration, "for which the widows and all concerned ought to be grateful."

For this service, Munro, without any prior authority from his committee, paid Mackenzie six guineas — twice the amount he had paid, also without authority, to his own employee and cousin, Walter Rose, for the audit the Central Committee refused to accept.

Around the same time, Munro made another payment which suggests that either he, or his master, was unsure of the legality of what they had done. A sum of £5.9.6. was paid for "Opinion of Counsel as to division of Funds among proper parties."

The discrimination between the widows who had remarried, and those who had not, caused a good deal of jealousy in Ness. Who had a better claim on the fund, a widow with six orphans, who had found a new husband, prepared to "adopt" so large a family, or a widow with one orphan who had remained unmarried?

Munro paid no attention to the complaints of injustice from Ness, but the inference is that Counsel's opinion supported the complaint of those who had remarried and been struck off the list.

In any event, whether acting on Counsel's opinion, or responding to some other pressure, Munro, this time with the consent of his Committee, decided to pay out the whole remaining balance in one great bonanza, and in doing so to equalise the payment to the two groups.

On the 30th November, 1874, Ryrie, by advertisement in the *Times*, convened a meeting of all the subscribers to the fund, who had answered his own personal appeal. It is not recorded how many attended, but two resolutions were passed.

The first resolution called on the Central and Local Committees to furnish full accounts, showing "the authority under which drafts" were made, with a full list of all the widows and orphans originally placed on the Fund, and another list of those who were still in receipt of assistance.

The second resolution authorised Ryrie to send a copy of the first resolution to each member of the two committees, personally and individually; to continue his investigations; and to publish his findings.

The very next day — not knowing the London meeting had taken place, but knowing that it had been called — Munro set off from Stornoway, in a snowstorm, with nearly six hundred pounds in a bag, to distribute to the bewildered widows and orphans riches of which they had never dreamed.

He carried in his pocket two loaded revolvers, because the crofters of Swainbost were marching to Stornoway, to complain to Sir James Matheson that Munro had unjustly deprived them of their summer grazings.

The story of the Ness Disaster Fund, which began in tragedy, ended in farce.

To ensure that the final distribution was properly vouched, Munro arranged for the presence of the two local ministers and the catechist.

The whole remaining balance of the Fund — apart from £5.3.2 retained to meet the cost of a final audit — was handed over, in sums ranging from £4.10 to £26. Most of the payments were nearer the higher than the lower end of the scale, because they included sums, described as arrears, paid to those who for many years had received nothing at all, because they had husbands who could pay the rent.

When the distribution was completed a strange ceremony took place.

According to Munro's final report to the Central Committee, the beneficiaries passed a resolution in the following terms:

"In taking payment of our final division of the Ness Widows Fund ... we heartily tender our best thanks to Sir James Matheson, for the great kindness and liberality evinced by him in being the mainspring of securing a large Fund for our benefit; and we also beg to offer our best thanks to the Chamberlain for his great trouble, without fee or reward, over a period of twelve years; and to the Central and Local Committees for the aid and great interest taken by them on our behalf; and finally, we approve of all past actings, and of the Treasurer's intromissions."

According to Munro's report, this comprehensive and curious resolution was then, "signed by 22 widows and 15 dependants," and witnessed by the two clergymen and the catechist.

Leaving aside the fact that more than half the so-called "widows" had remarried, the mystery remains how 37 people, few of whom could read, write or speak a word of English, were able to compose, between them, so elegant a testimonial, and set it down in proper form.

As Ryrie tersely comments, the internal evidence is that it was composed by Munro himself.

In due course, Munro laid the "testimonial" before a meeting of the Central Committee, presided over by Sir James, together with his own final report.

Two members of the Committee — Norman MacIver, a banker and shipowner, and the minister from Ness — refused to pass the accounts until they had access to the detailed papers. No one supported them, and the books were closed.

The Committee endorsed Munro's "whole actings and intromissions," and recorded their thanks to him "for his long and gratuitous services."

Whereupon Munro sent a copy of the minute to Ryrie and upbraided him, for his failure "to look into the administration of the funds for upwards of eleven years."

"Surely there is some culpability here, if you had any locus standi in the business."

Having put his inquisitor in his place, Munro concluded, "I feel satisfied that all manner of justice has been done to parties interested."

Despite the Bernera Riot, despite the scandalous manner in which the Ness Disaster Fund was handled, Munro still, clearly, enjoyed the confidence of Sir James, who resisted, for another six months, the mounting pressure to get rid of the tyrant.

According to Rev Norman C. Macfarlane, a native of Lewis, who was minister for many years at Juniper Green in Edinburgh, Sir James was eventually persuaded to get rid of Munro by Lady Matheson, whose Society friends in London asked snide questions about affairs in Lewis.

It is ironic that the fate of Lewis may thus have been decided around the tea table in Stornoway House, the Matheson's magnificent London home, rather than in the Island capital from which it took its name.

Much of the history of the Highlands is encapsulated in that fact.

16. THE ARROW

In 1874, when Munro and Ross were still at the height of their power, but just before the senior partner was swept away by the Bernera Riot, my mother's family became involved in another legal entanglement, which was deeply embarrassing, although it was not as long drawn out as the notorious Stephen case.

The litigation about the *Arrow* might have little significance if it stood alone. It involved no greater degree of injustice than is often inflicted on an unfortunate debtor by an uncompromising creditor, or by the dilatory actions of a slipshod solicitor.

However, as part of the general pattern I have been examining, and especially in light of the relationship already existing between my mother's family and the "mafia", it has other overtones.

As with the web of legal entanglement which enmeshed George Stephen, the difficulty over my grandfather's ship, the *Arrow*, began with a simple act of family generosity.

Almost every house along the seafront of Stornoway, at that time, was the home of a ship's captain. In some houses there were two. On more than one occasion my uncle and my aunts, who lived at 29 Newton, have enumerated them for me, although, regrettably I did not note them, as I should have done.

They spoke of men who sailed to Melbourne in the Gold Rush; helped to lay the first submarine cables across the Atlantic and the Behring Straits; were mistakenly mourned as dead when they were ice-fast for a winter in the Dvina at Archangel; encountered pirates on the Barbary coast and in the China seas; ran the blockade in the American civil war; perished mysteriously in the Bay of Biscay, or were swept to their deaths by angry seas, as they rounded the Horn.

One of their neighbours boasted that the British navy sailed between his legs, because a wooden stump did duty for a limb that had been buried many years before on the island of Java.

"Old shipmasters were almost, if not altogether, in the front rank of our gentry," according to a local writer of the time. To be anything of consequence one must own "at least a schooner, which, by dint of attentive pumping, could be kept afloat between Stornoway and Cronstadt."

My grandfather did not belong to either group. He was not in any sense a man of property. He was not even a master mariner, although he was, by courtesy, known as Captain, because he frequently commanded

Roderick Mackenzie of the 'Iris' whose generosity to his brother-in-law involved the family in a great legal wrangle with Munro and Ross. The original is now in the possession of Roderick's great grand nephew, Sandy Matheson, formerly Convenor of Comhairle nan Eilean.

small vessels in the coastal trade, for which a full certificate was not essential, and, in emergency, commanded foreign-going ships as well.

I do not know why he never took his master's ticket. It may have been diffidence: he was not a pushing man. Or the claims of a large young family may have prevented him from taking time ashore to join the mature students — weather-beaten seamen! — among the boys in the Navigation Class run by John Mackay, whose famous academy was absorbed, after his death, into the Nicolson Institute.

Mackay was generally known as "Toy", because of his dapper figure. He was often to be seen, in an outdated Regency frock-coat and stove-pipe hat, on Sandwick Beach, demonstrating the use of the sextant to men who knew the Bay of Fundy or the Straits of Malacca almost as well as they knew the mouth of the River Creed in their own home port.

On the voyage before the *Arrow* entered his life — and his soul! — my grandfather was mate on the *Perilla*, part-owned by his brother-in-law, George Stephen, who commanded the vessel.

At the end of the outward voyage, George Stephen died of malaria, on the Gold Coast. The story has passed into the oral tradition of the family.

"Did you shoot the sun, Rory?" asked the dying man.

"Yes," replied my grandfather.

"Give me the figures and I'll work out our position."

Having completed his calculation, Stephen said, "I think we'll anchor here, Rory!" And they did. A short time later he was dead.

My grandfather took command and brought the ship back safely to Britain, but, when he paid off, the family connection with the ship was at an end. For six months he was unemployed, with a wife and a family of seven to feed

Then, quite unexpectedly, he became owner of the *Arrow*. The manner in which it came into his life tells us a great deal about the close family ties in a seaport town, and the attitude of the little island capital to the larger island across the Minch, which dominated its life and interfered in its affairs.

One day in May, 1873, my grandfather made his way to the Crown Inn, on the North Beach, accompanied by Capt Roderick Mackenzie, his wife's brother, who was a close neighbour in Newton, and Donald Macrae, his wife's brother-in-law, a ship's carpenter. There they took part in a rather unusual ceremony.

Formally, in the presence of a number of local businessmen, who might have dropped in for a casual drink, or may have been there by pre-arrangement, they intimated that Capt Mackenzie — generally known as Roderick the *Iris*, after one of his best known ships — had purchased a half share in the schooner *Arrow* from his brother-in-law, Donald Macrae for £70, and had sold it, together with his own half share, to my grandfather for a total of £140.

It was, in effect, a free gift by Capt Mackenzie to his youngest sister, Johanna, my grandmother. My grandfather was only to repay the £140 when (and if) he could, and there was no interest on the loan.

Captain Mackenzie handed the *Arrow*'s papers to my grandfather in a little tin box.

"There's the vessel for you," he said. "Make the best of it. Pay me if you can, but if you cannot, I'll never ask you for the money."

The *Arrow* was then lying opposite the foot of Church Street, in full view from the door of the Crown Inn. It was a small vessel, just over 83 tons gross, with two masts, Hermaphrodite rigged, with a square stern and a male bust figurehead. It was built in Bridport, in Dorset, but was well known in Stornoway. Capt Mackenzie and Donald Macrae had owned it for ten years, and had traded with it between Stornoway and the Baltic.

They bought it from the Rev Roderick Nicolson, minister of Applecross, who inherited it from his father Rory Nicolson, one of the most prosperous shipowners in the port: prosperous enough to have had at least one of his sons educated in the High School of Glasgow.

A native of Uig, Rory Nicolson was reputed to have presented the bell from a pirate ship to the Parish Church at Balnakil, a story which seems unlikely but is probably true. The bell, I have been told, came from the infamous *Jane*.

It was just three months before the transaction in the Crown Inn, that the Nicolson Institute opened its doors. It was endowed under the will of one of Rory's sons, Alexander Morison Nicolson, a marine engineer, who was killed on board ship in Shanghai, when the boiler exploded. The School was further endowed by Rory's other sons: a farmer in Queensland, a cotton-planter in Mississippi, a mill-owner in Skipton, and the Rev Roderick himself, who later moved from Applecross to London, to become Scottish Chaplain to the Brigade of Guards.

With a pedigree like that the *Arrow* was a rare prize for a working mate, above all it freed my grandfather — or so he vainly hoped — from the drudgery of long ocean voyages which had separated him for months, or even years, from his family, taking him to the Great Lakes when Chicago

Great credit is given to Sir James Matheson for the schools he built. The Matheson's interest in education was not, however, unique. An even more important contribution to Island education was made at the same period by the five sons of Roderick Nicolson, the shipowner, who quarrelled with the people of Coll about seaweed. They were an engineer in Shanghai, a mill-owner in Yorkshire, a sheep farmer in Queensland, a cotton planter in Mississippi and a chaplain to the Brigade of Guards.

and Duluth were little more than shanty towns, to Sevastopol during the Crimean War, where he picked up, at Balaclava, the Russian bayonet my granny used to poke the fire, or to the far Pacific where he found the huge, richly coloured conches I was taught to hold to my ear as a child, so that I could hear the ocean breakers on tropical beaches I had never seen.

In the eyes of his fellow townsmen my grandfather was the owner of the *Arrow* as soon as he and his brothers-in-law, in the presence of their peers, had shaken hands on the bargain. He did not think it necessary to inform the Board of Trade.

Capt Mackenzie and Donald Macrae had registered the transfer from the Rev Roderick Nicolson to themselves but, with the islanders' disregard of time and bureaucracy, they had only done so five years after they acquired the vessel.

My grandfather might well have got round to the legal niceties in the same leisurely way, but he was too preoccupied at the time with the practical problems of fitting out the *Arrow* for a voyage to Stettin.

Some essential repairs had to be carried out, and the herring fishing season was drawing to a close before the *Arrow* was ready, but by the end of July he was able to buy tar, yarn, rope, marlin spikes, pack sheet, butter, tea, coffee, sugar and barley, and set out on the great adventure: now one of the minor gentry of the town — the owner of a schooner at last! .

There was one problem. Although he was owner, he could not sail as master. He solved it by appointing a neighbour, Kenneth Maciver, captain, and signing on, himself, as boatswain.

The voyage to Stettin, with a cargo of cured herring, was uneventful. There my grandfather loaded a cargo of timber for a consignee in Sunderland. On the voyage home the *Arrow* was shattered in the equinoctial gales and limped into Elsinore a sorry, and an uninsured, wreck.

The bill for repairing and refitting the *Arrow* came to £145: more than the nominal value placed on the ship by Captain Mackenzie, when he gave it to my grandfather, more even than the market value when Mackenzie bought it ten years before.

Whether the Danes took advantage of my grandfather's predicament to "lay it on," I cannot say. Probably not. My uncle, Rev Roderick Morison, minister of the High Church in Stornoway, who just missed his hundredth birthday, and was still preaching eloquent sermons when he was ninety, remembered hearing that the vessel had been carried up the beach by tide and storm. A channel had to be cut, at great cost, to refloat it. His recollection is confirmed by the fact that among the items replaced in Elsinore were the ship's anchors, all of which had been lost.

Forgetting his modest role as boatswain, my grandfather had now to assume his true position, as owner of the damaged vessel, and chaffer with the bankers and money-lenders of Elsinore to buy the freedom to go home.

A commission agent, Theodore Lund, advanced him the money, against three bills, one for £40, one for £50 and the third for £55. My grandfather explained to Lund that he was a relatively poor man, with no capital apart from the vessel. For this reason, the bills were made payable on different dates, to give him a chance to earn some freight. He met the first without difficulty, but was unable to meet the others as they fell due.

The bills were drawn on 18th December 1873, which indicates that my grandfather must have spent two months in Elsinore getting his ship repaired.

It would have been Christmas, or even into the New Year before he got back to Stornoway. When, eventually, the *Arrow* tied up at the pier on North Beach, just opposite the Crown Inn, where fortune seemed to have smiled on him so recently, my grandfather was in a much worse position, financially, than he had been before his brother-in-law's generosity was lavished on him.

There was no way in which he could earn enough, in three winter months, by the vessel's freight, to clear the debt.

He tried, but the Elsinore bills caught up with him.

Lund transferred them to William Anderson, a shipowner in Lossiemouth, and he employed Munro and Ross to recover the debt.

Immediately, they nailed an arrestment notice on the *Arrow*'s mast. My uncle could remember seeing it there as a boy. He would have been thirteen at the time, and, no doubt, made his way to the quay to have a look, because of anxious conversations overheard at home.

If the *Arrow* had been sold at once, Theodore Lund would have got his money, but Munro and Ross had other fish to fry.

Seizing on my grandfather's failure to record his acquisition of the vessel with the Board of Trade, they raised an action against all three parties to the transaction in the Crown Inn, maintaining that Capt Roderick Mackenzie and Donald Macrae were still the real owners of the vessel, and responsible for all its debts.

It was a juicy morsel. A case which would inevitably be contested in the Sheriff Court, creating work and fees for the local partners, and might, with luck, spill over into the Court of Session, where William Ross Skinner could join the gravy train.

The *Arrow* languished at the North Beach Quay while Munro and Ross pursued their own, rather than their client's, interests.

Rev Norman C. Macfarlane wrote a series of articles for the *Stornoway Gazette* about his youth in Lewis. He recalls the *Arrow* "when it lay beside the North Beach Quay and boys fancied themselves sailors as they climbed her rigging. It was a delightful play to climb to the cross yards and picture oneself at "Toy's" navigational feat."

The lawyers argued, the boys made a playground of the *Arrow*, the vandals and the thieves moved in, while my grandfather was stranded ashore, unable to earn a penny for the maintenance of his family, or the payment of his debts. Eventually he took the only course open to him: he abandoned the *Arrow* and signed on as mate, on a long foreign voyage.

On 18th November 1874, the Record in the case was closed, which means, in effect, that the lines of battle had been drawn, and the parties were ready to go to proof before the Sheriff Substitute, Charles Grey Spittal.

Proof was fixed for 11th December but there were difficulties. My grandfather was, by this time, in Sunderland, waiting to join a ship, and no one knew the whereabouts of his brother in law, Capt Roderick Mackenzie, who had been last heard of in Liverpool.

Sheriff Spittal decided that Capt Mackenzie, who was on a coastal voyage, could reasonably be expected to come to Stornoway for the hearing, once he had been located, but made arrangements for my grandfather's evidence to be taken, on commission, by the Town Clerk of Sunderland.

William Ross argued that there was no need for the case to go to proof at all. The Register of the Board of Trade was conclusive: whatever anyone might say in evidence, Capt Mackenzie and Donald Macrae were the registered owners of the *Arrow* and his client had redress against them, for the cost of any repairs carried out to their ship. He appealed against the Sheriff Substitute's decision.

Ross seems to have put forward a formidable case against the three brothers-in-law, citing Acts of Parliament and legal precedents, but the Sheriff Principal decided against him. The Proof must proceed and the outcome would depend on the evidence.

By this time, however, my grandfather had left Sunderland for London, where he joined a vessel bound for the East Indies and beyond.

Before he sailed, he bought a Bible in Whitechapel, and inscribed on the fly leaf: "Wrote on the night of 28 of Jany laying in the Downs bound for Auckland Newzealand Barque E. Maclarin Greenock."

He remained on the vessel for nearly two years, taking his discharge in Amsterdam on 6th November 1876. The vessel may have been back in Britain briefly in the interval, but no one in Stornoway knew, at any moment, where precisely he was or when he might return. A long series of adjournments resulted.

On January 29th 1875, the case was adjourned because one witness was abroad and another was unwell. On 16th February, it was adjourned because my grandfather was "still abroad and Roderick Mackenzie was absent on a coasting voyage." On 9th March, it was adjourned because my grandfather was still abroad although "Mackenzie was expected home daily."

In November, a telegram was sent to the Greenock agents of the *Emily Mclaren* "Please wire me if it is possible to get Captain Roderick Morison's evidence as witness in important case by commission and where he can be found or how soon home."

The reply was not very helpful. "*Emily McLaren* trading between Australia and New Zealand, Captain Morison is not expected home before June. Any communication should be addressed Port Napier, New Zealand."

The *Arrow*, with William Ross's arrestment notice nailed to the mast, was still lying at the North Beach Quay, obstructing other shipping, and steadily deteriorating.

Eventually the Harbour Commissioners moved it from its berth, and beached it at Goat Island, where I saw it, still rotting away, more than forty years later, everytime I visited my granny's home.

On 26th March 1875, the Court considered a joint minute from the parties' solicitors, agreeing to the sale of the vessel.

It was a belated response to a letter written to William Ross by my grandfather before he went to sea: "As I have been told by the Sheriff Clerk whither (sic) he is correct or not that I cannot use my vessel *Arrow* ... I intimate that I must leave the place to support self and family and the vessel is at your risk from this date."

An auction was arranged, but, by this time, the *Arrow* had been "stripped of nearly all her furnishings." The best offer received was £45 for a vessel, which was said to be worth £300, when my grandfather had finished repairing and refitting it, after the transference of ownership at the ceremony in the Crown Inn.

Ross refused to accept the offer.

After the abortive sale, there was a lull in the legal proceedings until 28th March 1876, when Ross resumed his attempt to get, from Captain Mackenzie and Donald Macrae, the money which he clearly could not get from the real owner who had now, in effect, been ruined by Ross's own recalcitrance.

The case came before the Court in June, July and September, but was each time adjourned for lack of essential witnesses. On 3rd October 1876, my grandfather reappeared — in Falmouth! The Court granted a commission to Montague Bere, Esq, Judge of the County Court of Cornwall, to take his evidence there. The commission was never executed — presumably my grandfather's vessel had moved on once more.

His evidence was eventually heard on 20th December 1876.

He told the Court, as he had maintained from the start, "The debt is mine and no one else's."

He made it clear that Lund was in no doubt what the true position was. Lund had known him before, and there were other Stornoway captains in Elsinore at the time, to whom he could have referred, if he were in any doubt.

There was plenty of time for him to have telegraphed, or even written, to Stornoway while the *Arrow* was at Elsinore, but both Lund and his clerk were satisfied, having seen the Custom House papers relating to the voyage, which made it clear that my grandfather was owner and boatswain, although not the captain.

Even that was not the end of it. Ross now asked for a commission in favour of Otto Christian Reckling, magistrate in Elsinore, to take the evidence of Theodore Lund and his partner.

They were emphatic in their testimony that my grandfather had borrowed the money as Captain of the *Arrow* on the credit of the owners, whom he identified as Captain Mackenzie and Donald Macrae.

Sheriff Spittal does not seem to have been impressed by this new testimony.

On 16th May 1877, he gave his decision in favour of Captain Mackenzie and Donald Macrae, and awarded them substantial expenses against Ross's clients.

"The fault of the delay in this case lies with the Pursuer, who by appealing the case just when Morison was about to leave the Kingdom on a long voyage, prevented his examination at that time, and hung up the case until Morison returned recently from abroad," he commented.

My grandfather was not affected by the decision. He had never denied the debt nor defended the action. The bills against him were still outstanding, although they could have been settled at any time, if Ross had been content to take what he could get.

The Sheriff, no doubt, had this in mind when he restricted the expenses awarded against my grandfather. He was held liable only "up to the first calling of the case" — a total of just over £3.

Ross was still unwilling to give up.

For the second time he took the case to the Sheriff Principal.

According to Ross, my grandfather quite deliberately lied to Lund, concealed the fact that he owned the vessel, and borrowed money on the credit of his brother-in-law, Captain Mackenzie, who was known to Lund by reputation as "a man of means."

The transfer of the *Arrow* to my grandfather was attended with considerable suspicion and not worthy of credence.

"That was a curious scene in the Crown Inn," Ross argued. "Here were Mackenzie and Macrae, the one ready to sell, and the other ready to purchase, his share of the ship, and here also was Morison, ready, on the completion of that transaction, to receive a gift of the whole ship from his brother-in-law, Mackenzie. And not least important, here was an array of persons to bear witness, if needful, afterwards to the genuineness and good faith of the whole. Whether these witnesses were there by accident which was, to say the least of it, a remarkable coincidence, or whether they were so by arrangement is of little consequence ...

"One notable feature in the transaction is the simultaneous development in Mackenzie of the resolution to buy up his co-owner, and the generous, not to say affectionate, impulse to hand over instantly the good old craft to her skipper Morison. Is the story in the least probable? All the parties were admittedly in humble circumstances, and the gift, for virtually it was a gift, by Mackenzie to Morison of a vessel worth at least £140 (which must have been a little fortune to one in the donor's circumstances) is in the highest degree incredible.

"The other part of the transaction is no less so, for it is not easy to understand how Mackenzie (looking to his circumstances) could have the command of some £70 to purchase his co-owner, and, not only so, but to make a gift of that £70 worth, and as much more, to one who, although a brother-in-law, appears to have had no special claim upon his generosity.

"The whole affair was too dramatically arranged to have the appearance of *bona fide* dealing. On the theory that it was a simulated transaction for the benefit of two at least of the chief actors, the whole affair is at once intelligible, and especially the presence of the cloud of witnesses... The arrangement, of course, was that Morison should afterwards appear to be the owner in order to protect the true owners from all liability connected with the ship .

"Another curious thing is that, while the gift of the *Arrow* was avowedly made to Morison because of his poverty, he immediately set to work to have the vessel thoroughly repaired, and, although he seems to have paid for the repairs, it does not appear how he obtained the funds for the purpose, unless from Mackenzie and Macrae, on the theory that they were still the owners."

Ross supported his conspiracy theory by pointing out that my grandfather received no written title to the ship, that the Custom House book showed that, when he signed himself on as boatswain, the ship's papers, which he produced, still named Mackenzie and Macrae as owners, and the bills which he was asked to sign in Elsinore described him as Captain, not owner, but he still subscribed his signature.

Most damning of all, according to Ross, was the fact that the parties to the pretended transaction stood in a close relationship to one another.

The Sheriff Principal took a very different view.

Having listened to the arguments and heard the witnesses, he wrote in a Note to his Interlocutor, dated 4th July 1877: "There was nothing suspicious in these transactions leading to the inference that they were entered into by the Defenders with the view of getting rid of any liability existing at that time."

"That Morison was the true owner and acted as such in the transaction with Lund is apparent, and he admits that he did so and does not defend the action. Lund must have known the position of Morison from the ship's papers and from his granting a Bill against the freight to be earned by the vessel."

In dismissing the appeal, the Sheriff Principal awarded further substantial expenses to Capt Mackenzie and Donald Macrae against Ross's clients, to be added to those already awarded in the lower court.

Ross's obsession with the idea that there was a conspiracy between the brothers-in-law, to defraud anyone who might have a claim against the *Arrow,* had cost his clients the equivalent in modern money of several thousand pounds, over and above his own bill for his very unprofitable services to them.

Mackenzie and Macrae were now off the hook at last, but my grandfather was still saddled with a debt he was much less able to pay than he had been when he incurred it: the law's delays had wrecked his vessel much more effectively than the equinoctial gales had ever done.

Jobs were hard to come by, but eventually he got a berth as mate of the *Grecian Band*, a tiny ship, about half the size of the *Emily Maclaren*.

The smallness of the ship, and the fact that he joined it at Cardiff and left at Liverpool six months later, suggests that he had to settle for a job in the coastal trade.

Six days after he paid off from the *Grecian Band*, he engaged on the *Gananoque*, a vessel of 783 tons, the largest he had ever sailed on, for a voyage to Miramichi in New Brunswick.

The lapse of time, between leaving one vessel and joining the other, was too short to have permitted a visit to Stornoway, although he had an urgent reason to see his family, if he had known of it.

The family home had been destroyed in a violent gale.

The story was told me by my auntie Bella not long before she died in her hundred and first year.

There had been a week of unusually violent storms, lasting from one Sunday to the next, almost without intermission.

At the height of the first storm, Bella heard a great commotion just outside their house. She peered into the darkness. Vaguely she made out the figure of Aeneas Mackenzie, one of the principal shipowners in the town, struggling through the gale shouting, "*Gilsland* ahoy! *Gilsland* ahoy!" Then she saw a vessel looming over her, driven up the beach, almost to the front door. By morning the vessel had disappeared, smashed by the gale. The beach was littered inches deep with her cargo of wheat. Bella gave me a vivid description of the women of Newton, combing the shore with buckets to gather the precious grain, then trekking to the mill, at the other end of the town, to have it ground.

On the following Sunday, the gale was even worse.

At midnight Bella, her oldest brother, Roddie, and her mother, were sitting by the fire, afraid to go to bed, because of the violence of the wind. Suddenly there was a tearing noise. Bella looked up and shrieked. She could see the sky!

The wind had ripped the thatching off the little house.

Roddie grabbed my mother from her cot. She was just a few months old. Through the long night my granny, her two sons and five daughters, sheltered as best they could in the roofless house.

At daybreak — but not before! — they roused my granny's sister, Kate, who lived a few doors along the street, and sought sanctuary in her

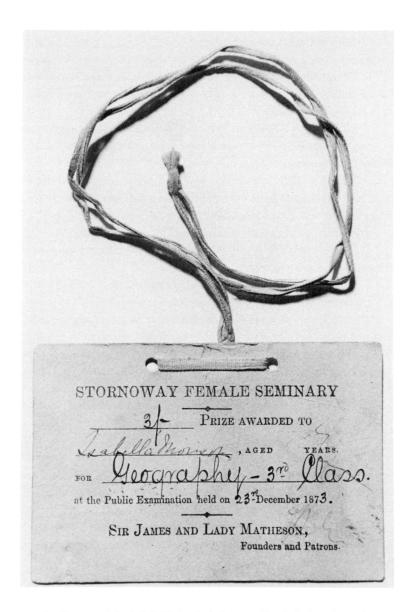

STORNOWAY FEMALE SEMINARY

3/- PRIZE AWARDED TO

Isabella Morison , AGED   YEARS.

FOR *Geography - 3rd Class.*

at the Public Examination held on 23rd December 1873.

SIR JAMES AND LADY MATHESON,
Founders and Patrons.

Certificate awarded to Isabella Morison in the Stornoway Female Seminary founded by Sir James and Lady Matheson. She received it in the same week as her father, Roderick Morison, signed the bonds in Elsinore after the 'Arrow' had been damaged in a storm. Bella was the source of much of the family information used in the book.

house; now occupied by Kate's great-grandson, Sandy Matheson, formerly Convener of Comhairle nan Eilean.

There seems to have been a special bond between the sisters. The whole family was close knit, and mutually supportive, as their brother's gift of the *Arrow* testifies, but, when my granny had been ill with fever, Kate was the one who went boldly into the house and nursed her, while the others kept a discreet distance, in case they caught the fever too.

Kate was a seaman's widow. Her husband, Capt John Smith, was drowned at sea when his ship, the *Rover*, Stornoway owned, was lost with all hands on a foreign voyage, around the time my grandfather's troubles in the court began.

He used to say afterwards that he once sailed over the spot where John Smith perished. I never heard on what particular voyage the incident happened but, from the dates, it must have been his voyage on the *Emily Mclaren*, just after he had bought the Bible, in Whitechapel, when his brother-in-law's death was still fresh in his mind.

In the Bay of Biscay, he dreamt that John Smith appeared to him, urging him in Gaelic "Tell Tarmod Ruadh it was no fault of mine."

Tarmod Ruadh was Norman Maciver, the local banker, and the *Rover's* owner.

When my grandfather got back from Miramichi, in August 1878, he returned to Stornoway, presumably to see how the family was faring in its new predicament.

He would have come reluctantly because hanging over him now was the very real threat of imprisonment for debt.

The dismissal of Donald Munro from his two principal appointments, might have made the partners more cautious than they had been in the heyday of their power, but that was a circumstance my grandfather would not have relied on. The experience of the family, in the Stephen case, was much too bitter to take any risks.

Munro, moreover, was still active as a solicitor, and, as we shall see in a later chapter, busy manufacturing litigation to make good the loss of his salaried posts.

My grandfather had one advantage over the earlier victims in the family, however. There was now an independent lawyer in the town, in competition with the partners.

Napier Campbell was somewhat inhibited, as we have seen, by the £1000 award for libel hanging over his head, but he was able to act within limits. On his advice, my grandfather did not wait for Ross to strike. He went to Court himself and raised an action of *cessio bonorum*.

Cessio bonorum means, in effect, a voluntary surrender of goods by a debtor to his creditors. It is an old principle of Roman law for the protection of honest debtors, overtaken by misfortune. It was assimilated into Scots Law, at a very early date, and survived until 1913, when it was superceded by new procedures. It protected the debtor from the risk of imprisonment, and assured him he would not be stripped of the bare necessities of life; everything else was at the disposal of his creditors, and, if his goods were not sufficient to discharge his debts, anything he acquired in future could also be seized.

For a man with a wife and seven children, only one of whom was earning, the protection offered by the procedure was important, but it still left my grandfather sunk in a morass of debt, artificially created by Munro and Ross.

Before he could avail himself even of that limited protection, he had to find someone prepared to sign a bond of caution, which the court fixed at £100: the equivalent of £4,000 or £5,000 in modern money.

The bond was eventually signed by his uncle, Colin Morison, whose own financial problems, many years before, sparked off the Stephen case.

Colin also found work in his little pub for my grandfather's eldest son, my uncle Roddie. Roddie tholed the job because the family could not live without the money, but he hated it. For the rest of his life he was a strict teetotaler, and an eloquent, crusading prohibitionist.

The caution of £100 was lodged but Napier Campbell botched the case.

When it came before the Court, William Ross protested that the procedure prescribed by the new Sheriff Court Act, which had come into force that year, had not been followed.

Campbell had to begin all over again, including the time-wasting and costly business of advertising at length in the *Edinburgh Gazette* so that any other creditors would know that my grandfather's modest possessions were up for grabs.

Sheriff Spittal, by this time, seems to have decided that my grandfather was suffering more than need be at the hands of the lawyers, on both sides of the case. In any event he reduced the caution to £50.

Apart from Theodore Lund in Elsinore my grandfather had only three creditors: he owed about £20 to a ship-chandler and a carpenter for fitting out the *Arrow* on its ill-fated voyage, and a few pounds to the butcher for the family's Sunday joint.

According to the *Encyclopaedia Britannica* one purpose of the procedure of *cessio bonorum* was to protect the debtor from infamy: to let him show the world that he was not a rogue but an honest citizen struggling against adversity.

Just what an ordeal these public proceedings must have been for a family that liked to hold its head high, came through to me for the first time when I found, among the papers in the Scottish Record Office, the official note of my grandfather's examination before Sheriff Spittal, on 10th December 1878, signed on every page in his stravaging seaman's hand, and vouched at the end as "truth, as the Deponent shall answer to God."

"I am not able to pay the debt. I am ready to surrender my whole estate to my creditors. I attribute my difficulties to the arrestment of my vessel, which in consequence of not being attended to has now become a total wreck ... I could not find caution to loose the arrestment and I could obtain no use of the vessel after the arrestment was laid ... I am married and have seven children all under seventeen years. When I went as mate, after my own vessel was arrested, my wage was from £5 to £6 a month ... Only one of my family is earning money for his support. I have been out of employment for three months. Before my last engagement I was out of employment for nine months."

In his cross-examination, William Ross pressed my grandfather about his little bit of real estate in Newton: the family feu he had inherited from his father, another Roderick Morison, who had been drowned at sea.

The situation surrounding the feu was typical of the casual pragmatic island approach to property which Munro and Ross delighted to exploit.

Although his father had been dead for forty-five years, and he was the eldest son, and his family had been living in the house until the roof blew off a few months before the hearing, he had never completed the legal formality of having himself "served heir" to his father.

As he explained to the Court, "My father left two sons besides myself, and a daughter." He might be legal heir, but his mother, his brothers and his sister had need of a home, as surely as he, until, with the passage of time, they provided for themselves.

On one point he was precise, indeed emphatic. The *Arrow* after being arrested "was neglected by Mr Anderson's agent." In other words by William Ross, the man who was pressing the questions.

"It was patent to observation that she was neglected," he added. The Harbour Commissioners had ordered the removal of the *Arrow* to Goat Island "as a wreck."

He offered to produce the letter from the Commissioners, if Ross wanted to see it.

Ross did not take up the offer. He knew very well what the letter said. He had written it himself as secretary to the Harbour Commission.

At the end of his ordeal, my grandfather had to take a comprehensive oath that the list of furniture and possessions he had produced was "true and correct," that he had "no lands, heritages, debts, sums of money, goods or gear" which were not included in the list, that he had not disposed of any of his effects, that he had not "put out of his hands any money, goods or gear" nor "cancelled, concealed or put away any writs or documents," to the prejudice of his creditors.

A week later, Sheriff Spittal issued an Interlocutor declaring himself satisfied that my grandfather had "complied with the requisites of the statute" "and that his inability to pay his debts has not been occasioned by fraud but has arisen solely from misfortunes and losses, and that he is therefore entitled to the benefit of the process of *Cessio bonorum*."

In order that he might enjoy the "benefit," his whole estate and effects were placed in the hands of a trustee for the satisfaction of his creditors. The low point in the family fortune had been reached!

I find it difficult to reconcile this picture with my granny's home as I knew it: a substantial two storey house, with handsome iron railings enclosing a little paved area, which today we might even dignify with the name of patio, and a row of outhouses at the back including a well equipped workshop, a commodious byre and a coal shed. I can vaguely remember great bowls of milk in the pantry from which my aunts drew off the cream with a scallop shell, the churn with which the family made their own butter, and my grandfather's navigational instruments hanging in the workshop, a constant source of wonder to a growing boy, especially the sextant with which he must have "shot" the sun, when George Stephen lay dying on the Gold Coast.

By the time I first knew the house, one of my uncles was a minister, the other a doctor, with an excellent practice in the North of England. Both of them contributed to my granny's maintenance and the maintenance of the unmarried daughters, who looked after her as she climbed into her nineties, but there must have been a very difficult period before the sons were established in their chosen professions.

In the early period, immediately after the loss of the *Arrow* and the destruction of the house, the members of the wider family rallied round.

At first my granny and her children had found refuge with my grand aunt Kate, but later, when they were stripped of all their possessions, they moved into the "big house": the substantial home, at 21 Newton, built by my granduncle, Capt Roderick Mackenzie, whose generosity to my grandfather so excited the scorn and disbelief of William Ross.

Roderick Mackenzie was a deeply unhappy man. His only child died in infancy. He wife, on whom he had lavished an abounding natural generosity, deserted him. He did everything in his power to win her back, but without avail. The great house he built for her was deserted when he returned from a long foreign voyage. She was in her mother's home, "looking after the lodgers."

It may be that she was gregarious by nature, quite unfitted for the long absences of a sailor husband. On the other hand, in a seaport town, the phrase might well have been a euphemism for something else.

In any event, when he finally got round to divorcing her, nearly thirty years after she left him, the judge who heard the case, in the Court of Session, commiserated with him on the "slow poison" which had blighted his life.

Unable to lavish his generosity on his wife, Capt Roderick lavished it on his blood relations.

My mother remembered from her childhood the great excitement when he paid one of his infrequent visits to the home which had such sombre associations for him. Barrels of apples — an exotic fruit in Lewis in the mid-nineteenth century — and other gifts were poured out on his innumerable nephews and nieces. More substantial gifts were made to their elders: like the *Arrow* handed over to my grandfather in a pub, presumably because he was the least well-to-do among the Captain's brothers-in-law, and the husband of the woman who had once been the baby of the family, the particular delight of her only brother.

The knowledge of the history of the *Arrow*, which I now have, explains something which puzzled me as a child.

I used to visit my granny every Sunday afternoon and have tea with her. Occasionally, in the fishing season, there would be a stranger present: John Smith, a burly, friendly man, with a round red face like a Lewis sunset, who, I gathered, was owner of a fishing boat from somewhere on the Moray Firth, or a lean, wiry, sallow man, a fishcurer, named Mitchell.

If either of them was present, my normal play was restrained. I couldn't hide in the old box bed beside the living room fire, or pretend I was a cooper trundling barrels on the quay, using as my barrel the hard cylindrical cushion from the horse-hair sofa at the back of the room.

Roderick Morison, owner of the 'Arrow' with his wife and family, photographed around the time of Donald Munro's death. In the back row, second from the right, is his eldest son, later Rev Roderick Morison, who was an eye witness of the arrival of the Bernera marchers at Goathill, and at the end of the row, Bella, who described the storm that took the roof off the house.

On the other hand, in compensation, we got a Scottish high tea.

I can still feel the deep embarrassment which almost choked me, when my aunt placed a huge helping of sausages before John Smith and he dumped them on to my already loaded plate, saying as he did so, "Thankee, Bella, but I canna manage. I'm full o' beef."

I looked in despair at my granny, whose "waste not: want not" philosophy demanded that children clear their plates.

They spoke as if they knew the house and had actually lived in it, but the friendship was not so close as to have brought them there, at any time, on holiday. Now I realise that they were former lodgers, returning to visit a landlady who had become a friend.

My grandmother was a capable woman. In the crisis she took control. While my grandfather went back to sea, she superintended the building of the new house — the house which still exists — and did her best to augment the family income. I am astonished in retrospect at the meagre economic base on which the family was brought up, apparently in comfort, if not in modest affluence.

In 1880, my grandfather was appointed skipper of the *Princess Royal* a cutter so small he did not need a master's ticket.

It belonged to an eccentric English mine-owner, Bankes of Letterewe, whose attempts to rid one of the lochs on his estate of a water kelpie provide some of the most amusing passages in Osgood Mackenzie's book *A Hundred Years in the Highlands*.

Having failed to catch the kelpie by draining the loch with a pump, specially brought from Liverpool, he employed the vessel's crew to pour tons of quicklime in to poison it. The crew did as they were commanded, but they also took soundings of the loch with their oars and satisfied themselves it was too shallow to hide anything.

Bankes paid my grandfather £6.10/- a month and gave him 1/9- per man, per day, to feed the crew, who were to be engaged, "as low as possible."

It was not a princely salary, but it was better than nothing, and the job kept him almost within sight of home.

This comfortable billet he owed, like so much else, to his brother-in-law, Captain Roderick Mackenzie, who commanded another of Mr Bankes's vessels, the *Iris*, and acted as commodore for the little fleet.

The family were now in quieter waters, literally and figuratively, but, every time they went in or out of doors, they saw the wreckage of the *Arrow*, like the death's head at a feast, reminding them of the family's second encounter with Donald Munro and William Ross.

17. "CUIRIDH MI AS AN FHEARANN THU!"

On 19th May, 1875, Sir James Matheson formally ended the Factorship of Donald Munro.

On that day the appointment of Hugh Mackay Matheson, merchant in London, as his Baron Bailie, Factor and Commissioner, was engrossed in the records of Stornoway Sheriff Court.

Hugh Mackay Matheson's lengthy commission was drafted by Sir James's Edinburgh agents, Stuart and Cheyne, and was signed at Lews Castle in the presence of the butler and valet as witnesses.

Munro was let down as lightly as possible. The appointment of Hugh Mackay Matheson was ostensibly made "considering that Donald Munro Esq ... who has for a considerable period past acted as my Chamberlain, Factor and Baron Bailie .. has resigned, or is about to resign, the said office."

Hugh Mackay Matheson was not a direct replacement for Munro. He was given much wider power to run the estate, without reference to Sir James, including the power of appointing a local factor to deal with day to day administration.

It would be wrong to assume that Sir James was placing an extra layer of bureaucracy between himself and events in Lewis, so that he could not be held personally accountable for any local friction. He was making provision for the future, because of his own declining health.

The only restraint placed on the Commissioner was that "it shall not be in the power of the said Hugh Mackay Matheson to appoint any factor under him while and so long as William Mackay, residing in Stornoway, whom I have of even date nominated and appointed Factor and local Manager ... under Hugh Mackay Matheson, shall continue to hold that office under my direct appointment."

William Mackay was protected in this way because he was a relative of Sir James. He had been Donald Munro's assistant. The clear signal was that the general policy of the estate was unchanged, although the instrument through which it was implemented had been replaced by a much less abrasive one.

On 8th July, 1875, the Sheriff Court Minute Book records that Munro's final accounting with the estate had been completed, and Sir James had agreed to "exoner, acquit and discharge (him), ... his heirs, executors and representatives of his actings as Factor, Chamberlain and Baron Bailie."

258.

At Cromarty on the 8th October next at noon
At Fortrose on the 25th September next at noon.
　　　　(Signed) Geo. Dingwall Fordyce
Edin 12 August 1874.

To John Ross Esqre
S.C. Depute, Stornoway

　　　　　　　Edinburgh 5 Forres Street
　　　　　　　　18 August 1874.
Dear Sir, I hereby appoint you to insert
the following order in the Books of Court
on receipt & I am
　　　　　Yours truly,
　　　　　(Signed) Geo Dingwall Fordyce

Order
Cancelling
Mr D Munro's
appointment
as
Proct. P. Fiscal
of
the Lews
　Order referred to —
Edinburgh 18th August 1874. The Sheriff
with reference to his Suspension of the
appointment of Mr D. Munro as joint
Procurator Fiscal of the Lews, in April
last, now Cancels the said appointment
& directs this order to be engrossed in the
Books of Court
　　　(Signed) Geo Dingwall Fordyce
　　　　　Sheriff of Ross, Cromarty
　　　　　and Sutherland
Written & Collated by John Ross Sheriff Clerk
Depute, on the 20th August 1874.

At Stornoway the Twenty second day of August
1874 years the following Commission or
appointment was presented and is
recorded

*This entry in the books of the Stornoway Sheriff Court, in the handwriting of "little Ross"
the Sheriff Clerk Depute, who was not related to Munro, records his removal from the post of Fiscal.
His removal from the post of Factor came in the following year.
(Photograph by courtesy of the Scottish Record Office.)*

From that point on, Munro was dependent on his earnings as a solicitor, without a salaried appointment.

A month later he and his cousin William Ross appeared in the Sheriff Court, on opposite sides in the same case, although they were still partners with a joint bank account.

This equivocal arrangement continued for at least another decade, according to the evidence of Napier Campbell to the Napier Commission in 1882. Munro at first threatened to sue Campbell but thought better of it.

It became even more complicated for a period, when William Ross's son John returned to Stornoway, and the three cousins engaged in an extraordinary dance around each other, appearing now as individuals — Donald Munro, solicitor; William Ross, solicitor, and John Ross, solicitor — and again as partnerships — W & J Ross, solicitors, or Munro and Ross, solicitors.

The Rosses had the Estate business, from which Munro was now excluded, but, from time to time, he would muscle in, on the opposite side, as a "born again" champion of the crofters.

Whether he was seeking revenge on the master who had dismissed him, or was driven by his own financial problems, does not appear, but, on one occasion his behaviour was so outrageous the Sheriff Substitute banned him from the Court for a year.

The trouble began in July 1877, when the new Factor sought an interdict against a number of tenants in Tong, to prohibit them from using a road through Goathill Farm which, at certain states of the tide, gave them a valuable short-cut to Stornoway, and which also gave them access to "Mackenzie's Well."

I was very familiar with both road and well in my childhood. Stornoway children used the farm road, unhindered, to gain access to the Cockle Ebb, where we dug for shell fish in the sand, and sometimes caught small flounders under our feet, on the incoming tide.

It was part of the ritual of the expedition to stop at Mackenzie's Well — or rather spring — to drink the cold, pure water.

The ritual of my childhood, and the anxiety of some of the Tong crofters to have access to the spring in 1877, suggest that it was believed to have health-giving properties, although I have no recollection of hearing that mentioned in my childhood.

The Tong crofters did not resist the interdict. In fact some of those involved didn't even know they were being interdicted, although summonses were delivered at their homes by a Sheriff Officer.

The story, as it emerges from a series of lengthy Interlocutors by Charles Grey Spittal, then Sheriff Substitute at Stornoway, gives us another insight into the character of Donald Munro, and, at the same time, illustrates the irrelevance of the whole legal process to the needs of a Gaelic-speaking community, the great majority of whom, at that time, were illiterate.

A few days after the Court granted the interdict, Donald Munro hired a gig and made his way to Tong, accompanied by Alexander Gerrie, who had been, at one time, farmer in Goathill.

As Sheriff Spittal put it afterwards, with heavy sarcasm, it was "pure philanthropy which took him to Tong. No one had sent for him."

Munro stopped first at the home of Malcolm Macleod, an old soldier, who was one of those interdicted. True to the principle he had enunciated in the Bernera trial — "I don't go to the people. They come to me." — he sent the driver of the gig to fetch Macleod.

Munro asked the old soldier to sign a piece of paper he had with him. Macleod could write his name after a fashion, although he could not read. Obedient to the ex-Factor's command — long established habits die hard — he scrawled his name across the page, although he told the Court afterwards he had no idea what the signature was for, and the paper was blank.

Sheriff Spittal believed Macleod had no idea what the paper was for, but doubted whether it had been blank, commenting, "It often happens that illiterate men, like Macleod, who cannot read and can barely scrawl their names, cannot say if there is any writing on paper to which they have put their names."

That seems a bit implausible and unduly kind to Munro but, whether the writing was added afterwards or not, Munro now had in his possession a mandate, signed by Macleod, engaging him as solicitor to fight the interdict.

Munro, not unnaturally, gave a very different account of what had happened at his meeting with Macleod but Sheriff Spittal refused to believe him. Munro's evidence was so unreliable, he said, it must be set aside completely.

Gerrie told the Court Munro had read the mandate to Macleod, and explained it to him; but he couldn't say what the explanation was. That suggests Gerrie was concealing something, or that Munro had spoken in Gaelic and Gerrie had no idea what the conversation was about.

After the interview by the roadside, Macleod was sent round the houses to collect the "papers", meaning the summonses served by the Sheriff Officer in the action for interdict.

When the incident came under scrutiny, Kenneth Macleod, the first person visited, could tell the Court nothing about the matter. He was at the fishing, in Peterhead, when the summons was served. His wife forgot to tell him about it, and, when Malcolm Macleod called, she gave it to him without question, "as they wanted it back again."

"They," presumably, were the mysterious powers, behind the English curtain, who ruled the crofters' lives as effectively, but even more impersonally, than the gods ruled Greece.

Roderick Smith admitted getting the summons, but no one in the house could read it, and he had no idea what it was about. He went out and spoke to Munro, who explained that he wanted the paper back, so that he could get Smith "the privilege of going to Mackenzie's well."

Smith replied that he could do without access to the well, and he didn't want Munro to take any trouble on his behalf. But he handed "over the paper:" because Munro wanted it.

Murdo Maciver was fishing, at Wick, when the summons was delivered. When Malcolm Macleod asked for it, Maciver said he never heard of such a paper. His elderly mother-in-law then searched for it, and gave Macleod part of the document, believing that he wanted it for the new Factor, William Mackay.

After the visitors left, Maciver puzzled over the piece of the document which was still in his possession, but could make nothing of it, because he had no English and could not read. He had no conversation at all with Donald Munro.

Henrietta Macleod, an old lady of 75, told the Court she had never seen the summons said to have been served on her. The Sheriff Officer had taken it to her daughter's house next door. She was told there was a paper there for her, but she had no idea what it was and wasn't interested anyway.

When he heard the paper was next door, Gerrie sent a boy to fetch it but didn't explain whom it was wanted by, or why.

Ann Macinnes, aged 70, told the Court she got a paper from the Sheriff Officer, who explained to her that she was to avoid the Goathill Road. She said she would, and put the paper in a chest.

When Malcolm Macleod called on her, she took the paper out of the chest, and handed it to Munro, who was waiting some distance from the house.

Munro didn't explain why he wanted the paper but asked if she liked "the short road."

She handed over the paper without hesitation. She assumed it had come from Munro in the first place.

Catherine Macdonald also got a summons, but could not read it, had no idea what it was about, and handed it back to Munro, without asking questions or receiving an explanation.

Finlay Macinnes and Malcolm Smith never saw the paper at all. They were away from home when it arrived. They were later told, by their wives, it had been given them by the Sheriff Officer, but Munro wanted it back, so they let him have it.

A few days after this expedition to Tong, Munro presented himself in the Sheriff Court to intimate that he had been retained by the crofters in Tong, to oppose the interdict which the Court had just granted.

He produced, as his mandate, the piece of paper Malcolm Macleod had signed. He explained that his other clients could not write their names, but had given him the "doubles" of the summonses, as authority to act for them as well.

The Sheriff agreed to reopen the case, but, when it next came before the Court, a document was handed to the bench signed — presumably by crosses — by five of the so-called defenders, denying they had ever authorised Donald Munro to represent them.

The five were present in Court. Sheriff Spittal said he would examine them on the question whether they had given authority to Donald Munro to act for them. At that point, Munro rose and made to leave the Court.

Sheriff Spittal told him to wait. Munro said he had to go. Sheriff Spittal told him to return within fifteen minutes. Munro said that was not convenient and walked out.

The Sheriff waited for half an hour and then took statements from the five crofters present, as to the manner in which Munro had acquired the "doubles."

Later in the day, when the Court had gone on to deal with criminal business, Munro returned and took his seat, as if nothing unusual had happened.

Sheriff Spittal told him five of the crofters had been examined, and the others would be examined at noon the following day.

"At which time I order you, in open court, to attend!"

Munro did not attend and sent neither excuse nor explanation.

The Sheriff sent a messenger to Munro's office. The messenger found Munro alone but, when he delivered the message, Munro told him he was engaged and could not attend the Court.

At that point Sheriff Spittal ordered Munro to return the Interdict Process and gave him twelve hours to comply.

Munro returned the process, and asked that the question, whether or not the crofters had authorised him to represent them, should go to proof.

He was given the opportunity of a proof but the only witnesses he could produce were Gerrie and the driver of the gig. Their evidence proved nothing.

At that point Munro dropped the case.

But that, said the Sheriff, was not the end of it.

Munro had been given ample opportunity to cross-examine the crofters on the question of agency but he declined to do so. The only conclusion possible was that he was afraid to question them.

Various parts of Munro's own evidence were described by the Sheriff as "glaringly and knowingly false" or "a tissue of falsehoods." His conduct throughout the case had "not only been unprofessional but thoroughly disgraceful." His persistence in leaving Court, against an express order to remain, was a grave contempt.

It was a painful case, said the Sheriff, but the only course open was to suspend Munro from appearing in Court, as a solicitor, for a year.

Munro appealed to the Sheriff Principal who rather ducked the issue. As Munro had been suspended, said the Sheriff Principal, in effect, he couldn't act as a solicitor, even on his own behalf, until the suspension had been lifted by a competent court.

It was unnecessary, therefore, to go into the merits of the suspension, but the Sheriff Principal hoped there would be no further attempt by Munro to "assume the functions of a procurator as long as he is judicially debarred from exercising them."

At that point Munro invoked the help of his cousin, William Ross Skinner, and an appeal was lodged with the Court of Session. The Lord Advocate appeared for Munro, and their Lordships swept the problem under the carpet.

As the *Scotsman* reported it, the Lord President "said it was undesirable to enter into any critical survey of the conduct of the process which had brought about the suspension ... The Court was, however, of the opinion that the circumstances were not such as to justify the Interlocutor of the Sheriff Substitute."

Clearly what happened in Lewis was of little concern in Edinburgh and Munro was back in business.

Not long afterwards, he appeared in Court to defend a group of fishermen from Lochs, whose boat was being sold for debt, at the instance of a Stornoway ship chandler, Charles Morrison.

Napier Campbell, who was acting for Charles Morrison, handed the Court a letter from the skipper, John Kennedy, stating that neither he nor his crew had engaged Munro to represent them.

As in the Tong case, Munro had possession of the "doubles" as evidence that he was acting for the defenders, but how he obtained them does not appear from the record.

Sheriff Spittal referred the case to the Sheriff Principal, who clearly thought he was taking it all too seriously. The fact that Munro held the "doubles" was, in the Sheriff Principal's view, a sufficient mandate for him to appear in Court and lodge defences, but the defenders were free at any time to recall the instructions they had given him.

He did, however, comment that, when the crew of the fishing boat withdrew the authority they had given Munro to represent them, it would "have been becoming and respectful" for Munro to have attended the Court and made his excuses. "Indeed it was his duty to have done so."

The activities of the senior partner must have been very irksome to his cousins at times, but they all came together quickly under the threat of competition. In that situation, they even made common cause with their inveterate critic, Napier Campbell.

In April 1882, there was a meeting of the Procurators in Stornoway. Donald Munro was in the chair. Napier Campbell was clerk. In the body of the room was John Ross, a sort of trinity, representing himself, his father and the firm of W. & J. Ross.

The business of the meeting was to curb the activities of John Norrie Anderson, who called himself an accountant, and was said to be transacting law business, although he had no qualifications.

They appear to have succeeded for a time, but, eventually, Anderson was permitted to practise and his name is still preserved in the firm of Anderson Macarthur & Co.

Apart from the stresses caused by Munro's downfall between the Stornoway cousins, the relationship with William Ross Skinner, in Edinburgh, was also entering a new phase.

Donald Munro, William Ross and William Ross Skinner, were jointly trustees, under the will of another cousin, William Munro, a surveyor of taxes in Glasgow, who died in 1871, leaving his estate to two unmarried daughters. One of the daughters, Janetta Munro, died, shortly after her father, leaving her estate to the other, Thomasina Munro, Tinto Bank, Tantallon Place, Edinburgh.

In 1876, Thomasina raised an action of "accounting and denuding", against the three Trustees. Her agent argued that, as the settlement contained no trust purposes or directions, it was the duty of the Trustees to have handed over the proceeds to the sole beneficiary, once they had gathered in the estate.

The three defenders, who were still in control of all the funds, five years after William Munro's death, argued that they had a duty to hold the trust estate, at least until Thomasina's marriage: to ensure that, in the marriage settlement, the *jus mariti*, and right of administration by a husband, should be excluded.

Thomasina won her case, but no expenses were awarded against the Trustees.

There was no suggestion that they had used the money improperly. Payments from the interest were made, at regular intervals, to the beneficiaries. It did, however, emerge that the Trustees, or one of them, had borrowed £200 from Janetta's share, shortly before her death, and the £200, plus the interest applicable to it, was still outstanding when the action was raised.

The members of the "mafia" in this, as in other matters, seemed very reluctant to release their hold on any funds they were entrusted with.

We know, from the Stephen case, that William Ross Skinner, around that time was short of money, while Donald Munro, after his dismissal from his salaried appointments, must have been living more or less from hand to mouth.

The very next year, Munro and Skinner fell out over a transaction Munro was involved in, jointly with George Macleay, a solicitor in Tain.

The details of the transaction are not clear but Skinner appears to have been engaged as a W.S. to transact some business in the Court of Session for the other two. At the end of the case, he billed Munro for £65.9.4. of expenses.

Munro asked for "a handsome reduction." Skinner said it was difficult to see what reduction he could make, "until you pay my account."

Munro temporised by saying he was in communication with Macleay about the account.

Skinner also demanded the return of certain papers he had sent to Munro.

Munro again temporised saying the papers had been sent to Macleay.

When he got the papers back from Macleay, Munro offered to return them to Skinner, if he would drop the bill for expenses.

Skinner responded by giving Munro until 10 a.m. next day to deliver the papers to his old rival, Napier Campbell, whom Skinner had engaged to pursue him for debt in the Stornoway Sheriff Court.

When the case came before the Court, the Sheriff found against Munro, but commented that it was "very trifling litigation between persons who seem to have been old friends." He awarded no expenses to either party.

Skinner appealed on the question of expenses and the Sheriff Principal decided against him. After thirty years together, the "mafia" was falling apart.

Munro, however, was still active when the Napier Commission visited Lewis, and was still apparently in partnership with William Ross.

Thereafter his health began to deteriorate and he appears to have suffered a stroke.

My mother used to see him, when she was on her way to school, shuffling along the street, with a crowd of boys dancing round him, singing out his old threat to the crofters, *"Cuiridh mi às an fhearann thu"* — "I'll take the land from you."

Munro would lunge at his tormentors with his walking stick, and shout back at them, "Put your feet in a bag and walk."

When he died, in 1890, the death was registered by John Ross. As if distancing himself from the corpse, Ross designated himself "neighbour" rather than "cousin," on the death certificate.

Munro left no estate. Whatever one may say about his conduct, he certainly did not enrich himself.

18. THE LOVE OF HIS LIFE

It was easy for Sir James Matheson to "exoner" Donald Munro at their final accounting. He had served his master faithfully, although not, perhaps, well.

The question whether one can exonerate him at the bar of history raises more complex issues.

Sir James Matheson was not an old style Highland Chief, bound to his clansmen by well recognised, if unwritten, obligations.

Nor was he that common hybrid of the period: the Highland Chief remodelled in an English mould; deracinated in a public school; the old empathy evaporated, but a borrowed sense of *noblesse oblige* still restraining the almost limitless power of a great landowner in mid nineteenth century Britain.

Equally he was not a ruthlessly commercial owner of property, evicting his tenants mercilessly, to add a few coppers to the rent.

He was a product of his upbringing. A Chinese mandarin. An Eastern potentate. Absolute in attitude, but benevolent in intention: doing everything with, as he saw it, a high moral purpose, but strictly on his own terms, and in his own way.

The clue can be found in the Conditions of Let drafted for the management of the Lewis Estate, by his Edinburgh agents, in 1849.

Most of the clauses are standard for the period, oppressive though they seem to us today.

The clue is not so much in the imposition of double rent for a year on crofters caught poaching, over and above any fines imposed by the Courts.

Nor the rule that "in going to kirk and market, or to ferry, or other place of resort," they must stick to the roads or footpaths the proprietor, or his factor, designated.

Nor the thirlage to estate mills, even when crofters had mills of their own, and the mills they were thirled to were a day's hard travel away.

Nor the prohibition on married couples from living in their parents' home.

Nor the obligation to make three tons of kelp per annum, at a price dictated by the Factor, under the threat that, if the kelp was not to the Factor's liking, or anything happened to it before it was safe on board ship, the full market value would be added to the rent.

The tone of the Matheson administration is best reflected in the final condition: "The proprietor, being very desirous of promoting education ... and having provided ... various schoolhouses and schoolmasters at his own expense, ... the parents or guardians ... of any child who may be absent from school for fourteen days continuously, without being able to assign a reason for such absence, ... shall be held to have incurred the proprietor's grave displeasure, which shall be considered as excluding (them) from those marks of grace and favour which he is always desirous of dispensing to his well-conducted tenantry."

Sir James's interest in education was real enough. But so, too, was his appetite for lavish praise and obsequious crofters.   He was not so much proprietor as god.

He got the praise, in certain quarters, but not the obsequious crofters.

In a series of articles on Lewis, shortly after the dismissal of Donald Munro, the *Scotsman*, dilating on Sir James's benevolence, described the people of Lewis as "incapable of gratitude, but capable of suicidal indolence."

The comment is significant. The *Scotsman* was, to a very large extent, the voice of the Edinburgh establishment. If that view prevailed in the capital, even after the Bernera Riot and the exposure of Donald Munro, it is not surprising the activities of the "mafia," in their role as procurators, was tolerated for so long by those who, alone, had the power to remedy it.

The *Scotsman* articles provoked a long and closely argued reply from Daniel MacKinlay, the man who alerted William Ryrie to the scandalous misapplication of the Ness Disaster Fund.

MacKinlay was a native of Stornoway and was educated in one of the schools established during the Seaforth regime. He became managing partner of a large Indian mercantile firm, which, he liked to boast, was older than Jardine Matheson & Co. At the time of his retirement, he was President of the Bengal Chamber of Commerce.

MacKinlay took a lease of the Gress shootings and fishings in 1874. With his numerous local connections, he had ample opportunity to learn, from the inside, what was going on in Lewis.

It is necessary to treat his comments with some caution, because he had his own personal quarrel with the estate, and, in particular with Donald Munro, but, even when allowance is made for that, his criticism is devastating.

Central government was at fault, he points out, in that the crofters in Lewis were less well protected than small tenants in Ireland.

In 1870, Irish tenants were given a legal entitlement to compensation for capricious disturbance, and unexhausted improvements. Highland crofters did not win similar protection until 1886.

He blames Sir James Matheson for the neglect of the fishing industry. Not only did he fail to provide harbours, he actively discouraged those who were prepared to invest in the industry. Fish-curers who built store houses in remote rural areas, on land of little value, were charged ground rents two or three times higher than those prevailing in the burgh of Stornoway.

For want of safe harbours, the lives of men were put at risk, although, as John Munro Mackenzie had revealed, when he was factor, more than twenty years before, the fishermen were, in effect, paying a toll on their catches. Rents in fishing villages were much higher than a farmer would have paid for the agricultural use of the land.

Even Sir James's record on education is criticised, despite the contribution he made to the establishment of schools, and the pride he took in it. When the Education Act of 1872 came into force, a minimum of 25 additional schools was required in Lewis. The census of the previous year showed that more than 50% of the children were receiving no instruction of any kind. There were more than 4,000 able young boys and girls, in Lewis, in 1874, who never, in the whole course of their lives, saw the inside of a classroom.

Sir James's fault was of omission, perhaps, rather than commission. MacKinlay's main charge against him was that he left the management of the estate almost entirely to his Factor, who, in turn, listened only to the ground-officers and constables, who were themselves, "frequently very tyrannical personages."

Comparing one factor with another, he blamed Scobie, who preceded John Munro Mackenzie, for having charged against the crofters' rents the cost of the meal distributed during the famine years.

As a result, "the sufferings of the crofters were beyond description; they had to part gradually with everything they possessed — their sheep, their cattle, their pigs and their poultry — so as to enable them pay for the meal and keep body and soul together."

During this period, the crofters became demoralised. John Munro Mackenzie, who succeeded Scobie, had the task of clearing up the mess. In Lewis tradition, as revealed by evidence given to the Napier Commission in 1882, Mackenzie was regarded as a hard factor, because of his part in re-lotting the island, and organising the mass emigration of 1851.

MacKinlay, who was much closer to the emigration of 1851 than we are now, or the crofters themselves were in 1882, came to the conclusion that Munro Mackenzie was "respected by everyone who knew him." He was even-handed in his dealings with the crofters, genuinely interested in their welfare, and, as we have seen in an earlier chapter, he realised that the key to the Lewis problem lay in developing the fishings. On that crucial issue, Sir James rejected his advice.

Mackenzie was succeeded by Donald Munro who "so wormed himself into the confidence of the proprietor that he was allowed to manage the people, and the estate, without any control, and ruled them with a rod of iron."

"The crofter tenants at will were quite at his mercy and nothing was done to improve their material condition ...

"Not a shilling has been expended on improving the dwellings or buildings of the crofters, or the several fishing stations of the island," on which the payment of their rents depended.

After the passing of the Education Act in 1872, Munro became chairman of the four Island School Boards, "but he did nothing to accelerate the building of schools, or the appointment of certificated teachers, as contemplated by the Act."

MacKinlay quotes an unnamed Stornoway gentleman for the comment, "Mr Munro took no interest whatever in the education of the people — his great aim was to keep them in thorough ignorance. It was very different with his predecessor — for Mr Munro Mackenzie, during his reign, took the greatest possible interest in all our schools, and had them regularly examined in his own presence."

Donald Munro's attitude to education also brought him into conflict with Sheriff Spittal.

When the Nicolson Institute was established, in 1873, Munro was clerk to the Trustees and Sheriff Spittal chairman. When a headmaster was appointed, the Trustees decided that he should be clerk, to save expense.

Munro was reluctant to relinquish his authority and refused to hand over the Minute Book and other papers relating to the school.

Sheriff Spittal asked Sir James to call his unruly servant to heel. Reluctantly, Munro handed over the Minute Book.

When Sheriff Spittal examined it, he found Munro had tampered with the record, making marginal additions of his own, which altered the Trustees' decisions.

In a rage, he tore the offending pages out and re-wrote the minutes in his own hand.

Later, Munro, in circumstances which are not explained, got the Minute Book back again, and filled nine pages with his own account of the incident, accusing the Sheriff, with some justification, of having committed a worse offence than his own, by defacing the Minute Book.

While Munro was pilloried, by MacKinlay and the Sheriff, for his attitude to education, his partner William Ross, who was, for many years, clerk to all the Island School Boards, was remembered, at his death in 1894, as the man who "built" the Lewis Schools.

The interests and activities of the two partners were closely intertwined but they were regarded very differently by the people of Lewis.

Munro was seen as an unmitigated tyrant. Ross was seen rather as an honest man doing his, at times unpleasant, duty. Even those who suffered at his hands do not seem to have borne so deep a grudge as they did against Munro.

According to the record, Ross was much more active than Munro in the legal harassment of my mother's family, but I have only once heard his name mentioned in that connection.

The fact that Munro was Factor, and had much more direct contact with his "victims", and had dealings with almost everyone in the island, accounts in part for the distinction drawn. I do not think it is the whole story.

The hatred with which Donald Munro is regarded, a hundred years after his death, is due less to the fact of what he did, than the style in which he did it. As Benjamin Franklin has pointed out, many men are capable of forgiving an injury, but no one ever forgave contempt.

To get the real flavour of Donald Munro's factorship, it is necessary to turn to a three-decker Victorian romance, *The Love of His Life* by Cosmo Cumming, published in 1880, by Moxon Saunders & Co, of Covent Garden.

The Love of His Life is "Dedicated to Donald Munro Esq., Lews, In Grateful Remembrance of His Constant and Valuable Sympathy."

The dedication is ironic. Donald Munro stalks through the first volume of the book — entitled *Israel in Egypt* — lightly disguised as Donald Black, and behaving precisely as the oral tradition in Lewis would lead one to expect.

Cosmo Cumming was the *nom de plume* used by John Macrae, a

Harrisman, educated in Inverness, who worked for a number of years as a clerk in Donald Munro's office.

The Love of His Life failed as a novel. The writing is turgid, the story convoluted and the characters wooden, but there are passages which spring to life. Incidents involving the Factor, and those describing the life of the hero as a student in Glasgow University, are drawn from Macrae's own experience, and read like reportage rather than fiction. More than a century after it disappeared without trace as a work of literature, it re-emerges from obscurity as a social document.

Macrae was clearly influenced by William Black's best seller, *A Princess of Thule*, and he follows Black's example in making his Hebrideans speak in a brogue which has never existed on earth or in heaven — "It iss a fwet tay you fwill gett for the rents" — reducing tragic figures to ridicule and farce.

Macrae knew well enough what he was doing. Conversations which would have taken place in Gaelic are not rendered into this pseudo-Hebridean patois, and, in one passage, he writes of the dignity and eloquence of an old man, talking in his own tongue, at his own fireside, to someone who could understand him.

Even the occasional use of a grossly exaggerated patois, however, illustrates the pressure of the assertive, at times arrogant, majority culture, which treated every deviation from the norm as a butt to be mocked, seducing even native writers by its commercial power; undermining the self-confidence and dignity of the Gael.

To remove this distorting mirror, I have changed the spelling, but not the words, in Macrae's description of a rent day in Lewis, in the reign of Donald Munro.

"Towards the middle of spring, when the snow had all melted away and the land presented a black barren aspect, the cottars of Shittim were waking out of their polar rest, and getting their spades and other agricultural implements ready for the season's labour.

"At this time Mr Donald Black, the factor, was wont to make a tour round the land over which he was the real king, with the object of collecting rents from those who might not have been able to settle arrears at the more important autumn collection. The past season had been memorably bad. The crops had entirely failed; there had been little or no fishing; and, to crown all, a disease came among the sheep and cattle, which destroyed many of them. But these circumstances had no softening influence upon the native severity of the tyrant factor. A vicious laugh of brutal joy came

THE

LOVE OF HIS LIFE.

A Novel.

BY COSMO CUMMING.

VOL. I.

Dedicated

TO

DONALD MUNRO, ESQUIRE,

LEWS,

IN GRATEFUL REMEMBRANCE

OF

HIS CONSTANT AND VALUABLE

SYMPATHY.

LONDON:
MOXON, SAUNDERS, & CO., 22, HENRIETTA STREET,
COVENT GARDEN, W.C.

[1877]

The title page of 'The Love of His Life', a three decker Victorian novel written by a Harrisman, John Macrae, over the nom de plume "Cosmo Cumming."
(Photograph by courtesy of the National Library of Scotland.)

The dedication of 'The Love of His Life' to Donald Munro is ironic. The author worked in Munro's offices as a young man and Munro, lightly disguised, figures in the book.
(Photograph by courtesy of the National Library of Scotland.)

from him as he stood in his coach-yard, wrapped up in a coat made of several grey seal-skins, and coughing through an immense comforter that covered the lower and the redder half of his face.

"'Hogh! hogh! it is a furious day to drive on, Tom. But so much the better; the scoundrels will get wet enough. I'll pay them for their confounded impudence. All ready there? Look sharp, confound you.'

"'All ready, Mr Black; step in, sir, please.'

"'Step in, you fool? Where is that idiot Campbell? Ho! there, you lazy idiot; be here at once, or you can walk to Rossy. Look sharp!'

"'Yes, sir,' said the servile Campbell as he stepped into his accustomed seat behind, after waiting an hour for his majesty's pleasure.

'Now drive on and make quick work of it. Take care of the horses,' the master shouted to Tom, who had the advantage of being dull of hearing ...

"The thirty or forty men who had come up to give their utmost farthing to the inexorable factor, had arrived at the time stated in his notice, and had now been more than an hour waiting for him. The pompous little inn-keeper at Rossy would not hear of giving them shelter, because they did not sufficiently patronise his poisonous taps, and because he feared a storm from his patron and colleague the factor, if he dared to show so much leniency to 'the scoundrels'.

"When he had made himself fairly comfortable, and got seated in his chair of state in the 'commercial' of the little inn, with his meek scribe before him, Mr Donald Black summoned a few of the dripping cottars to appear.

"The first who came to the table, cap in hand, and saluted his factor with becoming respect, was an elder of the church and knew a little English.

"'Good morning, Mr Black. It is a wet day you will get for the rents.'

"'Hush! What's your name? Where do you come from? Campbell, turn him up. Kenneth Smith, Barney. Number 26. Have you got the rent? Why did you not pay this before? Eh? Look sharp with it and stand back. You were smoking, man. Stand off. Hush! I don't want to hear any nonsense. Next man there.'

"The next man came up like his friend and imitated him in giving respect.

"'Good morning? Do you call this a good morning, man? Stupid brutes. Watcher. I saw you before. What's your name again? Number what? Speak out, man. Less noise, there. Any arrears there, Campbell?'

"'Yes, Mr Black,' and Campbell read some pencil notes on the margin of the rent sheets: 'Sold a cow to a drover at Christmas; has plenty of money. A rogue and a scoundrel.'"

"'I thought so. Well? What have you to say for yourself, Alexander Thompson? Eh? Sold a cow? Where's the money? Look sharp! Do you think I have nothing to do but wait here all day for you?'

"'Well, Mr Black,' the man commenced to explain, 'I had no potatoes; I was unsuccessful in the fishing, and my wife and family were starving; what could I do?'

"'Confound your wife and children. That's always the cry. Wife and children!. Why do you have a wife and children? I'll manage every one of you. Double his rent, Campbell. I'll see that you have no more children. A fine thing for you to spend his Lordship's money feeding too many children. Deacons and rubbish in a church, too! Fine Pharisees and rogues you make. But I'll sort you. Campbell, mark opposite his name — Summons, sell out, too many children; lazy scoundrel. Next there.'

"A widow next approached the tribunal. She was wet and shivering with cold.

'Well, who are you? A poor widow indeed! Not you. How much money have you? Look alive! What are you crying for? There's plenty of rain today. What! Twenty shillings to pay seven pounds? Confounded impertinence! Summons and evict. What do you mean? Why don't you pay your rents? Eh? Can you speak?'

"'We tried to pay as long as he who is no more was here to earn it,' the poor widow said, sobbing piteously. 'What can a poor widow with four children do more, when everything is against us? If you have a little patience, we shall pay it all. My oldest boy is going to the militia, and we can sell a cow.'

"'Hush your talk, woman. You must go. I'll put you out of the land, and you can go where you like. I have given your lot to another tenant.'

"'But I can sell the cattle now, and pay it if I must. God knows I have no place to go to.'

"'Hush your noise, woman, and go out. Next there.'

"The next was a tottering old man who advanced, leaning heavily upon his staff. At first sight one could see he was a great sinner. Traces of snuff were, alas! too conspicuous upon his face. The factor himself carried his snuff loose in his pocket; but that was no consideration, for the people were to do as he said, no matter what his own private habits were.

'Ah! here is an old divine to be sure; with plenty of snuff about him, too. What do you mean, sir, by coming in my presence in that state? Go out this moment and wash your face.'

'Och-a-nis! Mr Black; I am an old man, and snuff I have only taken lately to make me think less of my sorrows.'

"'Damn your sorrows, every one of you!'"

Later, when another old man comes in, Macrae writes: "In his extreme weakness (he) required to rest upon his stick before he could straighten his bent back in order to see and salute his superior. Impatient with this movement, which the wildest savage in mid Africa would have beheld with pity and reverence, the factor sprung at him and, violently pulling his cap off, flung it through the doorway."

That incident could well relate to something Macrae had actually witnessed, but the scene moves away from reportage when some of the tenants stand up to the Factor. One has the feeling, here, Macrae is recording what they said behind the Factor's back, rather than what they said to his face. And we pass into the realm of wishful thinking when the Factor's gig is waylaid on the homeward journey and he is dumped in an old quarry "where the slime had developed into that emerald semi-liquid, classically called 'green granny'."

The astonishing feature of Munro's reign in Lewis is that assaults on him did not occur. The windows of his home were smashed on one occasion but that was pure chance. A drunk had gone along the street breaking all the glass in sight, in a sort of geometric progression: one pane in the first house, two in the second, four in the third.

One of the victims of this haphazard vandalism was Peter Pope, a sailmaker, from Devon via Rothesay, whose son married George Stephen's daughter, and whose great grandson was my closest friend at school and university: Stephen MacLean, who is, in a sense, the author of this book.

Macrae, in other passages, draws a sharp distinction between Munro and his master, Lord Shittim, although the latter is a far from estimable character, and, indeed, turns out to be the villain of the story.

"The one is a good and benevolent proprietor, the other the most unworthy creature in Scotland," is the summing up of Helen, the first character in the book to mention the Factor. Later she comments, "When the master would give money to a helpless cottar to prop up his fallen roof, the fierce hireling would double the already heavy rent."

The Factor's method of answering prayer, she suggests, was to punish the petitioner.

Helen, Macrae's spokeswoman in these matters, might be

regarded as the heroine of his tale were it not for the fact that there is no heroine in the romantic tradition.

The story ends with the hero returning to his native parish, a confirmed bachelor, in order to set up a school. That, perhaps, gives us an indication what the establishment of the Nicolson Institute meant to the abler young men in Lewis of John Macrae's generation.

Many passages in the novel quite clearly reflect the interests and attitudes of the young men in the Stornoway Literary and Debating Society which blackballed Munro for so many years, and in which Macrae was one of the leading figures.

It is, in modern parlance, a committed novel; a piece of literary propaganda, unlike the novels of his model William Black.

In the fashion of his day, every chapter is headed by a verse of poetry. That chosen for the description of the rent collection is:
"And wherefore do the poor complain?
The rich man asked of me.
Come walk abroad with me, I said,
And I will answer thee."

There may be a sub-conscious Freudian reason for the decision to call the villain Lord Shittim, but, at the conscious level, it derives from Macrae's intense but, perhaps, naive idealism.

The name is applied only derivatively to the landlord. It is primarily the name of his estate, where the story is located, and which stands for Macrae's native Island of Lewis and Harris.

It is taken from the passage in Joel which looks forward to the day when "the Lord shall roar out of Zion ... and the heavens and the earth shall shake: but the Lord will be the hope of his people...

"And it shall come to pass in that day, that the mountains shall drop down new wine, and the hills shall flow with milk, and all the rivers of Judah shall flow with waters, and a fountain shall come forth of the house of the Lord, and shall water the valley of Shittim."

The name chosen for the Factor, on the other hand, is quite deliberately offensive.

The forename, Donald, links him directly with Munro, while the full name, Donald Black, is an English rendering of a popular Gaelic appellation for the devil.

19. A BOOK THAT WROTE ITSELF

This book has been creeping up on me for many years. It has almost written itself.

I was familiar with my grandfather's ship the *Arrow* from my early childhood. The wreckage was still mouldering on the beach at Goat Island where the slipway is today. I saw it whenever I visited my granny's, and I remember vividly the first time I stood beside it, looking up at the green and slimy timbers with childish awe.

You could approach it only at the bottom of the spring tide, when a path dried out between Newton and the Island, opposite Number 1, which, as I learned the facts, became even more significant than the *Arrow* itself.

I was taken to Goat Island by my eldest aunt, Bella, then in her early fifties. It was a great adventure, walking dry shod across the harbour, like the Israelites crossing the Red Sea with Pharaoh's chariots thundering at their heels. I knew there was no one pursuing us, but my aunt, afraid that I might wander, had filled me with terror of the incoming tide: the fear we might be trapped.

I asked about the wreck and was told, "Oh! That's the *Arrow*," as if that explained everything. There was something in the way it was said which, even to my childish mind, was loaded. It was clearly a question which should not have been asked.

Many years later, during the war, I had occasion to call on the Procurator Fiscal, Colin Scott Mackenzie, the middle member of a family dynasty, which has discharged the duties of the office, with impartiality and efficiency, for almost a century.

There was a drive to gather wastepaper at the time, and, when I called, the Fiscal was busy sorting out everything that could be sacrificed from the great stacks of paper with which his office was crammed.

My eye alighted on the word *Arrow* written boldly on a legal document lying on the top of the discard pile. I thought it might refer to my grandfather's vessel, and picked it up. It was the draft of William Ross's appeal from the Sheriff Substitute's decision that my granduncles had nothing to do with the ship or its debts. For the first time, I learned of the gathering in the Crown Inn, the gift of the ship, the voyage to Stettin and the disaster at Elsinore.

Much of the legal detail was new even to my uncle, although he remembered seeing the *Arrow*, as a boy, with an arrestment nailed to the mast, and was able to draw me a rough sketch, showing how she was rigged.

Between my first acquaintance with the *Arrow* and my visit to the Fiscal's office, I had learned a good deal about Donald Munro. He was in the air in Lewis, so to speak. A legendary figure whose name cropped up from time to time in my elders' reminiscences, or allusively, as the great exemplar, the bench mark against which lesser tyrannies could be assessed.

The Bernera Riot was often mentioned, particularly around the jubilee in 1924, when I was still a boy at school.

Shortly after I took over the *Stornoway Gazette*, on my father's death, an uncle in Durham, who, as a medical student in Edinburgh, had been active in the Land League movement, sent me a bundle of pamphlets, including the contemporary account of the trial of the Bernera men, and, even more importantly, Ryrie's exposure of the misapplication of the Ness Disaster Fund, of which I had not previously heard.

There had been some vague talk at home about the Stephen case, in the early twenties, when Rev Norman C. Macfarlane wrote his article about old sea captains for the *Gazette* in which he referred, not quite accurately, to the death of the twins. By that time, even within the family, the story was imprecise and blurred, and, anyway, I was then too young to be really interested.

The final nudge towards writing this book came from George Stephen's great grandson, Stephen MacLean, who was, in fact, named after him.

Stephen and I were cousins. We lived just a few doors apart in Stornoway. We went through school together. We shared a room for two years as students at Glasgow University. We had interminable discussions about work and play, a wide variety of current interests, and family affairs, but we never mentioned the Stephen case, until he brought the matter up, briefly, a few days before his death.

When I left the University, Stephen stayed on to take an honours degree in Mathematics, with a view to becoming an actuary. He had the promise of a post with the Sun Life Assurance Company in Montreal, and spent one of his long vacations there, working in the Head Office.

In his final year, when he was running neck and neck at the top of the honours class, he contracted tuberculosis, and spent some years in a sanatorium at Bridge of Weir.

When he had recovered sufficiently, he returned to the University but switched to Law, finally taking his LLB with distinction in most of his

Stephen M. Maclean, George Stephen's great-grandson, who died in the house once occupied by Donald Munro, and who first suggested the writing of this book.

classes. He served his apprenticeship with a well known Glasgow firm, but aimed to become an advocate and had actually paid his admission fees when his health broke down a second time.

After a long spell in the Lewis Sanatorium, he began to run a solicitor's business from his sick bed, in his parents' home on Lewis Street. He also played an active part in the pioneering work, in community development, being done by the Lewis Association, writing some of the Association's pamphlets single handed.

He was only once able to take a case in court. Although the Courthouse was less than a hundred yards from his home, I had to take him there by car: he wasn't strong enough to walk.

One day, shortly before he died, at the early age of 36, he told me he had occasion to look at the title deeds to Number 1 Newton, the old Stephen home, then occupied by his aunt, a retired school teacher, Mary Pope.

He referred briefly to the manner in which his great grandparents had been harassed and, much to my surprise, spoke of William Ross, rather than Donald Munro, as the culprit. I t was the first time I had heard William Ross's name mentioned in connection with the case, but it reminded me of the old document about the *Arrow* drafted by William Ross, which was then lying, almost forgotten, in a drawer in my desk.

Stephen was proud of the manner in which his family stood up to the "mafia". He declared his intention, as soon as his health was restored and he was back in Edinburgh, of looking out the old legal processes, to see for himself precisely what had happened.

A few days later I was sent for, urgently. His condition had suddenly deteriorated. He was being kept alive with oxygen and wanted to see me, before he died.

When I got to his bedside, he took off the oxygen mask, and calmly dictated his will, directing me how to complete it in proper legal form.

He was worried about the work he was doing for the large number of clients who had come to him for legal advice, ranging from a professional man threatened with prosecution for a minor poaching offence which, trivial though it was, might have ruined his career, to a retired business-man, negotiating his divorce from a wife he had left behind in South America.

Stephen's mother, by that time, was dead. His father was suffering from Alzheimer's disease, although we did not know it by that name. He wanted to make sure that I was in a position to secure his papers, when the need arose, and arrange with his old firm in Glasgow to complete outstanding business.

As soon as his will was ready, he put the oxygen mask on again.

Before morning he was dead.

I have always felt, since then, that I must one day dig out the records in the Stephen case, and write it up, as he would have done, although I lack his knowledge of the law.

When finally I got round to it, I found I was engaged in something much wider than a bit of family history.

To understand what had happened to my great-grandmother, her daughter and her son-in-law, I had to have a look at the maladministration of the law, in Lewis, over a long period of time, and I found that the events of a hundred and fifty years ago still had contemporary relevance.

The basic problem with the law in Lewis, in the 1840s and 1850s, was that the provision of solicitors was left to the free play of market forces, and the market failed to deliver.

When I became a member of the Highlands and Islands Development Board in 1970, the same problem still existed, in a modern form. Development in the remoter areas was seriously impeded by a lack of local solicitors and accountants. The Board had to make good the deficiencies of the market, by enabling professional men to go where they would not otherwise have been.

Since the Board was established, conditions in the Highlands and Islands have greatly improved, but central government still applies urban solutions to rural problems with unfortunate results.

While some of the problems which affected Lewis, in the period I am concerned with, arose from the unrestrained operation of market forces, the situation under the benevolent dictatorship of Sir James Matheson, as applied through a hierarchy of bureaucrats presided over by Donald Munro, has many parallels with the situation, under communism, in Eastern Europe. The repressive, debilitating effect on the people and the economy was precisely the same as we have seen in our own day in Poland, East Germany and Czechoslovakia.

There are warning lessons in the Lewis experience for dogmatists at both ends of the political spectrum.

The Lewis experience is also relevant to the problems of linguistic and racial minorities in almost every country in the world.

The fact that Donald Munro was both a Highlander and a Gaelic speaker makes his open contempt for the crofters all the more significant.

Repression of cultural minorities is often most virulent among those who are closest to them in time and space. The implications of this for the structures of government, both local and national — and for the interpretation of history in a country like Scotland — are immense.

Donald Munro was a living caricature of an arrogant assumption of superiority to which many of us, on the English-speaking side of the divide, succumb, but which we camouflage from other people, and often conceal even from ourselves.

In a wry sort of way, we owe him a debt of gratitude, for exemplifying, and discrediting, our own original sin.

In a sense this book is a memorial to a friend who died more than forty years ago. It is also an attempt to trace the inter-connectedness of events; the ironies which become apparent in a small community where almost everything about everyone is known.

It was on the day of Stephen's funeral, for instance, my uncle told me that Donald Munro had lived, in his declining years, in the house on Lewis Street later owned by the MacLeans.

Stephen MacLean and Donald Munro died in the same house, and, most probably, in the same bedroom.

How differently they are remembered!